"AN UNFORGETTABLE TOUR OF THE WORLD WITH THEROUX ...

[His] powers of description and knack at turning a phrase are arresting. . . . Wonderful."
—*The Flint Journal*

"A unique view of our global village as experienced through a unique writer's eyes and ears ... Like a modern Ulysses ... His writings are proof that getting there may be most of the fun."
—*Houston Chronicle*

"An enticing selection of travel writings by one of the premier travel writers in the English language ... Theroux has the ability of penetrating to the heart of wherever he journeys. . . . [He's] a top-notch travel writer."
—*Magill Book Reviews*

"Scintillating . . . Theroux will never tell you about the best hotel in town because, chances are, he's never stayed there. He *has*, however, stayed in working class residences here and there, absorbing local color, prevailing attitudes and prejudices of the inhabitants. TO THE ENDS OF THE EARTH offers selections from some truly unique, exotic travel adventures. . . . [It's] a super book, a collection of journeys to some strange places, described by a fine writer who couldn't write a dull, trite line if he tried. Extremely well done."
—*Coast Book Review Service*

TO THE ENDS OF THE EARTH

The Selected Travels of

Paul Theroux

IVY BOOKS • NEW YORK

Ivy Books
Published by Ballantine Books
Copyright © 1990, 1991 by Paul Theroux
Photographs copyright © 1991 by Carin Riley

This work was originally published in different form in Great Britain as *Traveling the World* by Sinclair-Stevenson Limited, London, in 1990. Portions of this work were previously published separately in *The Great Railway Bazaar, Sunrise with Seamonsters, The Old Patagonian Express, The Kingdom by the Sea,* and *Riding the Iron Rooster.*

Grateful acknowledgment is made to the following for permission to reprint previously published material:

EMI MUSIC PUBLISHING AND CAREERS—BMG MUSIC PUBLISHING, INC.: Excerpt from "Oh, Carol" by Neil Sedaka and Howard Greenfield. Copyright © 1959, 1960 by Screen Gems—EMI Music, Inc. Copyright renewed 1987, 1988 by Screen Gems—EMI Music, Inc./Careers—BMG Music Publishing, Inc. All rights reserved. Reprinted by permission.

HARCOURT BRACE JOVANOVICH, INC., AND FABER AND FABER, LIMITED: Excerpt from "East Coker" from *Four Quartets* by T. S. Eliot. Copyright 1943 by T. S. Eliot. Copyright © renewed 1971 by Esme Valerie Eliot. Rights throughout the world excluding the United States are controlled by Faber and Faber Limited. Reprinted by permission.

Library of Congress Catalog Card Number: 91-9533

ISBN 0-8041-1122-7

This edition published by arrangement with Random House, Inc.

Printed in Canada

First Ballantine Books Edition: May 1994

10 9 8 7

To Anne Theroux,
who made it possible for me
to go on these journeys.

"My father was full of Sayings," the Hawaiian said. "He told me once, 'Kaniela, remember this. No matter where you go, that's where you are.' "

Contents

Introduction

I HAD BEEN TRAVELING FOR MORE THAN TEN YEARS—IN Europe, Asia, and Africa—and it had not occurred to me to write a travel book. I had always somewhat disliked travel books: they seemed self-indulgent, unfunny, and rather selective. I had the idea that the travel writer left a great deal out of his or her book and put all the wrong things in. I hated sight-seeing, and yet that was what constituted much of the travel writer's material: the pyramids, the Taj Mahal, the Vatican, the paintings here, the mosaics there. In an age of mass tourism, everyone set off to see the same things, and that was what travel writing seemed to be about. I am speaking of the 1960s and early 1970s.

The travel book was a bore. A bore wrote it and a bore read it—I could just imagine the sort of finger-wetting spud in carpet slippers who used his library card as bookmark, and called himself an armchair traveler. As for the writer, it annoyed me that a traveler would suppress his or her moments of desperation or fear or lust. Or the time he or she screamed at a taxi driver, or was picked up by a plausible local, or slept until noon. And what did they eat, what books did they read to kill time, and what were the toilets like? I had done enough traveling to know that half of travel was delay or nuisance—buses breaking down and hotel clerks being rude and market traders being rapacious. The truth of travel was unexpected and off-key, and few people ever wrote about it.

Now and then one would find this reality in a book—Evelyn Waugh being mistaken for his brother Alec in *Labels*, or the good intentions and bad temper in parts of

Naipaul's *An Area of Darkness*, a superbly structured book, deeply personal and imaginative and informative, but wayward, too. I saw it in the humor and the dialogue in Trollope's *The West Indies and the Spanish Main.*

An unlikely source, Nabokov's *Laughter in the Dark*, vividly illustrates this sort of travel writing. One of the characters says, "A writer for instance talks about India which I have seen, and gushes about dancing girls, tiger hunts, fakirs, betel nuts, serpents: the Glamour of the Mysterious East. But what does it amount to? Nothing. Instead of visualizing India I merely get a bad toothache from all these Eastern delights. Now, there's the other way, as for instance, the fellow who writes: 'Before turning in, I put out my wet boots to dry and in the morning I found that a thick blue forest had grown on them ("Fungi, Madam," he explained) . . .' and at once India becomes alive for me. The rest is shop."

When something human is recorded, good travel writing happens.

The trip—the itinerary—was another essential; and so many travel books I read had grown out of a traveler's chasing around a city or a little country—*Discovering Portugal*, that kind of thing. It was not travel at all, but rather a form of extended residence that I knew well from having myself lived in Malawi and Uganda and Singapore and England. I had come to rest in those places, I was working, I had a local driver's license, I went shopping every Saturday. It had never occurred to me to write a travel book about any of it. Travel had to do with movement and truth, with trying everything, offering yourself to experience and then reporting it. And I felt that television had put the sight-seers out of business.

Choosing the right itinerary—the best route, the correct mode of travel—was the surest way, I felt, of gaining experience. It had to be total immersion, a long deliberate trip through the hinterland rather than flying from one big city to another, which didn't seem to me to be travel at all. The travel books I liked were oddities—not simply Trollope and Naipaul but Henry Miller's *The Air-Conditioned Nightmare* (America, coast to coast, by car), or Mark Twain's *Follow-*

ing the Equator (a lecture tour around the world). I wanted my book to be a series of long train journeys, but where to?

All this speculation took place in the autumn of 1972, when I was teaching for a semester at the University of Virginia. I was working on a novel, *The Black House*, and awaiting the publication of *Saint Jack*. In those days I began a new book as soon as I finished the one I was working on. My wife, Anne, was in London with our two children, and she was working—indeed, earning a good living—but I still felt I was the breadwinner and that I was not earning enough. My British advance for *Saint Jack* came to about $500, and I assumed I would not get much more for *The Black House*. I kept thinking to myself, *Now what?*

Money is rather a clumsy subject, but it was a crucial factor in my decision to write my first travel book—simply, I needed the money. And when I mentioned the possibility of such a book to my American editor, she was delighted. She said, "We'll give you an advance for it." I had never before received an advance at this stage. Normally, I wrote a book and submitted it and then was paid; I had never asked for, nor been given, money or a contract on an unwritten book.

It is often the case that only when someone asks you very specific questions do you begin to think clearly about your intentions. In my mind this travel book had something to do with trains, but I had no idea where I wanted to go—only that it should be a long trip. I saw a thick book with lots of people in it and lots of dialogue and no sightseeing. But my editor's questioning made me think hard about it, and I thought, *Trains Through Asia.* I was determined to start in London, and to take the Orient Express, and when I looked at this route, I saw that I could continue through Turkey, into Iran, and after a short bus ride in Baluchistan, I could catch a train in Zahedan, go into Pakistan, and more or less chug through Asia.

My original idea had been to go to Vietnam, take the train to Hanoi, and then continue through China, Mongolia, and the Soviet Union. Much of this, on closer examination, proved impractical or impossible. The man at the Chinese Embassy in 1972 abruptly hung up on me when I said I wanted a visa to take trains through China. I had to wait fourteen years before I was able to take the trip I described in *Riding the Iron Rooster*. Then I discovered there was a war in progress in Baluchistan. I rerouted myself through Afghanistan. I decided to include Japan and the whole of the Trans-Siberian. I didn't mind where I went as long as it was in Asia and had a railway system and visas were available. I saw myself puffing along, changing countries by changing trains.

Meanwhile, I was finishing my novel *The Black House*. It was set in rural England and it was rather ghostly and solemn. I wanted my next to be a sunny book. I had just about decided on my travel itinerary when I delivered my novel to my British publisher. He suggested we have lunch. Almost before we had started eating he told me how much he disliked *The Black House*. "It will hurt your reputation" was how he put it. "But I want to publish your travel book." I had told him that I had signed a contract for this with my American publisher. I said that if he brought out my novel he could have the travel book. "If you twist my arm I'll publish your novel," he said. That did it. It made me want to leave him immediately.

For dropping me from his list—after all, what was I costing him?—he became rather a laughingstock. But that was later. I think of the circumstances surrounding my first travel book, *The Great Railway Bazaar*, rather than the trip itself. I hated leaving my family behind in London, I had never taken such a deliberate trip before, I felt encumbered by an advance on royalties, modest though it was; and my writer friends, stick-in-the-mud English writers, generally mocked my idea. I never got around to worrying about the trip itself, though I was beset by an obscure ache that was both mental and physical—the lingering anxiety that I was doomed: I was going to die on this trip.

I had always had the idea and still do that my particular exit would be made via an appointment in Samarra: I would go a great distance and endure enormous discomfort and expense in order to meet my death. If I chose to sit at home and eat and drink in the bosom of my family, it would never happen—I'd live to be a hundred. But of course I would head for the hinterland, and pretty soon there would be some corner of a foreign field that would be forever Medford, Mass. And I imagined my death would be a silly mistake, like that of the monk and mystic Thomas Merton, who at last left his monastery in Kentucky after twenty-five secure years, and popped up in Singapore (while I was there), and accidentally electrocuted himself on the frayed wires of a fan in Bangkok a week later. All that way, all that trouble, just to yank a faulty light switch in a crummy hotel!

I left London on September 19, 1973. It was a gray day. I had a cold. My wife waved me good-bye. Almost immediately I felt I had made an absurd decision. I hadn't the slightest idea of what I was doing. I became very gloomy. To cheer myself up and give myself the illusion that this was real work I began to take voluminous notes. Every day, from the time I left until the moment I arrived back in England four months later, I wrote down everything I saw and heard, filling one notebook after another. I recorded conversations, descriptions of people and places, details of trains, interesting trivia, even criticism of the novels I happened to be reading. I still have some of those paperbacks—Joyce's *Exiles*, Chekhov's stories, Endo's *Silence*, and others—and on the blank back pages are scribbled small insectile notes, which I amplified when I transferred them to my large notebooks. I always wrote in the past tense.

The trip recorded in *The Great Railway Bazaar* was the trip I took, and the manner of my journey and my way of writing about it became my method in all my future travel books. I changed the names of some people I wished to protect, but many of the names I left as was. My problem in writing the book was finding a form for it — a structure. In the end I simply hung it on a series of train journeys. I had never read a book quite like the one I was writing. This worried me, as well as making me hopeful. The writing of the book took the same amount of time as the trip itself, four months.

That was more than seventeen years ago. The book is still in print and still sells well. Some people think it is the only book I have ever written (which annoys me) or is my best (which is equally untrue). I think the writing in *The Old Patagonian Express* is more fluent, *The Kingdom by the Sea* funnier and more knowledgeable, and *Riding the Iron Rooster* more prescient. For example, in *The Great Railway Bazaar*, my train passed through Nis in Yugoslavia. I mentioned this but I never bothered to discover anything about Nis. I have just located a copy of *The Blue Guide to Yugoslavia* and found that it was the birthplace of Emperor Constantine. Reading on, I came to the sentence "Though not a pleasant place in itself, Nis has several interesting monuments" and I realized, perhaps, why I did not linger in Nis.

It has been a satisfaction to me that my *Railway Bazaar* (I got the title from a street name in Kanpur, India) and the rest of my travel books have fared well. I did not realize when I wrote my first one that every trip is unique. My travel book is about my trip, not yours or anyone else's. Even if someone had come with me and written a book about the trip, it would have been a different book. This is true of life in general. It bothers me, as it bothers the Borges character Ireneo Funes, "that the dog at three fourteen (seen from the side) should have the same name as the dog at three fifteen (seen from the front)."

Another thing I did not know was that every trip has a historical dimension. Not long after I traveled through those countries there were political changes. (It seems to happen every time.) The shah was deposed and Iran became very dangerous for the traveler. Afghanistan went to war with itself. India and Pakistan restored their rail link. Laos shut its borders to foreigners and exiled its royalty. Vietnam fixed its railway, so that now it is possible to travel by train from Ho Chi Minh City (Saigon) to Hanoi. Many of the individual trains were taken out of service, most notably the Orient Express. The train that plies from London to Venice under that name is for rich, idle people who have selfish, sumptuous fantasies about travel that bear no relation to the real thing. However awful my old Orient Express was, at least I can say that all sorts of people took it—rich and poor, old and young, rattling back and forth between East and West.

It was cheap and friendly, and like all great trains, it was like the world on wheels.

Attempting to write my travel experiences for the first time, I was groping in the dark—although I was careful to disguise the fact. I am told that I often seem self-assured in my travel writing, but that is usually my way of whistling to keep my spirits up. I know that I have hijacked a venerable form, the travel book about a grand tour, and am steering it my own way, to suit myself, and my peculiar trip and temperament. Whatever else travel writing is, it is certainly different from writing a novel: fiction requires close concentration and intense imagining, a leap of faith, magic almost. But a travel book, I discovered, was more the work of my left hand, and it was a deliberate act—like the act of travel itself. It took health and strength and confidence. When I finished a novel I never knew whether I would be able to write another one. But I knew, when I finished my first travel book, that I would be able to do it again.

Someday I hope to complete a shelf of travel books, which, between bookends, will encompass the world. In the meantime, this selection, drawn from six of my books, can stand as a set of traveler's tales.

—Paul Theroux
East Sandwich
May 1991

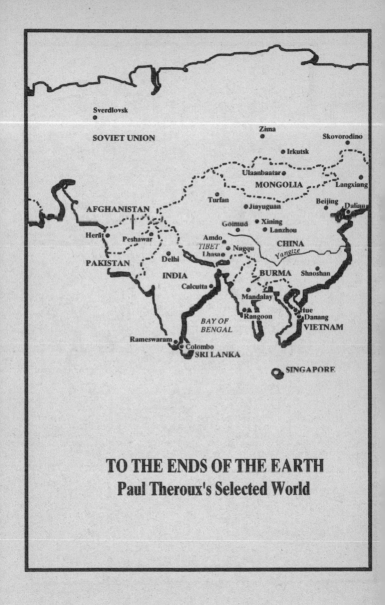

TO THE ENDS OF THE EARTH
Paul Theroux's Selected World

The Great
Railway Bazaar

The Mysterious
Mister Duffill

I REMEMBER MISTER DUFFILL BECAUSE HIS NAME LATER BE-
came a verb—Molesworth's, then mine. He was just ahead
of me in the line at Platform 7 at Victoria, "Continental Departures." He was old and his clothes were far too big for
him, so he might have left in a hurry and grabbed the
wrong clothes, or perhaps he'd just come out of the hospital. He walked treading his trouser cuffs to rags and carried
many oddly shaped parcels wrapped in string and brown
paper—more the luggage of an incautiously busy bomber
than of an intrepid traveler. The tags were fluttering in the
draft from the track, and each gave his name as *R. Duffill*
and his address as *Splendid Palus Hotel, Istanbul.* We
would be traveling together. A satirical widow in a severe
veil might have been more welcome, and if her satchel was
full of gin and an inheritance, so much the better. But there
was no widow; there were hikers, returning Continentals
with Harrods shopping bags, salesmen, French girls with
sour friends, and gray-haired English couples who appeared
to be embarking, with armloads of novels, on expensive literary adulteries. None would get farther than Ljubljana.
Duffill was for Istanbul—I wondered what his excuse was.
I was doing a bunk, myself. I hadn't nailed my colors to the
mast; I had no job—no one would notice me falling silent,
kissing my wife, and boarding the 15:30 alone.

The train was rumbling through Clapham. I decided that
travel was flight and pursuit in equal parts, but by the time
we had left the brick terraces and coal yards and the narrow
back gardens of the South London suburbs and were passing Dulwich College's playing fields—children lazily exer-
cising in neckties—I was tuned to the motion of the train

3

and had forgotten the newspaper billboards I had been reading all morning: BABY KRISTEN: WOMAN TO BE CHARGED and PLAN TO FREE STAB GIRL AGED NINE—none lettered NOVELIST VANISHES, and just as well. Then, past a row of semidetached houses, we entered a tunnel, and after traveling a minute in complete darkness we were shot wonderfully into a new setting, open meadows, cows cropping grass, farmers haying in blue jackets. We had surfaced from London, a gray sodden city that lay underground. At Sevenoaks there was another tunnel, another glimpse of the pastoral, fields of pawing horses, some kneeling sheep, crows on an oasthouse, and a swift sight of a settlement of prefab houses out one window. Out the other window, a Jacobean farmhouse and more cows. That is England: The suburbs overlap the farms. At several level crossings the country lanes were choked with cars, backed up for a hundred yards. The train passengers were gloating vindictively at the traffic and seemed to be murmuring, "Stop, you bitches!"

The sky was old. Schoolboys in dark blue blazers, carrying cricket bats and schoolbags, their socks falling down, were smirking on the platform at Tonbridge. We raced by them, taking their smirks away. We didn't stop, not even at the larger stations. These I contemplated from the dining car over a sloshing carton of tea, while Mr. Duffill, similarly hunched, kept an eye on his parcels and stirred his tea with a doctor's tongue depressor. He had that uneasy look of a man who has left his parcels elsewhere, which is also the look of a man who thinks he's being followed. His oversized clothes made him seem frail. A mouse-gray gabardine coat slumped in folds from his shoulders, the cuffs so long they reached to his fingertips and answered the length of his trampled trousers. He smelled of bread crusts. He still wore his tweed cap, and like me was fighting a cold. His shoes were interesting, the all-purpose brogans country people wear. Although I could not place his accent—he was asking the barman for cider—there was something else of the provinces about him, a stubborn frugality in his serviceable clothes, which is shabbiness in a Londoner's. He could tell you where he bought that cap and coat, and for how much, and how long those shoes had lasted. A few minutes later I passed by him in a corner of the lounge and saw that he had opened one of his parcels. A knife, a length of French bread, a tube of mustard, and disks of bright red salami were spread before him. Lost in thought, he slowly chewed his sandwich.

At the Gare du Nord my car was shunted onto a different engine. Duffill and I watched this being done from the platform and then we boarded. It took him a long time to heave himself up, and he panted with effort on the landing. He was still standing there, gasping, as we pulled out of the station for our twenty-minute trip to the Gare de Lyon to meet the rest of the Direct-Orient Express. It was after eleven, and most of the apartment blocks were in darkness. Duffill, on boarding the Direct-Orient Express, had put on a pair of glasses, wire-framed and with enough Scotch tape on the lenses to prevent his seeing the Blue Mosque. He assembled his parcels and, grunting, produced a suitcase, bound with a selection of leather and canvas belts as an added guarantee against its bursting open. A few cars down we met again to read the sign on the side of the wagon-lit: DIRECT-ORIENT and its itinerary, PARIS-LAUSANNE-MILANO-TRIESTE-ZAGREB-BEOGRAD-SOFIYA-ISTANBUL. We stood there, staring at this sign; Duffill worked his glasses like binoculars. Finally he said, "I took this train in 1929."

It seemed to call for a reply, but by the time a reply occurred to me ("Judging from its condition, it was probably this very train!") Duffill had gathered up his parcels and his strapped suitcase and moved down the platform. It was a great train in 1929, and it goes without saying that the Orient Express is the most famous train in the world. Like the Trans-Siberian it links Europe with Asia, which accounts for some of its romance. But it has also been hallowed by fiction: restless Lady Chatterley took it; so did Hercule Poirot and James Bond; Graham Greene sent some of his prowling unbelievers on it, even before he took it himself ("As I couldn't take a train to Istanbul the best I could do was buy a record of Honegger's Pacific 231," Greene writes in the introduction to *Stamboul Train*). The fictional source of the romance is *La Madone des Sleepings* (1925) by Maurice Dekobra. Dekobra's heroine, Lady Diana ("the type of woman who would have brought tears to the eyes of John Ruskin"), is completely sold on the Orient Express: "I have a ticket for Constantinople. But I may step off at Vienna or Budapest. That depends absolutely on chance or on the color of the eyes of my neighbor in the compartment."

My compartment was a cramped two-berth closet with an intruding ladder. I swung my suitcase in and, when I had done this, there was no room for me. The conductor showed me how to kick my suitcase under the lower berth. He hesitated, hoping to be tipped.

"Anybody else in here?" It had not occurred to me that I would have company; the conceit of the long-distance traveler is the belief that he is going so far, he will be alone—inconceivable that another person has the same good idea.

The conductor shrugged, perhaps yes, perhaps no. His vagueness made me withhold my tip. I took a stroll down the car: a Japanese couple in a double couchette—it was the first and last time I saw them; an elderly American couple next to them; a fat French mother breathing suspicion on her lovely daughter; a Belgian girl of extraordinary size—well over six feet tall, wearing enormous shoes—traveling with a chic French woman; and (the door was shutting) either a nun or a plump diabolist. At the far end of the car a man wearing a turtleneck, a seaman's cap, and a monocle was setting up bottles on the windowsill: three wine bottles, Perrier water, a broad-shouldered bottle of gin—he was obviously going some distance.

Duffill was standing outside my compartment. He was out of breath; he had had trouble finding the right car, he said, because his French was rusty. He took a deep breath and slid off his gabardine coat and hung that and his cap on the hook next to mine.

"I'm up here," he said, patting the upper berth. He was a small man, but I noticed that as soon as he stepped into the compartment he filled it.

"How far are you going?" I asked gamely, and even though I knew his reply, when I heard it I cringed. I had planned on studying him from a little distance; I was counting on having the compartment to myself. This was unwelcome news. He saw I was taking it badly.

He said, "I won't get in your way." His parcels were on the floor. "I just have to find a home for these."

A half hour later I returned to my compartment. The lights were blazing, and in his upper berth Duffill was sleeping; his face turned up to the overhead light gave him a gray corpse-like look, and his pajamas were buttoned to his neck. The expression on his face was one of agony; his features were fixed and his head moved as the train did. I turned out the lights and crawled into my berth. But I couldn't sleep at first; my cold and all that I'd drunk—the fatigue itself—kept me awake. And then something else alarmed me: it was a glowing circle, the luminous dial of Duffill's watch, for his arm had slipped down and was swinging back and forth as the train rocked, moving this glowing green dial past my face like a pendulum.

Then the dial disappeared. I heard Duffill climbing down the ladder, groaning on each rung. The dial moved sideways to the sink, and then the light came on. I rolled over against the wall and heard the clunk of Duffill dislodging the chamber pot from the cupboard under the sink; I waited, and after a long moment a warbling burble began, changing in pitch as the pot filled. There was a splash, like a sigh, and the light went out and the ladder creaked. Duffill groaned one last time and I slept.

IN THE MORNING DUFFILL WAS GONE. I LAY IN BED AND worked the window curtain up with my foot; after a few inches it shot up on its roller, revealing a sunny mountainside, the Alps dappled with light and moving past the window. It was the first time I had seen the sun for days, this first morning on the train, and I think this is the place to say that it continued to shine for the next two months. I traveled under clear skies all the way to southern India, and only then, two months later, did I see rain again, the late monsoon of Madras.

At Vevey I restored myself with a glass of fruit salts, and at Montreux felt well enough to shave. Duffill came back in time to admire my rechargeable electric razor. He said he used a blade and on trains always cut himself to pieces. He showed me a nick on his throat, then told me his name. He'd be spending two months in Turkey, but he didn't say what he'd be doing. In the bright sunlight he looked much older than he had in the grayness of Victoria. I guessed he was about seventy. But he was not in the least spry, and I could not imagine why anyone except a fleeing embezzler would spend two months in Turkey.

He looked out at the Alps and said, "They say if the Swiss had designed these mountains, um, they'd be rather flatter."

Duffill ate the last of his salami. He offered me some, but I said I was planning to buy my breakfast at an Italian station. Duffill lifted the piece of salami and brought it to his mouth, but just as he bit into it we entered a tunnel and everything went black.

"Try the lights," he said. "I can't eat in the dark. I can't taste it."

I groped for the light switch and flicked it, but we stayed in darkness.

Duffill said, "Maybe they're trying to save electricity."

His voice in the darkness sounded very near to my face. I moved to the window and tried to see the tunnel walls, but I saw only blackness. The sound of the wheels' drumming seemed louder in the dark and the train itself was gathering speed, the motion and the dark producing in me a suffocating feeling of claustrophobia and an acute awareness of the smell of the room, the salami, Duffill's woolens, and bread crusts. Minutes had passed and we were still in the tunnel; we might be dropping down a well, a great sinkhole in the Alps that would land us in the clockwork interior of Switzerland, glacial cogs and ratchets and frostbitten cuckoos.

Duffill said, "This must be the Simplon."

I said, "I wish they'd turn the lights on."

I heard Duffill wrapping his uneaten salami and punching the parcel into a corner.

I said, "What do you aim to do in Turkey?"

"Me?" Duffill said, as if the compartment was crammed with old men bound for Turkey, each waiting to state a reason. He paused, then said, "I'll be in Istanbul for a while. After that I'll be traveling around the country."

"Business or pleasure?" I was dying to know and in the confessional darkness did not feel so bad about badgering him; he could not see the eagerness on my face. On the other hand, I could hear the tremulous hesitation in his replies.

"A little of both," he said.

This was not helpful. I waited for him to say more, but when he added nothing further, I said, "What exactly do you do, Mr. Duffill?"

"Me?" he said again, but before I could reply with the sarcasm he was pleading for, the train left the tunnel and the compartment filled with sunlight and Duffill said, "This must be Italy."

Duffill put on his tweed cap. He saw me staring at it and said, "I've had this cap for years—eleven years. You dry-clean it. Bought it in Barrow-on-Humber." And he dug out his parcel of salami and resumed the meal the Simplon tunnel had interrupted.

At nine thirty-five we stopped at the Italian station of Domodossola, where a man poured cups of coffee from a jug and sold food from a heavily laden pushcart. He had fruit, loaves of bread and rolls, various kinds of salami, and lunch bags that, he said, contained, *"tante belle cose."* He also had a stock of wine. An Englishman, introducing himself as Molesworth, bought a Bardolino and ("just in case") three bottles of Chianti; I bought an Orvieto and a Chianti; and Duffill had his hand on a bottle of claret.

Molesworth said, "I'll take these back to my compartment. Get me a lunch bag, will you?"

I bought two lunch bags and some apples.

Duffill said, "English money, I only have English money."

The Italian snatched a pound from the old man and gave him change in lire.

Molesworth came back and said, "Those apples want washing. There's cholera here." He looked again at the pushcart and said, "I think *two* lunch bags, just to be safe."

While Molesworth bought more food and another bottle of Bardolino, Duffill said, "I took this train in 1929."

"It was worth taking then," said Molesworth. "Yes, she used to be quite a train."

"How long are we staying here?" I asked.

No one knew. Molesworth called out to the train guard, "I say, George, how long are we stopping for?"

The guard shrugged, and as he did so the train began to back up.

"Do you think we should board?" I asked.

"It's going backward," said Molesworth. "I expect they're shunting."

The train guard said, *"Andiamo."*

"The Italians love wearing uniforms," said Molesworth. "Look at him, will you? And the uniforms are always so wretched. They really are like overgrown schoolboys. Are you talking to us, George?"

"I think he wants us to board," I said. The train stopped going backward. I hopped aboard and looked down. Molesworth and Duffill were at the bottom of the stairs.

"You've got parcels," said Duffill. "You go first."

"I'm quite all right," said Molesworth. "Up you go."

"But you've got parcels," said Duffill. He produced a pipe from his coat and began sucking on the stem. "Carry on." He moved back and gave Molesworth room.

Molesworth said, "Are you sure?"

Duffill said, "I didn't go all the way, then, in 1929. I didn't do that until after the second war." He put his pipe in his mouth and smiled.

Molesworth stepped aboard and climbed up—slowly, because he was carrying a bottle of wine and his second lunch bag. Duffill grasped the rails beside the door and as he did so the train began to move and he let go. He dropped his arms. Two train guards rushed behind him and held his arms and hustled him along the platform to the moving stairs of Car 99. Duffill, feeling the Italians' hands, resisted the embrace, went feeble, and stepped back; he made a half-turn to smile wanly at the fugitive door. He looked a hundred years old. The train was moving swiftly past his face.

I never saw Mr. Duffill again. When we were buying more food on the platform at Milan, Molesworth said, "We'd better get aboard. I don't want to be duffilled." I left his suitcase and his paper bags at Venice with a note, and I wondered whether he caught up with them and continued to Istanbul.

One of the few things Mr. Duffill had told me was that he lived in Barrow-on-Humber, in Lincolnshire.

It was a tiny place—a church, a narrow High Street, a manor house, and a few shops. It had an air of rural monotony that was like the drone of a bee as it bumbled slowly from flower to flower. No one ever came here; people just went away from it and never returned.

I walked down the street and saw a man.

"Excuse me, do you know a Mr. Duffill?"

He nodded. "The corner shop."

The corner shop had a small sign that said DUFFILL'S HARDWARE. But it was locked. A square of cardboard in the window was lettered GONE ON HOLIDAY. I said out loud, "Goddamn it."

A lady was passing. She saw that I was exasperated. She wondered if I needed directions. I said I was looking for Mr. Duffill.

"He won't be back for another week," she said.

"Where has he gone this time?" I asked. "Not Istanbul, I hope."

She said, "Are you looking for *Richard* Duffill?"

"Yes," I said.

Her hand went to her face, and I knew before she spoke that he was dead.

"HIS NAME WAS RICHARD CUTHBERT DUFFILL. HE WAS A most unusual man," said his sister-in-law, Mrs. Jack Duffill. She lived at Glyndbourne, a bungalow just beyond the churchyard. She did not ask who I was. It seemed only natural to her that someone should be inquiring about the life of this strange man, who had died two years before, at the age of seventy-nine. He had been as old as the century—seventy-three the year he had stepped off the Orient Express at Domodossola. Mrs. Jack said, "Do you know about his adventurous life?"

I said, "I don't know anything about him." All I knew was his name and his village.

"He was born right here in Barrow, in the Hall cottages. The Hall was one of the grand houses. Richard's father was the gardener and his mother was a housemaid. Those were the days of servants. The Hall was the manor—Mr. Uppleby was the Lord of the Manor—and of course the Duffills were servants, and rather poor. . . ."

But Richard Duffill was brilliant. At the age of eleven he was encouraged by the headmaster of the village school to go to the Technical College in Hull. He excelled at math, but he was also a gifted linguist. He learned French, Latin, German, Russian, and Spanish while still a teenager at Hull. But he had become somewhat introspective, for when Richard was twelve his father died. Mr. Uppleby took an interest, but the young boy usually just stayed inside and read and did his lessons, or else he went for long solitary walks.

His main recreation was swimming, and his skill in this resulted in his becoming a local hero. One summer day in 1917 he was on a swimming expedition with some friends at a quarry called the Brick Pits, near the Humber Bank. One of the boys, a certain Howson, began to struggle. He shouted, and then he disappeared beneath the murky water. Duffill dived repeatedly after him and finally surfaced with Howson and dragged him to shore, saving the boy's life. A few days later, the Hull newspaper reported the story under the headline A PLUCKY BARROW BOY.

For this, Duffill, a Boy Scout, was awarded the Silver Cross for Bravery. It was the first time this honor had ever come to a Lincolnshire scout. Some months afterward, the Carnegie Heroes' Fund presented Duffill with a silver watch "for gallantry," and gave him a sum of money "to help him in his education and future career."

In 1919, still young, and fluent in half a dozen languages, he joined the Inter-Allied Plebiscite Commission and was sent to Allenstein, in what was then East Prussia, to deal with the aftermath of World War One—sorting out prisoners and helping at the Special Court of Justice. In the following few years he did the same in Klagenfurt (Austria) and Oppeln (Opole, Upper Silesia—now Poland). Berlin was next. Duffill got a job with the celebrated firm of Price, Waterhouse, the international accountants. He stayed in Berlin for ten years, abruptly resigning in 1935 and leaving—fleeing, some people said—for England.

Politically, he was of the left. His friends in Berlin thought he might be gathering information for the British secret service. ("One felt he would have made the ideal agent," an old friend of Duffill's told me.) In any case, he left Germany so suddenly, it was assumed that he was being pursued by Nazi agents or wolves from the Sturm Abteilung. He made it safely home, and he was also able to get all his money out of Germany ("an exceedingly clever and daring feat," another friend told me. "His fortune was considerable.").

He may have had a nervous breakdown then; there was some speculation. He sank for a year, reemerging in 1936 as a chief accountant for an American movie company. Two years later, a letter of reference said that Duffill was "thoroughly acquainted with various sides of the film trade." In 1939 there was another gap, lasting until 1945: the war certainly—but where was Duffill? No one could tell me. His brother said, "Richard never discussed his working life or his world traveling with us."

In the late forties, he apparently rejoined Price, Waterhouse and traveled throughout Europe. He went to Egypt and Turkey; he returned to Germany; he went to Sweden and Russia, "for whose leaders he had the greatest admiration."

After his retirement he continued to travel. He had never married. He was always alone. But the snapshots he kept showed him to be a very stylish dresser—waistcoat, plus fours, cashmere overcoat, homburg, stickpin. A characteristic of natty dressers is that they wear too many clothes. Duffill's snapshots showed this; and he always wore a hat.

He wore a rug-like wig, I was told. "It stuck out in the back." He had had brain surgery. "He once played tennis in Cairo." He had gone on socialist holidays to Eastern Europe. He hated Hitler. He was very "spiritual," one of his old friends said. He became interested in the philosophy of George Ivanovich Gurdjieff and was a close friend of the great Gurdjieff scholar John Godolphin Bennett. "And after a while Richard got frightfully steamed up about dervishes," Bennett's widow told me. That was why Duffill was on his way to Istanbul, she said—to renew his acquaintance with some whirling dervishes!

But what I wanted to know was what had happened to him after the Orient Express pulled out of Domodossola.

Mrs. Jack said, "He got out at a station. He didn't tell me where. He had left his luggage on the train. Then the train pulled out. He had inquired when the next train was, and they told him the time—five o'clock. Only a few hours, he thought. But he had got mixed up. He thought they meant P.M. and they actually meant A.M.—five the next morning. He had a very bad night, and the next day he went to—where was it? Venice? Yes, he collected his luggage"—the paper bags I had left with the *controllore*—"and eventually got to Istanbul."

So he had made it!

I told Mrs. Jack who I was and how I had met Mr. Duffill.

She said, "Oh, yes, I read your book! My neighbor's son is an avid reader. He told us about it. He said, 'I think you should see this—I think this is our Mr. Duffill.' And then everyone in Barrow read it."

I was eager to know whether Mr. Duffill himself had read it.

"I wanted him to see it," Mrs. Jack said. "I put a copy aside. But when he came over, he wasn't too good. He didn't see it. The next time he came over I forgot about the book. That was the last time, really. He had his stroke and just deteriorated. And he died. So he never saw it—"

Thank God for that, I thought.

What an interesting man that stranger had been! He had seemed frail, elderly, a little crazy and suspicious on the Orient Express. Typical, I had thought. But now I knew how unusual he had been—brave, kind, secretive, resourceful, solitary, brilliant. He had slept and snored in the upper berth of my compartment. I had not known him at all, but the more I found out about him, the more I missed him. It would have been a privilege to know him personally, and yet even in friendship he would never have confirmed what I strongly suspected—that he had almost certainly been a spy.

Looking out the Window at Yugoslavia

THERE WERE WOMEN, BUT THEY WERE OLD, SHAWLED against the sun and yoked to green watering cans in trampled cornfields. The landscape was low and uneven, barely supporting in its dust a few farm animals, maybe five motionless cows, and a herdsman leaning on a stick watching them starve in the same way the scarecrows—two plastic bags on a bony crosspiece—watched the devastated fields of cabbages and peppers. And beyond the rows of blue cabbage, a pink pig butted the splintery fence of his small pen and a cow lay under goalposts of saplings in an unused football field. Red peppers, as crimson and pointed as clusters of poinsettias, dried in the sun outside farm cottages in districts where farming consisted of men stumbling after oxen dragging wooden plows and harrows, or occasionally wobbling on bicycles loaded with hay bales. Herdsmen were not simply herdsmen; they were sentries, guarding little flocks from marauders: four cows watched by a woman, three gray pigs driven by a man with a truncheon, scrawny chickens watched by scrawny children. "In Yugoslavia we have three things," I was told, "freedom, women, and drinking." A woman in a field tipped a water bottle to her mouth; she swallowed and bent from the waist to continue tying up cornstalks. Large ocher squashes sat plumply in fields of withering vines; people priming pumps and swinging buckets out of wells on long poles; tall narrow haystacks, and pepper fields in so many stages of ripeness I first took them for flower gardens. It is a feeling of utter quietness, deep rural isolation the train briefly penetrates. It goes on without a change for hours, this afternoon in Yugoslavia, and then all people disappear and the effect is eerie: roads without cars or bicycles, cottages with empty windows at the fringes of empty fields, trees heavy with apples and no one picking them. Perhaps it's the wrong time— three-thirty; perhaps it's too hot. But where are the people who stacked that hay and set those peppers so carefully to dry? The train passes on—that's the beauty of a train, this heedless movement—but it passes on to more of the same. Six neat beehives, a derelict steam engine with wildflowers garlanding its smokestack, a stalled ox at a level crossing. In the heat haze of the afternoon my compartment grows dusty, and down at the front of the train Turks lie all over their seats, sleeping with their mouths open and children wakeful on their stomachs. At each river and bridge there were square brick emplacements, like Croatian copies of Martello towers, pocked by bombs. Then I saw a man, headless, bent over in a field, camouflaged by cornstalks that were taller than he; I wondered if I had missed all the others because they were made so tiny by their crops.

There was a drama outside Nis. At a road near the track a crowd of people fought to look at a horse, still in its traces and hitched to an overloaded wagon, lying dead on its side in a mud puddle in which the wagon was obviously stuck. I imagined its heart had burst when it tried to free the wagon. And it had just happened: children were calling to their friends, a man was dropping his bike and running back for a look, and farther along a man pissing against a fence was straining to see the horse. The scene was composed like a Flemish painting in which the pissing man was a vivid detail. The train, the window frame holding the scene for moments, made it a picture. The man at the fence flicks the last droplets from his penis and, tucking it in his baggy pants, begins to sprint; the picture is complete.

"I HATE SIGHT-SEEING," SAID MOLESWORTH. WE WERE AT THE corridor window and I had just been reprimanded by a Yugoslav policeman for snapping a picture of a steam locomotive that, in the late afternoon sun and the whirling dust the thousands of homeward-bound commuters had raised crossing the railway lines, stood amidst a magnificent exhalation of blue vapors mingling with clouds of gold gnats. Now we were in a rocky gorge outside Nis, on the way to Dimitrovgrad, the cliffs rising as we moved and holding occasional symmetries, like remainders of intelligent brickwork in the battlements of a ruined castle. The sight of this seemed to tire Molesworth, and I think he felt called upon to explain his fatigue. "All that tramping around with guidebooks," he said after a moment. "In those horrible crocodiles of tourists, in and out of churches, museums, and mosques. I just like to be still, find a comfortable chair, absorb a country."

Dusk in Central Turkey

IT IS DUSK, THE SERENEST HOUR IN CENTRAL TURKEY: A FEW bright stars depend from a velvet blue sky, the mountains are suitably black, and the puddles near the spigots of village wells have the shimmering color and uncertain shape of pools of mercury. Night falls quickly, and it is all black, and only the smell of the dust still settling reminds you of the exhausting day.

"Mister?" It is the green-eyed Turkish conductor on his way to lock the sleeping-car door against the marauders he imagines in the rest of the train.

"Yes?"

"Turkey good or bad?"

"Good," I said.

"Thank you, mister."

Hippies lay on their seats lengthwise, hogging half the

compartment, and humped under the astonished eyes of Turkish women who sat staring in dark *yashmaks*, their hands clasped between their knees. Occasionally, I saw an amorous pair leave their compartment hand in hand to go copulate in a toilet.

Most were on their way to India and Nepal, because

*The wildest dreams of Kew are the facts of Khatmandhu,
And the crimes of Clapham chaste in Martaban.*

But the majority of them, going for the first time, had that look of frozen apprehension that is the mask on the face of an escapee. Indeed, I had no doubt that the teenaged girls who made up the bulk of these loose tribal groups would eventually appear on the notice boards of American consulates in Asia, in blurred snapshots or retouched high school graduation pictures; MISSING PERSON and HAVE YOU SEEN THIS GIRL? These initiates had leaders who were instantly recognizable by the way they dressed: the faded dervish outfit, the ragged shoulder bag, the jewelry—earrings, amulets, bracelets, necklaces. Status derived solely from experience, and it was possible to tell from the ornaments alone—that jangling in the corridor—whose experience had made him the leader of his particular group. All in all, a social order familiar to the average Masai tribesman.

I tried to find out where they were going. It was not easy. They seldom ate in the dining car; they often slept; they were not allowed in the fastness of the de luxe sleeping car. Some stood by the windows in the corridor, in the trance-like state the Turkish landscape induces in travelers. I sidled up to them and asked them their plans. One did not even turn around. He was a man of about thirty-five, with dusty hair, a T-shirt that read MOTO-GUZZI, and a small gold earring in the lobe of his ear. I surmised that he had sold his motorcycle for a ticket to India. He held the windowsill and stared at the empty reddish yellow flatlands. In reply to my question he said softly, "Pondicherry."

"The ashram?" Auroville, a kind of spiritual Levite town dedicated to the memory of Sri Aurobindo and at that time ruled over by his ninety-year-old French mistress (the "Mother"), is located near Pondicherry, in South India.

"Yes. I want to stay there as long as possible."

"How long?"

"Years." He regarded a passing village and nodded. "If they let me."

It was the tone of a man who tells you, with a mixture of piety and arrogance, that he has a vocation. But Moto-Guzzi had a wife and children in California. Interesting: he had fled his children and some of the girls in his group had fled their parents.

Another fellow sat on the steps of the coach, dangling his feet in the wind. He was eating an apple. I asked him where he was going. "Maybe try Nepal," he said. He took a bite of the apple. "Maybe Ceylon, if it's happening there." He took another bite. The apple was like the globe he was calmly apportioning to himself, as small, bright, and accessible. He poised his very white teeth and bit again. "Maybe Bali." He was chewing. "Maybe go to Australia." He took a last bite and winged the apple into the dust. "What are you, writing a book?"

Sadik

AGAIN I SHOWED THE CONDUCTOR MY TICKET. "FIRST-CLASS ticket," I said. "You give me first-class couchette."

"No couchette," he said. He pointed to my berth in a second-class compartment with three Australians in it.

"No," I said. I pointed to an empty compartment. "I want this one."

"No." He gave me a fanatical grin.

He was grinning at my hand. I held thirty Turkish liras (about two dollars). His hand appeared near mine. I dropped my voice and whispered the word that is known all over the East, *"Baksheesh."*

He took the money and pocketed it. He got my bag from the Australian compartment and carried it to another compartment in which there were a battered suitcase and a box of crackers. He slid the bag into the luggage rack and patted the berth. He asked if I wanted sheets and blankets. I said yes. He got them, and a pillow, too. He drew the curtains, shutting out the sun. He bowed and brought me a pitcher of ice water, and he smiled, as if to say, "All this could have been yours yesterday."

The suitcase and crackers belonged to a large bald Turk named Sadik, who wore baggy woolen trousers and a stretched sweater. He was from one of the wilder parts of Turkey, the Upper Valley of Greater Zap; he had boarded the train in Van; he was going to Australia.

He came in and drew his arm across his sweating face. He said, "Are you in here?"

"Yes."

"How much did you give him?"

I told him.

He said, "I gave him fifteen rials. He is very dishonest, but now he is on our side. He will not put anyone else in here, so now we have this big room together."

Sadik smiled; he had crooked teeth. It is not skinny people who look hungry, but rather fat ones, and Sadik looked famished.

"I think it's only fair to say," I said, wondering how I was going to finish the sentence, "that I'm not, um, queer. Well, you know, I don't like boys and—"

"And me, I don't like," said Sadik, and with that he lay down and went to sleep. He had the gift of slumber; he needed only to be horizontal and he was sound asleep, and he always slept in the same sweater and trousers. He never took them off; and for the duration of the trip to Teheran he neither shaved nor washed.

He was an unlikely tycoon. He admitted he behaved like a pig, but he had lots of money and his career was a successful record of considerable ingenuity. He had started out exporting Turkish curios to France and he seems to have been in the vanguard of the movement, monopolizing the puzzle ring and copper-pot trade in Europe long before anyone else thought of it. He paid no export duties in Turkey, no import duties in France. He managed this by shipping crates of worthless articles to the French border and warehousing them there. He went to French wholesalers with his samples, took orders, and left the wholesalers the headache of importing the goods. He did this for three years and banked the money in Switzerland.

"When I have enough money," said Sadik, whose English was not perfect, "I like to start a travel agency. Where you want to go? Budapesht? Prague? Romania? Bulgaria? All nice places, oh boy! Turkish people like to travel. But they are very silly. They don't speak English. They say to me, 'Mister Sadik, I want a coffee'—this is in Prague. I say, 'Ask the waiter.' They are afraid. They shout their eyes. But they have money in their packets. I say to the waiter, 'Coffee'—he understand. Everyone understand coffee, but Turkish people don't speak any language, so all the time I am translator. This, I tell you, drive me crazy. The people they follow me. 'Mister Sadik, take me to a nightclub'; 'Mister Sadik, find me a gairl.' They follow me even to the lavabo and sometime I want to escape, so I am clever and I use the service elevator.

"I give up Budapesht, Belgrade. I decide to take pilgrims to Mecca. They pay me five thousand liras and I take care of everything. I get smallpox injections and stamp the book—sometimes I stamp the book and don't get smallpox injections! I have a friend in the medical. Ha! But I take good care of them, buy them rubber mattresses, each person one mattress, blow them up so you don't have to sleep on the floor. I take them to Mecca, Medina, Jiddah, then I leave them. 'I have business in Jiddah,' I say. But I go to Beirut. You know Beirut? Nice place—nightclubs, gairls, lots of fun. Then I come back to Jiddah, pick up the *hajis*, and bring them back to Istanbul. Good profit."

I asked Sadik why, if he was a Muslim and he was so close to Mecca, he never made the *haj* himself.

"Once you go to Mecca you have to make promise—no

drinking, no swearing, no women, money to poor people."
He laughed. "Is for old men. I'm not ready!"

He was headed now for Australia, which he pronounced
"Owstraalia"; he had another idea. It had come to him one
day in Saudi Arabia when he was bored (he said as soon
as he began making money in a project he lost interest in
it). His new idea concerned the export of Turks to Australia. There was a shortage of workers there. He would go,
and, much as he had sold puzzle rings to the French, visit
Australian industrialists and find out what sort of skilled
people they required. He would make a list. His partner in
Istanbul would get up a large group of emigrants and deal
with the paperwork, obtaining passports, health cards, and
references. Then the Turks would be sent on a charter flight
that Sadik would arrange, and after collecting a fee from
the Turks he would collect from the Australians. He
winked. "Good profit."

It was Sadik who pointed out to me that the hippies were
doomed. They dressed like wild Indians, he said, but basically they were middle-class Americans. They didn't understand *baksheesh*, and because they were always holding
tight to their money and expecting to scrounge food and
hospitality they would always lose. He resented the fact that
the hippie chiefs were surrounded by such young pretty
girls. "These guys are ugly and I am ugly too, so why don't
the gairls like me?"

He enjoyed telling stories against himself. The best one
concerned a blonde he had picked up in an Istanbul bar. It
was midnight; he was drunk and feeling lecherous. He took
the blonde home and made love to her twice, then slept for
a few hours, woke up, and made love to her again. Late
the next day as he was crawling out of bed he noticed the
blonde needed a shave and then he saw the wig and the
man's enormous penis. " 'Only Sadik,' my friends say,
"only Sadik can make love to a man three times and think
it is a woman!' But I was very drunk."

Peshawar

PESHAWAR IS A PRETTY TOWN. I WOULD GLADLY MOVE THERE, settle down on a veranda, and grow old watching sunsets in the Khyber Pass. Peshawar's widely spaced mansions, all excellent examples of Anglo-Muslim Gothic, are spread along broad sleepy roads under cool trees: just the place to recover from the hideous experience of Kabul. You hail a *tonga* at the station and ride to the hotel, where on the veranda the chairs have swing-out extensions for you to prop up your legs and get the blood circulating. A nimble waiter brings a large bottle of Murree Export Lager. The hotel is empty; the other guests have risked a punishing journey to Swat in hopes of being received by His Highness the Wali. You sleep soundly under a tent of mosquito net and are awakened by the fluting of birds for an English breakfast that begins with porridge and ends with a kidney. Afterwards a *tonga* to the museum.

A little distance from the museum, when I was buying some matches at a shop, I was offered morphine. I wondered if I heard right and asked to see it. The man took out a matchbox (perhaps "matches" was a code word?) and slipped it open. Inside was a small vial marked MORPHINE SULPHATE, ten white tablets. The man said they were to be taken in the arm and told me that I could have the whole lot for twenty dollars. I offered him five dollars and laughed, but he saw he was being mocked. He turned surly and told me to go away.

I would have liked to stay longer in Peshawar. I liked lazing on the veranda, shaking out my newspaper, and watching the *tongas* go by, and I enjoyed hearing Pakistanis discussing the coming war with Afghanistan. They were

23

worried and aggrieved, but I gave them encouragement and said they would find an enthusiastic well-wisher in me if they ever cared to invade that barbarous country. My prompt reassurance surprised them, but they saw I was sincere. "I hope you will help us," one said. I explained that I was not a very able soldier. He said, "Not you in person, but America in general." I said I couldn't promise national support, but that I would be glad to put a word in for them.

Everything is easy in Peshawar except buying a train ticket. This is a morning's work and leaves you exhausted. First you consult the timetable, *Pakistan Western Railways*, and find that the Khyber Mail leaves at four o'clock. Then you go to the Information window and are told it leaves at nine-fifty P.M. The Information man sends you to Reservations. The man in Reservations is not there, but a sweeper says he'll be right back. He returns in an hour and helps you decide on a class. He writes your name in a book and gives you a chit. You take the chit to Bookings, where, for 108 rupees (about ten dollars), you are handed two tickets and an initialed chit. You go back to Reservations, and wait for the man to return once again. He returns, initials the tickets, examines the chit, and writes the details in a ledger about six feet square.

Nor was this the only difficulty. The man in Reservations told me no bedding was available on the Khyber Mail. I suspected he was angling for *baksheesh* and gave him six rupees to find bedding. After twenty minutes he said it had all been booked. He was very sorry. I asked for my bribe back. He said, "As you wish."

Later in the day I worked out the perfect solution. I was staying in Dean's Hotel, one in a chain of hotels that includes Faletti's in Lahore. I had to pester the clerk a good deal, but he finally agreed to give me what bedding I needed. I would give him sixty rupees and he would give me a chit. In Lahore I would give the bedding and chit to Faletti's and get my sixty rupees back. This was the chit:

Please refund this man Rs. 60/–(RS. SIXTY ONLY) if he produce you this receipt and One Blanket and One Sheet.

One Pillow and Credit it in Dean's Hotel Peshawar Account.

The Village in the Railway Station

THE SIGNS IN AMRITSAR STATION (THIRD-CLASS EXIT, SECOND-CLASS LADIES' WAITING ROOM, FIRST-CLASS TOILET, SWEEPERS ONLY) had given me a formal idea of Indian society. The less formal reality I saw at seven in the morning in the Northern Railways Terminal in Old Delhi. To understand the real India, the Indians say, you must go to the villages. But that is not strictly true, because the Indians have carried their villages to the railway stations. In the daytime it is not apparent—you might mistake any of these people for beggars, ticketless travelers (sign: TICKETLESS TRAVEL IS A SOCIAL EVIL), or unlicensed hawkers. At night and in the early morning the station village is complete, a community so preoccupied that the thousands of passengers arriving and departing leave it undisturbed: they detour around it. The railway dwellers possess the station, but only the new arrival notices this. He feels something is wrong because he has not learned the Indian habit of ignoring the obvious, making a detour to preserve his calm. The newcomer cannot believe he has been plunged into such intimacy so soon. In another country this would all be hidden from him, and not even a trip to a village would reveal with this clarity the pattern of life. The village in rural India tells the visitor very little except that he is required to keep his distance and limit his experience of the place to tea or a meal in a stuffy parlor. The life of the village, its interior, is denied to him.

But the station village is all interior, and the shock of this exposure made me hurry away. I didn't feel I had any right

to watch people bathing under a low faucet—naked among
the incoming tide of office workers; men sleeping late on
their *charpoys* or tucking up their turbans; women with
nose rings and cracked yellow feet cooking stews of begged
vegetables over smoky fires, suckling infants, folding bed-
rolls; children pissing on their toes; little girls, in oversized
frocks falling from their shoulders, fetching water in tin
cans from the third-class toilet; and, near a newspaper ven-
dor, a man lying on his back, holding a baby up to admire
and tickling it. Hard work, poor pleasures, and the scrim-
mage of appetite. This village has no walls.

Mr. Bhardwaj on the Railcar
to Simla

AT SEVEN-FIFTEEN, THE DRIVER OF THE RAILCAR INSERTED A
long-handled crank into the engine and gave it a jerk. The
engine shook and coughed and, still juddering and smoking,
began to whine. Within minutes we were on the slope,
looking down at the top of Kalka Station, where in the train
yard two men were winching a huge steam locomotive
around in a circle. The railcar's speed was a steady ten
miles an hour, zigzagging in and out of the steeply pitched
hill, reversing on switchbacks through the terraced gardens
and the white flocks of butterflies. We passed through several tunnels before I noticed they were numbered; a large
number 4 was painted over the entrance of the next one.
The man seated beside me, who had told me he was a civil
servant in Simla, said there were 103 tunnels all together. I
tried not to notice the numbers after that. Outside the car,
there was a sheer drop, hundreds of feet down, for the railway, which was opened in 1904, is cut directly into the hillside, and the line above is notched like the skidway on a
toboggan run, circling the hills.

After thirty minutes everyone in the railcar was asleep except the civil servant and me. At the little stations along the way, the postman in the rear seat awoke from his doze to throw a mailbag out the window to a waiting porter on the platform. I tried to take pictures, but the landscape eluded me: one vista shifted into another, lasting only seconds, a dizzying displacement of hill and air, of haze and all the morning shades of green. The meat-grinder cogs working against the rack under the railcar ticked like an aging clock and made me drowsy. I took out my inflatable pillow, blew it up, put it under my head, and slept peacefully in the sunshine until I was awakened by the thud of the railcar's brakes and the banging of doors.

"Ten minutes," said the driver.

We were just below a wooden structure, a doll's house, its window boxes overflowing with red blossoms, and moss trimming its wide eaves. This was Bangu Station. It had a wide complicated veranda on which a waiter stood with a menu under his arm. The railcar passengers scrambled up the stairs. I smelled eggs and coffee and heard the Bengalis quarreling with the waiters in English.

I walked down the gravel paths to admire the well-tended flower beds and the carefully mown lengths of turf beside the track; below the station a rushing stream gurgled, and signs there, and near the flower beds, read NO PLUCK ING. A waiter chased me down to the stream and called out, "We have juices! You like fresh mango juice? A little porridge? Coffee-tea?"

We resumed the rise, and the time passed quickly as I dozed again and woke to higher mountains, with fewer trees, stonier slopes, and huts perched more precariously. The haze had disappeared and the hillsides were bright, but the air was cool and a fresh breeze blew through the open windows of the railcar. In every tunnel the driver switched on orange lamps, and the racket of the clattering wheels increased and echoed. After Solon the only people in the railcar were a family of Bengali pilgrims (all of them sound asleep, snoring, their faces turned up), the civil servant, the postman, and me. The next stop was Solon Brewery, where the air was pungent with yeast and hops, and after that we passed through pine forests and cedar groves. On one stretch a baboon the size of a six-year-old crept off the tracks to let us go by. I remarked on the largeness of the creature.

The civil servant said, "There was once a *saddhu*—a holy man—who lived near Simla. He could speak to monkeys. A certain Englishman had a garden, and all the time the monkeys were causing him trouble. Monkeys can be very destructive. The Englishman told this *saddhu* his problem. The *saddhu* said, 'I will see what I can do.' Then the *saddhu* went into the forest and assembled all the monkeys. He said, 'I hear you are troubling the Englishman. That is bad. You must stop; leave his garden alone. If I hear that you are causing damage I will treat you very harshly.' And from that time onward the monkeys never went into the Englishman's garden."

"Do you believe the story?"

"Oh, yes. But the man is now dead—the *saddhu*. I don't know what happened to the Englishman. Perhaps he went away, like the rest of them."

A little farther on, he said, "What do you think of India?"

"It's a hard question," I said. I wanted to tell him about the children I had seen that morning pathetically raiding the leftovers of my breakfast, and ask him if he thought there was any truth in Mark Twain's comment on Indians: "It is a curious people. With them, all life seems to be sacred except human life." But I added instead, "I haven't been here very long."

"I will tell you what I think," he said. "If all the people who are talking about honesty, fair play, socialism, and so forth—if they began to practice it themselves, India will do well. Otherwise there will be a revolution."

He was an unsmiling man in his early fifties and had the stern features of a Brahmin. He neither drank nor smoked, and before he joined the civil service he had been a Sanskrit scholar in an Indian university. He got up at five every morning, had an apple, a glass of milk, and some almonds; he washed and said his prayers and after that took a long walk. Then he went to his office. To set an example for his junior officers he always walked to work, he furnished his office sparsely, and he did not require his bearer to wear a khaki uniform. He admitted that his example was unpersuasive. His junior officers had parking permits, sumptuous furnishings, and uniformed bearers.

"I ask them why all this money is spent for nothing. They tell me to make a good first impression is very important. I say to the blighters, 'What about *second* impression?' "

Blighters was a word that occurred often in his speech. Lord Clive was a blighter and so were most of the other viceroys. Blighters ask for bribes; blighters try to cheat the Accounts Department; blighters are living in luxury and talking about socialism. It was a point of honor with this civil servant that he had never in his life given or received *baksheesh*: "Not even a single paisa." Some of his clerks had, and in eighteen years in the civil service he had personally fired thirty-two people. He thought it might be a record. I asked him what they had done wrong.

"Gross incompetence," he said, "pinching money, hanky-panky. But I never fire anyone without first having a good talk with his parents. There was a blighter in the Audit Department, always pinching girls' bottoms. Indian girls from good families! I warned him about this, but he wouldn't stop. So I told him I wanted to see his parents. The blighter said his parents lived fifty miles away. I gave him money for their bus fare. They were poor, and they were quite worried about the blighter. I said to them, 'Now I want you to understand that your son is in deep trouble. He is causing annoyance to the lady members of this department. Please talk to him and make him understand that if this continues, I will have no choice but to sack him.' Parents go away, blighter goes back to work, and ten days later he is at it again. I suspended him on the spot, then I chargesheeted him."

I wondered whether any of these people had tried to take revenge on him.

"Yes, there was one. He got himself drunk one night and came to my house with a knife. 'Come outside and I will kill you!' That sort of thing. My wife was upset. But I was angry. I couldn't control myself. I dashed outside and fetched the blighter a blooming kick. He dropped his knife and began to cry. 'Don't call the police,' he said. 'I have a wife and children.' He was a complete coward, you see. I let him go and everyone criticized me—they said I should have brought charges. But I told them he'll never bother anyone again.

"And there was another time. I was working for Heavy Electricals, doing an audit for some cheaters in Bengal. Faulty construction, double entries, and estimates that were five times what they should have been. There was also immorality. One bloke—son of the contractor, very wealthy—kept four harlots. He gave them whisky and made them take their clothes off and run naked into a group of women and children doing *puja*. Disgraceful! Well, they didn't like me at all and the day I left there were four *dacoits* with knives waiting for me on the station road. But I expected that, so I took a different road, and the blighters never caught me. A month later two auditors were murdered by *dacoits*."

The railcar tottered around a cliffside, and on the opposite slope, across a deep valley, was Simla. Most of the town fits the ridge like a saddle made entirely of rusty roofs, but as we drew closer the fringes seemed to be sliding into the valley. Simla is unmistakable, for as *Murray's Handbook* indicates, "its skyline is incongruously dominated by a Gothic Church, a baronial castle and a Victorian country mansion." Above these brick piles is the sharply pointed peak of Jakhu (eight thousand feet); below are the clinging house fronts. The southerly aspect of Simla is so steep that flights of cement stairs take the place of roads. From the railcar it looked an attractive place, a town of rusting splendor with snowy mountains in the background.

"My office is in that castle," said the civil servant.

"Gorton Castle," I said, referring to my handbook. "Do you work for the Accountant General of the Punjab?"

"Well, I *am* the A.G.," he said. But he was giving information, not boasting. At Simla Station the porter strapped my suitcase to his back (he was a Kashmiri, up for the sea-

son). The civil servant introduced himself as Vishnu
Bhardwaj and invited me for tea that afternoon.

The Mall was filled with Indian vacationers taking their
morning stroll, warmly dressed children, women with cardi-
gans over their saris, and men in tweed suits, clasping the
green Simla guidebook in one hand and a cane in the other.
The promenading has strict hours, nine to twelve in the
morning and four to eight in the evening, determined by
mealtimes and shop openings. These hours were fixed a
hundred years ago, when Simla was the summer capital of
the Indian empire, and they have not varied. The architecture is similarly unchanged—it is all high Victorian, with
the vulgarly grandiose touches colonial labor allowed, ex-
travagant gutters and porticoes, buttressed by pillars and
steelwork to prevent its slipping down the hill. The Gaiety
Theatre (1887) is still the Gaiety Theatre (though when I
was there it was the venue of a "Spiritual Exhibition" I was
not privileged to see); pettifogging continues in Gorton
Castle, as praying does in Christ Church (1857), the Angli-
can cathedral; the viceroy's lodge (Rastrapati Nivas), a baronial mansion, is now the Indian Institute of Advanced
Studies, but the visiting scholars creep about with the diffi-
dence of caretakers maintaining the sepulchral stateliness of
the place. Scattered among these large Simla buildings are
the bungalows—Holly Lodge, Romney Castle, The Bricks,
Forest View, Sevenoaks, Fernside—but the inhabitants now
are Indians, or rather that inheriting breed of Indian that in-
sists on the guidebook, the walking stick, the cravat, tea at
four, and an evening stroll to Scandal Point. It is the Empire with a dark complexion, an imperial outpost that the
mimicking vacationers have preserved from change, though
not the place of highly colored intrigues described in *Kim*,
and certainly tamer than it was a century ago. After all,
Lola Montez, the *grande horizontale*, began her whoring in
Simla, and the only single women I saw were short red-
cheeked Tibetan laborers in quilted coats, who walked
along the Mall with heavy stones in slings on their backs.

I had tea with the Bhardwaj family. It was not the simple
meal I had expected. There were eight or nine dishes:
pakora, vegetables fried in batter; *poha*, a rice mixture with

peas, coriander, and turmeric; *khira*, a creamy pudding of rice, milk, and sugar; a kind of fruit salad, with cucumber and lemon added to it, called *chaat*; *murak*, a Tamil savory, like large nutty pretzels; *tikkiya*, potato cakes; *malai* chops, sweet sugary balls topped with cream; and almond-scented *pinnis*. I ate what I could, and the next day I saw Mr. Bhardwaj's office in Gorton Castle. It was as sparsely furnished as he had said on the railcar, and over his desk was this sign:

> I AM NOT INTERESTED IN EXCUSES FOR DELAY;
> I AM INTERESTED ONLY IN A THING DONE.
> —Jawaharlal Nehru

In Jaipur with Mr. Gopal

"WHAT'S THIS?" I ASKED MR. GOPAL, THE EMBASSY LIAI-son man, pointing to a kind of fortress.

"That's a kind of fortress."

He had ridiculed the handbook I had been carrying around: "You have this big book, but I tell you to close it and leave it at hotel because Jaipur is like open book to me." Unwisely, I had taken his advice. We were now six miles outside Jaipur, wading ankle-deep through sand drifts toward the wrecked settlement of Galta. Earlier we had passed through a jamboree of some two hundred baboons: "Act normal," said Mr. Gopal, as they hopped and chattered and showed their teeth, clustering on the road with a curiosity that bordered on menace. The landscape was rocky and very dry, and each rugged hill was capped with a cracked fortress.

"Whose is it?"

"The Maharajah's."

"No, who built it?"

"You would not know his name."

"Do *you*?"

Mr. Gopal walked on. It was dusk, and the buildings crammed into the Galta gorge were darkening. A monkey chattered and leaped to a branch in a banyan tree above Mr. Gopal's head, yanking the branch down and making a punkah's *whoosh*. We entered the gate and crossed a courtyard to some ruined buildings, with colored frescoes of trees and people on their façades. Some had been raked with indecipherable graffiti and painted over; whole panels had been chiseled away.

"What's this?" I asked. I hated him for making me leave my handbook behind.

"Ah," said Mr. Gopal. It was a temple enclosure. Some men dozed in the archways, others squatted on their haunches, and just outside the enclosure were some tea and vegetable stalls whose owners leaned against more frescoes, rubbing them away with their backs. I was struck by the solitude of the place—a few people at sundown, no one speaking, and it was so quiet I could hear the hooves of the goats clattering on the cobblestones, the murmuring of the distant monkeys.

"A temple?"

Mr. Gopal thought a moment. "Yes," he said finally, "a kind of temple."

On the ornate temple walls, stuck with posters, defaced with chisels, pissed on, and scrawled over with huge Devanagri script advertising Jaipur businesses, there was a blue enamel sign, warning visitors in Hindi and English that it was "forbidden to desecrate, deface, mark or otherwise abuse the walls." The sign itself had been defaced: the enamel was chipped—it looked partly eaten.

Farther along, the cobblestone road became a narrow path and then a steep staircase cut into the rock walls of the gorge. At the top of this was a temple facing a still, black pool. Insects swimming in circles on the pool's surface made minuscule ripples, and small clouds of vibrant gnats hovered over the water. The temple was an unambitious niche in the rock face, a shallow cave, lighted with oil lamps and tapers. On either side of its portals were seven-foot marble slabs, the shape of those handed down from Sinai but with a weight that would give the most muscular prophet a hernia. These tablets had numbered instructions cut into them in two languages. In the failing light I copied down the English.

1. The use of soap in the temple and washing clothes is strictly prohibited
2. Please do not bring shoes near the tank
3. It does not suit for women to take bath among male members
4. Spitting while swimming is quite a bad habit
5. Do not spoil others' clothes by splitting water while swimming
6. Do not enter the temple with wet clothes
7. Do not spit improperly to make the places dirty

"Splitting?" I said to Mr. Gopal. "What is splitting?"

"That does not say splitting."

"Take a look at number five."

"It says splashing."

"It says splitting."

"It says—"

We walked over to the tablet. The letters, two inches high, were cut deep into the marble.

"—splitting," said Mr. Gopal. "I've never run across that one before. I think it's a kind of splashing."

The Grand Trunk Express to the Real India

THE LUMBERING EXPRESS THAT BISECTS INDIA, A 1,400-mile slash from Delhi south to Madras, gets its name from the route. It might easily have derived it from the kind of luggage the porters were heaving on board. There were grand trunks all over the platform. I had never seen such heaps of belongings in my life, or so many laden people; they were like evacuees who had been given time to pack, lazily fleeing an ambiguous catastrophe. In the best of times there is nothing simple about an Indian boarding a train, but these people climbing into the Grand Trunk Express looked as if they were setting up house—they had the air, and the merchandise, of people moving in. Within minutes the compartments were colonized, the trunks were emptied, the hampers, food baskets, water bottles, bedrolls, and Gladstones put in place; and before the train started up its character changed, for while we were still standing at Delhi Station the men stripped off their baggy trousers and twill jackets and got into traditional South Indian dress: the sleeveless gym-class undershirt and the sarong they call a *lungi*. These were scored with packing creases. It was as if, at once—in expectation of the train whistle—they all dropped the disguise they had adopted for Delhi, the Madras-bound express allowing them to assume their true identity. The train was full of Tamils; and they had moved in so completely, I felt like a stranger among residents, which was odd, since I had arrived earlier than anyone else.

Tamils are black and bony; they have thick straight hair and their teeth are prominent and glister from repeated scrubbings with peeled green twigs. Watch a Tamil going over his teeth with an eight-inch twig and you begin to wonder if he isn't trying to yank a branch out of his stomach. One of the attractions of the Grand Trunk Express is that its route takes in the forests of Madhya Pradesh, where the best toothbrush twigs are found; they are sold in bundles, bound like cheroots, at the stations in the province. Tamils are also modest. Before they change their clothes each makes a toga of his bedsheet, and, hopping up and down and working his elbows, he kicks his shoes and trousers off, all the while babbling in that rippling speech that resembles the sputtering of a man singing in the shower. Tamils seem to talk constantly—only toothbrushing silences them. Pleasure for a Tamil is discussing a large matter (life, truth, beauty, "walues") over a large meal (very wet vege-tables studded with chilies and capsicums, and served with damp poori and two mounds of glutinous rice). The Tamils were happy on the Grand Trunk Express: their language was spoken; their food was served; their belongings were dumped helter-skelter, giving the train the customary clutter of a Tamil home.

I started out with three Tamils in my compartment. After they changed, unstrapped their suitcases, unbuckled bed-rolls, and had a meal (one gently scoffed at my spoon: "Food taken with hand tastes different from food taken with spoon—sort of metal taste"), they spent an immense amount of time introducing themselves to one another. In bursts of Tamil speech were English words like "re-posting," "casual leave," "annual audit." As soon as I joined the conversation they began, with what I thought was a high degree of tact and courage, to speak to one an-other in English. They were in agreement on one point: Delhi was barbarous.

"I am staying at Lodi Hotel. I am booked months ahead. Everyone in Trich tells me it is a good hotel. Hah! I cannot use telephone. You have used telephone?"

"I cannot use telephone at all."

"It is not Lodi Hotel," said the third Tamil. "It is Delhi."

"Yes, my friend, you are right," said the second.

"I say to receptionist, 'Kindly stop speaking to me in Hindi. Does no one speak English around this place? Speak to me in English if you please!'"

"It is really atrocious situation."

"Hindi, Hindi, Hindi. *Tcha!*"

I said I'd had similar experiences. They shook their heads and added more stories of distress. We sat like four fugitives from savagery, bemoaning the general ignorance of English, and it was one of the Tamils—not I—who pointed out that the Hindi speaker would be lost in London.

I said, "Would he be lost in Madras?"

"English is widely spoken in Madras. We also use Tamil, but seldom Hindi. It is not our language."

"In the south everyone has matric." They had a knowing

ease with abbreviations, "matric" for matriculation, "Trich" for the town of Tiruchchirappalli.

The conductor put his head into the compartment. He was a harassed man with the badges and equipment of Indian authority, a gunmetal puncher, a vindictive pencil, a clipboard thick with damp passenger lists, a bronze conductor's pin, and a khaki pith helmet. He tapped my shoulder.

"Bring your case."

Earlier I had asked for the two-berth compartment I had paid for. He had said they were overbooked. I demanded a refund. He said I'd have to file an application at the place of issue. I accused him of inefficiency. He withdrew. Now he had found a coupé in the next carriage.

"Does this cost extra?" I asked, sliding my suitcase in. I didn't like the extortionate overtones of the word *baksheesh*.

"What you want," he said.

"Then it doesn't."

"I am not saying it does or doesn't. I am not asking."

I liked the approach. I said, "What should I do?"

"To give or not to give." He frowned at his passenger lists. "That is entirely your lookout."

I gave him five rupees.

The compartment was gritty. There was no sink; the drop-leaf table was unhinged; and the rattling at the window, rising to a scream when another train passed, jarred my ears. Sometimes it was an old locomotive that sped by in the night, its kettle boiling, its whistle going, and its pistons leaking a hiss with the warning pitch of a blown valve that precedes an explosion. At about six A.M., near Bhopal, there was a rap on the door—not morning tea, but a candidate for the upper berth. He said, "Excuse me," and crept in.

The forests of Madhya Pradesh, where all the toothbrushes grow, looked like the woods of New Hampshire with the last faint blue range of mountains removed. It was green, uncultivated, and full of leafy bluffs and shady brooks, but as the second day wore on it grew dustier, and New Hampshire gave way to Indian heat and Indian air. Dust collected at the window and sifted in, covering my map, my pipe, my glasses and notebook, my new stock of paperbacks (Joyce's *Exiles*, Browning's poems, *The Narrow Corner* by Somerset Maugham). I had a fine layer of dust on my face; dust furred the mirror, made the plastic seat abrasive and the floor crunchy. The window had to be kept open a crack because of the heat, but the penalty for this breeze was a stream of choking dust from the Central Indian plains.

At Nagpur in the afternoon, my traveling companion (an engineer with an extraordinary scar on his chest), said, "There are primitive people here called Gondis. They are quite strange. One woman may have four to five husbands and vicey-versy."

I bought four oranges at the station, made a note of a sign advertising horoscopes that read MARRY YOUR DAUGHTERS BY SPENDING RS. 12 ONLY, shouted at a little man who was bullying a beggar, and read my handbook's entry for Nagpur (so-called because it is on the River Nag):

> Among the inhabitants are many aborigines known as Gonds. Of these the hill-tribes have black skins, flat noses and thick lips. A cloth round the waist is their chief garment. The religious belief varies from village to village. Nearly all worship the cholera and smallpox deities, and there are traces of serpent worship.

To my relief, the whistle blew and we were on our way. The engineer read the Nagpur paper, I ate my Nagpur oranges and then had a siesta. I awoke to an odd sight, the first rain clouds I'd seen since leaving England. At dusk, near the border of the South Indian province of Andhra Pradesh, broad blue-gray clouds, dark at the edges, hung on the horizon. We were headed for them in a landscape where it had recently rained: now the little stations were splashed with mud, brown puddles had collected at level crossings, and the earth was reddened by the late monsoon. But we were not under the clouds until we reached Chandrapur, a station so small and sooty it is not on the map. There, the rain fell in torrents, and signalmen skipped along the line waving their sodden flags. The people on the platform stood watching from under large black umbrellas that shone with wetness. Some hawkers rushed into the downpour to sell bananas to the train passengers.

A woman crawled into the rain from the shelter of the platform. She appeared to be injured: she was on all fours, moving slowly toward the train—toward me. Her spine, I saw, was twisted with meningitis; she had rags tied to her knees and woodblocks in her hands. She toiled across the tracks with painful slowness, and when she was near the door she looked up. She had a lovely smile—a girl's beaming face on that broken body. She propped herself up and lifted her free hand at me, and waited, her face streaming with rain, her clothes soaked. While I was fishing in my pockets for money the train started up, and my futile gesture was to throw a handful of rupees onto the flooded line.

At the next station I was accosted by another beggar. This was a boy of about ten, wearing a clean shirt and shorts. He implored with his eyes and said rapidly, "Please, sir, give me money. My father and mother have been at station platform for two days. They are stranded. They have no food. My father has no job, my mother's clothes are torn. We must get to Delhi soon and if you give me one or two rupees we will be able."

"The train's going to leave. You'd better hop off."

He said, "Please, sir, give me money. My father and mother—"

He went on mechanically reciting. I urged him to get off the train, but it was clear that apart from his spiel he did not speak English. I walked away.

It had grown dark, the rain was letting up, and I sat reading the engineer's newspaper. The news was of conferences, an incredible number of gatherings in the very titles of which I heard the clack of voices, the rattle of mimeographed sheets, the squeak of folding chairs, and the eternal Indian prologue: "There is one question we all have to ask ourselves—" One Nagpur conference was spending a week discussing "Is the Future of Zoroastrianism in Peril?" On the same page two hundred Indians were reported attending a "Congress of Peace-Loving Countries." "Hinduism: Are We at a Crossroads?" occupied another group, and on the back page there was an advertisement for Raymond's Suitings (slogan: "You'll have something to say in Raymond's Suitings . . ."). The man wearing a Raymond suit was shown addressing a conference audience. He was squinting, making a beckoning gesture; he had something to say. His words were, "Communication is perception. Communication is expectations. Communication is involvement."

A beggar's skinny hand appeared at my compartment door, a bruised forearm, a ragged sleeve. Then the doomed cry, *"Sahib!"*

At Sirpur, just over the border of Andhra Pradesh, the train ground to a halt. Twenty minutes later we were still there. Sirpur is insignificant: the platform is uncovered, the station has two rooms, and there are cows on the veranda. Grass tufts grow out of the ledge of the booking-office window. It smelled of rain and wood smoke and cow dung; it was little more than a hut, dignified with the usual railway signs, of which the most hopeful was TRAINS RUNNING LATE ARE LIKELY TO MAKE UP TIME. Passengers on the Grand Trunk Express began to get out. They promenaded, belching in little groups, grateful for the exercise.

"The engine has packed up," one man told me. "They are sending for a new one. Delay of two hours."

Another man said, "If there was a cabinet minister on this train they would have an engine in ten minutes' time."

The Tamils were raving on the platform. A native of Sirpur wandered out of the darkness with a sack of roasted chickpeas. He was set upon by the Tamils, who bought all the chickpeas and demanded more. A mob of Tamils gathered at the stationmaster's window to howl at a man tapping out Morse code with a little key.

I decided to look for a beer, but just outside the station I was in darkness so complete I had second thoughts. The smell of rain on the vegetation gave a humid richness to the air that was almost sweet. There were cows lying on the road: they were white; I could see them clearly. Using the cows as road markers I walked along until I saw a small orange light about fifty yards away. I headed toward it and came to a little hut, a low poky shack with mud walls and a canvas roof. There was a kerosene lantern hanging over the doorway and another inside lighting the surprised faces of half a dozen tea drinkers, two of whom recognized me from the train.

"What do you want?" one said. "I will ask for it."

"Can I buy a bottle of beer here?"

This was translated. There was laughter. I knew the answer.

"About two kilometers down the road"—the man pointed into the blackness—"there is a bar. You can get beer there."

"How will I find it?"

"A car," he said. He spoke again to the man serving tea. "But there is no car here. Have some tea."

We stood in the hut drinking milky tea out of cracked glasses. A joss stick was lit. No one said a word. The train passengers looked at the villagers; the villagers averted their eyes. The canvas ceiling drooped; the tables were worn shiny; the joss stick filled the room with stinking perfume. The train passengers grew uncomfortable and, in their discomfort, took an exaggerated interest in the calendar, the faded color prints of Shiva and Ganpati. The lanterns flickered in the dead silence as our shadows leaped on the walls.

The Indian who had translated my question said under his breath, "This is the real India!"

*"I Find You English Girl"—
Madras*

THIS WAS WHAT I IMAGINED: SOMEWHERE PAST THE BRICK-and-plaster mansions of Madras, arrayed along Mount Road like so many yellowing wedding cakes, was the Bay of Bengal, on which I would find a breezy seafront restaurant, palm trees, flapping tablecloths. I would sit facing the water, have a fish dinner and five beers, and watch the dancing lights of the little Tamil fishing smacks. Then I would go to bed and be up early for the train to Rameswaram, that village on the tip of India's nose.

"Take me to the beach," I said to the taxi driver. He was an unshaven, wild-haired Tamil with his shirt torn open. He had the look of the feral child in the psychology textbook: feral children—mangled, demented Mowglis—abound in South India. It is said they are suckled by wolves.

"Beach Road?"

"That sounds like the place." I explained that I wanted to eat a fish.

"Twenty rupees."

"I'll give you five."

"Okay, fifteen. Get in."

We drove about two hundred yards and I realized that I was very hungry: turning vegetarian had confused my stomach with what seemed an imperfect substitute for real food. Vegetables subdued my appetite, but a craving—a carnivorous emotion—remained.

"You like English girls?" The taxi driver was turning the steering wheel with his wrists, as a wolf might, given the opportunity to drive a taxi.

"Very much," I said.

"I find you English girl."

"Really?" It seemed an unlikely place to find an English whore—Madras, a city without any apparent prosperity. In Bombay I might have believed it: the sleek Indian business-men, running in and out of the Taj Mahal Hotel, oozing wealth, and driving at top speed past the sleepers on the sidewalk—they were certainly whore fodder. And in Delhi, city of conferees and delegates, I was told there were lots of European hookers cruising through the lobbies of the plush hotels, promising pleasure with a cheery swing of their hips. But in Madras?

The driver spun in his seat and crossed his heart, two slashes with his long nails. "*English* girl."

"Keep your eyes on the road!"

"Twenty-five rupees."

Three dollars and twenty-five cents.

"Pretty girl?"

"*English* girl," he said. "You want?"

I thought this over. It wasn't the girl but the situation that attracted me. An English girl in Madras, whoring for peanuts. I wondered where she lived, and how, and for how long; what had brought her to the godforsaken place? I saw her as a castaway, a fugitive, like Lena in Conrad's *Victory* fleeing a tuneless traveling orchestra in Surabaya. I had once met an English whore in Singapore. She said she was making a fortune. But it wasn't just the money: she preferred Chinese and Indian men to the English, who were not so quick and, worse, usually wanted to spank her.

The driver noticed my silence and slowed down. In the heavy traffic he turned around once again. His cracked teeth, stained with betel juice, were red and gleaming in the lights from the car behind us. He said, "Beach or girl?"

"Beach," I said.

He drove for a few minutes more. Surely she was Anglo-Indian—"English" was a euphemism.

"Girl," I said.

"Beach or girl?"

"Girl, *girl*, for Heaven's sake." It was as if he were trying to make me confess to an especially vicious impulse.

He swung the car around dangerously and sped in the opposite direction, babbling, "Good— nice girls—you like—little house—about two miles—five girls—"

"English girls?"

"*English* girls."

The luminous certitude had gone out of his voice but still he nodded, perhaps trying to calm me.

We drove for twenty minutes. We went through streets where kerosene lamps burned at stalls, and past brightly lit textile shops in which clerks in striped pajamas shook out bolts of yellow cloth and sequined saris. I sat back and watched Madras go by, teeth and eyes in dark alleys, nighttime shoppers with full baskets, and endless doorways distinguished by memorable signboards, SANGADA LUNCH HOME, VISHNU SHOE CLINIC, and the dark, funereal THOUSAND LIGHTS RESTAURANT.

He turned corners, choosing the narrowest unlighted lanes, and then we stayed on dirt roads. I suspected he was going to rob me, and when we came to the darkest part of a bumpy track—we were in the country now—and he pulled over and switched off the lights, I was certain he was a con man: his next move would be to stick a knife in my ribs. How stupid I'd been to believe his fatuous story about the twenty-five-rupee English girl! We were far from Madras, on a deserted road, beside a faintly gleaming swamp where frogs whistled and gulped. The taxi driver jerked his head. I jumped. He blew his nose into his fingers and flung the result out the window.

I started to get out of the car.

"You sit down."

I sat down.

He thumped his chest with his hand. "I'm coming." He slid out and banged the door, and I saw him disappear down a path to the left.

I waited until he was gone, until the *shush* of his legs in the tall grass had died out, and then I carefully worked the door open. In the open air it was cool, and there was a mingled smell of swamp water and jasmine. I heard voices on the road, men chattering; like me they were in darkness. I could see the road around me, but a few feet away it vanished. I estimated that I was about a mile from the main road. I would head for that and find a bus.

There were puddles in the road. I blundered into one, and, trying to get out, plopped through the deepest part. I had been running; the puddle slowed me to a ponderous shamble.

"Mister! *Sahib!*"

I kept going, but he saw me and came closer. I was caught.

"Sit *down*, mister!" he said. I saw he was alone. "Where you going?"

"Where *you* going?"

"Checking up."

"English girl?"

"No English girl."

"What do you mean, no English girl?" I was frightened, and now it seemed clearer than ever.

He thought I was angry. He said, "English girl—forty, fifty. Like this." He stepped close to me so that in the darkness I could see he was blowing out his cheeks; he clenched his fists and hunched his shoulders. I got the message: a fat English girl. "*Indian* girl—small, nice. Sit down, we go."

I had no other choice. A mad dash down the road would have taken me nowhere—and he would have chased me. We walked back to the taxi. He started the engine angrily and we bumped along the grassy path he had taken earlier on foot. The taxi rolled from side to side in the potholes and strained up a grade. This was indeed the country. In all that darkness there was one lighted hut. A little boy crouched in the doorway with a sparkler, in anticipation of *Diwali*, the festival of lights: it illuminated his face, his skinny arm, and made his eyes shine. Ahead of us there was another hut, slightly larger, with a flat roof and two square windows. It was on its own, like a shop in a jungle clearing. Dark heads moved at the windows.

"You come," said the taxi driver, parking in front of the door. I heard giggling and saw at the windows round black faces and gleaming hair. A man in a white turban leaned against the wall, just out of the light.

We went inside the dirty room. I found a chair and sat down. A dim electric bulb burned on a cord in the center of the low ceiling. I was sitting in the good chair—the others were broken or had burst cushions. Some girls were sitting on a long wooden bench. They watched me, while the rest gathered around me, pinching my arm and laughing. They were very small, and they looked awkward and a bit comic, too young to be wearing lipstick, nose jewels, earrings, and slipping bracelets. Sprigs of white jasmine plaited into their hair made them look appropriately girlish, but the smudged lipstick and large jewelry also exaggerated their youth. One stout, sulky girl held a buzzing transistor radio to the side of her head and looked me over. They gave the impression of schoolgirls in their mothers' clothes. None could have been older than fifteen.

"Which one you like?" This was the man in the turban. He was stocky and looked tough in a rather grizzled way. His turban was a bath towel knotted on his head.

"Sorry," I said.

A thin man walked in through the door. He had a sly, bony face and his hands were stuck into the top of his *lungi*. He nodded at one. "Take her—she good."

"One hundred rupees all night," said the man with the turban. "Fifty for one jig."

"He said it costs twenty-five."

"Fifty," said the grizzled man, standing firm.

"Anyway, forget it," I said. "I just came for a drink."

"No drink," said the thin man.

"He said he had an English girl."

"What English girl?" said the thin man, now twisting the knot on his *lungi*. "These Kerala girl—young, small, from Malabar Coast."

The man in the turban caught one by the arm and shoved her against me. She shrieked delightedly and hopped away.

"You look at room," said the man in the turban.

The room was right through the door. He switched on the light. This was the bedroom; it was the same size as the outside one, but dirtier and more cluttered. And it smelled horrible. In the center of the room was a wooden bed with a stained bamboo mat on it, and on the wall six shelves, each holding a small tin padlocked suitcase. In a corner of the room a battered table held some medicine bottles, big and small, and a basin of water. There were scorch marks on the beaverboard ceiling, newspapers on the floor and on the wall over the bed charcoal sketches of dismembered bodies, breasts, and genitals.

"Look!"

The man grinned wildly, rushed to the far wall, and threw a switch.

"Fan!"

It began to groan slowly over the filthy bed, stirring the air with its cracked paddles and making the room even smellier.

Two girls came into the room and sat on the bed. Laughing, they began to unwind their saris. I hurried out, into the parlor, through the front door, and found the taxi driver. "Come on, let's go."

"You not liking Indian girl? *Nice* Indian girl?"

Skinny was starting to shout. He shouted something in

Tamil to the taxi driver, who was in as great a hurry as I to leave the place: he had produced a dud customer. The fault was his, not mine. The girls were still giggling and calling out, and Skinny was still shouting as we swung away from the hut and through the tall grass onto the bumpy back road.

Mr. Wong the Tooth Mechanic

THE TRAIN FROM GALLE WINDS ALONG THE COAST NORTH TOward Colombo, so close to the shoreline that the spray flung by the heavy rollers from Africa reaches the broken windows of the battered wooden carriages. I was going third class, and for the early part of the trip sat in a dark, overcrowded compartment with people who, as soon as I became friendly, asked me for money. They were not begging with any urgency; indeed, they didn't look as if they needed money, but rather seemed to be taking the position that whatever they succeeded in wheedling out of me might come in handy at some future date. It happened fairly often. In the middle of a conversation a man would gently ask me if I had any appliance I could give him. "What sort of appliance?" "Razor blades." I would say no and the conversation would continue.

After nearly an hour of this I crawled out of the compartment to stand by the door and watch the rain dropping out of a dark layer of high clouds just off the coast—the distant rain like majestic pillars of granite. To the right the sun was setting, and in the foreground were children, purpling in the sunset and skipping along the sand. That was on the ocean side of the train. On the jungle side it had already begun to pour heavily, and at each station the signalman covered himself with his flags, making the red one into a kerchief, the green one into a skirt, flapping the green when the train approached and quickly using it to keep the rain off when the train had passed.

A Chinese man and his Singhalese wife had boarded the train in Galle with their fat dark baby. They were the Wongs, off to Colombo for a little holiday. Mr. Wong said he was a dentist; he had learned the trade from his father, who had come to Ceylon from Shanghai in 1937. Mr. Wong didn't like the train and said he usually went to Colombo on his motorcycle except during the monsoon. He also had a helmet and goggles. If I ever went back to Galle he would show them to me. He told me how much they cost.

"Can you speak Chinese?"

"*Humbwa*—go, *mingwa*—come. That's all. I speak Singhalese and English. Chinese very hard." He pressed his temples with his knuckles.

Simla had been full of Chinese dentists, with signboards showing horrible cross sections of the human mouth and trays of white toothcaps in the window. I asked him why so many Chinese I had seen were dentists.

"Chinese are very good dentists!" he said. His breath was spiced with coconut. "I'm good!"

"Can you give me a filling?"

"No, no stoppings."

"Do you clean teeth?"

"No."

"Can you pull them?"

"You want extraction? I can give you name of a good extractionist."

"What kind of dentist are you, Mr. Wong?"

"Tooth mechanics," he said. "Chinese are the best ones for tooth mechanics."

Tooth mechanics is this: you have a shop with a shelf of English putty, a pink semiliquid; you also have drawers filled with teeth in various sizes. A person comes in who has had two front teeth knocked out in a food riot or a quarrel over a coconut. You fill his mouth with pink putty and make a mold of his guns. A plate is made from this, and, when it is trimmed, two Japanese fangs are stuck to it.

Unfortunately, these plastic dentures are valueless for chewing food with and must be removed at mealtime. Mr. Wong said business was excellent and he was taking in between 1,000 and 1,400 rupees a month, which is more than a professor gets at Colombo University.

Inside the train the passengers were banging the windows shut to keep the rain out. The sunset's fire was tangled in leaden clouds, and the pillars of rain supporting the toppling thunderheads were very close; the fishermen were fighting their catamarans ashore through high surf. The train had begun to smell awful; Mr. Wong apologized for the stink. People were jammed in the compartments and pressed in the corridors. I was at the door and could see the more nimble ones clinging to the steel ladders, balanced on the coupling. When the rain increased—and now it was really coming down—they fought their way into the carriages and slammed the doors and stood in the darkness while the rain hit the metal doors like hail.

My door was still open, and I was against the wall, while blurred gusts of rain beat past me.

Mr. Chatterjee's Calcutta

FROM THE OUTSIDE, HOWRAH STATION LOOKS LIKE A SECRE-tariat, with its not quite square towers and many clocks— each showing a different time—and its impenetrable brickwork. The British buildings in India look as if they have been designed to withstand a siege—there are hornworks and cannon emplacements and watchtowers on the unlikeliest structures. So Howrah Station looked like a fortified version of a mammoth circumlocution office, an impression that buying a ticket there only confirms. But inside it is high and smoky from the fires of the people who occupy it; the ceiling is black, the floor is wet and filthy, and it is dark—the long shafts of sun streaming from the topmost windows lose their light in dust on the way down.

"It's much better than it was," said Mr. Chatterjee, seeing me craning my neck. "You should have seen it *before* they cleaned it up."

His remark was unanswerable. Yet at every pillar squatters huddled amid the rubbish they had created: broken glass, bits of wood and paper, straw, and tin cans. Some infants slept against their parents; others were curled up like changelings in dusty corners. Families sought refuge beside pillars, under counters and luggage carts: the hugeness of the station intimidated them with space and drove them to the walls. Their children prowled in the open spaces, combining their scavenging with play. They are the tiny children of tiny parents, and it's amazing how, in India, it is possible to see two kinds of people in the process of evolution, side by side, one fairly tall, quick, and responsive, the other, whose evolution is reduction, small, stricken, and cringing. They are two races whose common ground is the railway station, and though they come quite close (an urchin lies on his back near the ticket window watching the legs of the people in line) they do not meet.

I walked outside, into the midday chaos at the western end of the Howrah Bridge. In Simla, rickshaws were retained for their quaintness: people posed in them. In Calcutta, rickshaws, pulled by skinny running men in tattered clothes, are a necessary form of transport, cheap, and easy to steer in narrow back lanes. They are a crude symbol of Indian society, but in India all symbols are crude: the homeless people sleeping in the doorway of the mansion, the commuter running to his train accidentally trampling a station sleeper, the thin rickshaw-wallah hauling his plump passengers. Ponies harnessed to stagecoaches labored over cobblestones; men pushed bicycles loaded with hay bales and firewood. I had never seen so many different forms of transport: wagons, scooters, old cars, carts and sledges and odd, old-fashioned horse-drawn vehicles that might have been barouches. In one cart, their white flippers limp, dead sea turtles were stacked; on another cart was a dead buffalo, and in a third an entire family with their belongings—children, parrot cage, pots and pans. All these vehicles, and people surging among them. Then there was panic, and the people scattered as a tottering tramcar marked TOLLYGUNGE swayed down the bridge. Mr. Chatterjee said, "Too much of people!"

Mr. Chatterjee walked across the bridge with me. He was a Bengali, and Bengalis were the most alert people I had met in India. But they were also irritable, talkative, dogmatic, arrogant, and humorless, holding forth with malicious skill on virtually every subject except the future of Calcutta. Any mention of that brought them up short. But Mr. Chatterjee had views. He had been reading an article about Calcutta's prospects. Calcutta had been very unlucky: Chicago had had a great fire, San Francisco an earthquake, and London a plague as well as a fire. But nothing had happened to Calcutta to give planners a chance to redesign it. You had to admit, he said, it had vitality. The problem of pavement dwellers (he put the figure at a quarter of a million) had been "somewhat overdramatized," and when you considered that these pavement dwellers were almost exclusively engaged in ragpicking you could see how Calcutta's garbage was "most intensively recycled." It seemed an unusual choice of words, and it strayed close to claptrap; vitality in a place where people lay dead in the gutter ("But everyone dies eventually," said Mr. C.), the overdramatized quarter of a million, the recycling ragpickers. We passed a man who leaned at us and put his hand out. He was a monster. Half his face was missing; it looked as if it had been clumsily guillotined—he had no nose, no lips, no chin, and clamped in his teeth, which were perpetually exposed, was the bruised plug of his tongue. Mr. Chatterjee saw my shock. "Oh, *him*! He is always here!"

Before he left me at the Barabazar, Mr. Chatterjee said, "I *love* this city." We exchanged addresses and we parted, I to a hotel, Mr. Chatterjee to Strand Road, where the Hooghly was silting up so badly, soon all that would float on it would be the ashes of cremated Bengalis.

The Hopping Man

I WAS ON MY WAY WHEN I SAW THE HOPPING MAN IN THE crowd on Chowringhee. He was very strange: in a city of mutilated people only the truly monstrous looked odd. This man had one leg—the other was amputated at the thigh—but he did not carry a crutch. He had a greasy bundle in one hand. He hopped past me with his mouth open, pumping his shoulders. I went after him, and he turned into Middleton Street, hopping very fast on one muscular leg, like a man on a pogo stick, his head rising above the crowd, then descending into it. I couldn't run because of the other people, black darting clerks, swamis with umbrellas, armless beggars working their stumps at me, women proffering drugged babies, strolling families, men seeming to block the sidewalk with their wide flapping trousers and swinging arms. The hopping man was in the distance. I gained on him—I saw his head clearly—then lost him. On one leg he had outrun me, so I never found out how he did it. But afterward, whenever I thought of India, I saw him—hop, hop, hop—moving nimbly through those millions.

52

Memories of the Raj—
Mr. Bernard in Burma

THE OLD MAN NEXT TO ME ON THE LOCAL TO MAYMYO SAID, "How old do you think I am? Guess."

I said sixty, thinking he was seventy.

He straightened up. "Wrong! I am eighty. That is, I passed my seventy-ninth birthday, so I am in my eightieth year."

The train switched back and forth on curves as sharp as those on the way to Simla and Landi Kotal. Occasionally, for no apparent reason, it ground to a halt, starting up without a warning whistle, and it was then that the Burmese who had jumped out to piss chased after the train, retying their sarongs as they ran along the track and being whooped at by their friends in the train. The mist, the rain, and cold, low clouds gave the train a feeling of early morning, a chill and predawn dimness that lasted until noon. I put a shirt over my jersey, then a sweater and a plastic raincoat, but I was still cold, the damp penetrating to my bones. It was the coldest I had been since leaving England.

"I was born in 1894 in Rangoon," said the old man suddenly. "My father was an Indian, but a Catholic. That is why I am called Bernard. My father was a soldier in the Indian Army. He had been a soldier his whole life—I suppose he joined up in Madras in the 1870s. He was in the Twenty-sixth Madras Infantry and he came to Rangoon with his regiment in 1888. I used to have his picture, but when the Japanese occupied Burma—I'm sure you have heard of the Japanese war—all our possessions were scattered, and we lost so many things."

He was eager to talk, glad to have a listener, and he didn't need prompting questions. He spoke carefully, pluck-

53

ing at the cloth bundle, as he remembered a clause, and I hugged myself in the cold, grateful that all that was required of me was an occasional nod to show I was interested.

"I don't remember much about Rangoon, and we moved to Mandalay when I was very young. I can remember practically everything from 1900 onward. Mr. MacDowell, Mr. Owen, Mr. Stewart, Captain Taylor—I worked for them all. I was head cook in the Royal Artillery officer's mess, but I did more than cook—I did everything. I went all over Burma, in the camps when they were in the field. I have a good memory, I think. For example, I remember the day Queen Victoria died. I was in the second standard at Saint Xavier's School in Mandalay. The teacher said to us, 'The Queen is dead, so there is no school today.' I was— what?—seven years old. I was a good student. I did my lessons, but when I finished with school there was nothing to do. In 1910 I was sixteen and I thought I should get a job on the railways. I wanted to be an engine driver. I wanted to be in a loco, traveling to Upper Burma. But I was disappointed. They made us carry coal in baskets on our heads. It was very hard work, you can't imagine—so hot— and the man in charge of us, one Mr. Vander, was an Anglo-Indian. He shouted at us, of course, all the time; fifteen minutes for lunch and he still shouted. He was a fat man and not kind to us at all. There were a lot of Anglo-Indians on the railway then. I should say most of them were Anglo-Indians. I imagined I would be driving a loco and here I was carrying coal! The work was too much for me, so I ran away.

"I liked my next job very much. This was in the kitchen of the officers' mess in the Royal Artillery. I still have some of the certificates, with *RA* written on them. I helped the cook at first and later became a cook myself. The cook's name was Stewart and he showed me how to cut vegetables in various ways and how to make salad, fruit cup, the trifle, and all the different kinds of joints. It was 1912 then, and that was the best time in Burma. It will never be nice like that again. There was plenty of food, things were cheap, and even after the First World War started things were still fine. We never knew about the First World War in Burma; we heard nothing—we didn't feel it. I knew a little bit about it because of my brother. He was fighting in Basra—I'm sure you know it—Basra, in Mesopotamia.

"At that time I was getting twenty-five rupees a month. It doesn't sound so much, does it? But, do you know, it only cost me ten rupees to live—I saved the rest and later I bought a farm. When I went for my pay I collected one gold sovereign and a ten-rupee bank note. A gold sovereign was worth fifteen rupees. But to show you how cheap things were, a shirt cost four annas, food was plentiful, and life was very good. I married and had four children. I was at the officers' mess from 1912 until 1941, when the Japanese came. I loved doing the work. The officers all knew me and I believe they respected me. They only got cross if something was late: everything had to be done on time, and of course if it wasn't—if there was a delay—they were very angry. But not a single one was cruel to me. After all, they were officers—British officers, you know—and they had a good standard of behavior. Throughout that time, whenever they ate, they wore full-dress uniforms, and there were sometimes guests or wives in evening dress, black ties, and the ladies wore gowns. Beautiful as moths. I had a uniform too, white jacket, black tie, and soft shoes— you know the kind of soft shoes. They make no noise. I could come into a room and no one could hear me. They don't make those shoes anymore, the kind that are noiseless.

"Things went on this way for some years. I remember one night at the mess. General Slim was there. You know him. And Lady Slim. They came into the kitchen. General and Lady Slim and some others, officers and their wives.

"I stood to attention.

" 'You are Bernard?' Lady Slim asked me.

"I said, 'Yes, Madam.'

"She said it was a good meal and very tasty. It was glazed chicken, vegetables, and trifle.

"I said, 'I'm glad you liked it.'

" 'That is Bernard,' General Slim said, and they went out.

"Chiang Kai-shek and Madame Chiang came as well. He was very tall and did not speak. I served them. They stayed for two days—one night and two days. And the viceroy came—that was Lord Curzon. So many people came—the Duke of Kent, people from India, and another general—I will think of his name.

"Then the Japanese came. Oh, I remember that very well! It was like this. I was standing in the bush near my house—outside Maymyo, where the road forks. I wore a singlet and a *longyi*, as the Burmese do. The car was so huge, with a flag on the hood—the Japanese flag, rising sun, red and white. The car stopped at the fork. I didn't think they could see me. A man called me over. He said something to me in Burmese.

"I said, 'I speak English.'

" 'You are Indian?' says this Japanese gentleman. I said yes. He put his hands together like this and said, 'India-Japan. Friends!' I smiled at him. I had never been to India in my life.

"There was a very high official in the car. He said nothing, but the other man said, 'Is this the road to Maymyo?'

"I said it was. They drove on, up the hill. That was how the Japanese entered Maymyo."

Gokteik Viaduct

TOWARD NOON WE WERE IN THE ENVIRONS OF GOKTEIK. THE mist was heavy and noisy waterfalls splashed down through pipe thickets of green bamboo. We crawled around the upper edges of hills, hooting at each curve, but out the windows there was only the whiteness of mist, shifted by a strong wind to reveal the more intense whiteness of cloud. It was like traveling in a slow plane with the windows open, and I envied the opium-smoker seated across from me his repose.

"The views are clouded," said my escort, Security Officer U Sit Aye.

We climbed to nearly four thousand feet and then began descending into the gorge where, below, boat-shaped wisps of cloud moved quickly across from hillside to hillside and other lengths of vapor depended in the gorge with only the barest motion, like veils of threadbare silk. The viaduct, a monster of silver geometry in all the ragged rock and jungle, came into view and then slipped behind an outcrop of rock. It appeared again at intervals, growing larger, less silver, more imposing. Its presence there was bizarre, this man-made thing in so remote a place. Competing with the grandeur of the enormous gorge and yet seeming more grand than its surroundings, which were hardly negligible— the water rushing through the girder legs and falling on the tops of trees, the flights of birds through the swirling clouds and the blackness of the tunnels beyond the viaduct. We approached it slowly, stopping briefly at Gokteik Station, where hill people, tattooed Shans and straggling Chinese, had taken up residence in unused railway cars—freight cars and sheds. They came to the doors to watch the Lashio Mail go past.

There were wincing sentries at the entrance to the viaduct with rifles on their shoulders; the wind blew through their wall-less shelters and the drizzle continued. I asked U Sit Aye if I could hang out the window. He said it was all right with him, "but don't fall." The train wheels banged on the steel spans and the plunging water roared the birds out of their nests a thousand feet down. The cold had depressed me, and the journey had been unremarkable, but this lifted my spirits, crossing the long bridge in the rain, from one steep hill to another, over a jungly deepness, bursting with a river to which the monsoon had given a hectoring voice, and the engine whistling again and again, the echo carrying down the gorge to China.

The tunnels began, and they were cavernous, smelling of bat shit and sodden plants, with just enough light to illuminate the water rushing down the walls and the odd night-blooming flowers growing amid fountains of creepers and leaves in the twisted stone. When we emerged from the last tunnel we were far from the Gokteik Viaduct, and Naung-Peng, an hour more of steady traveling, was the end of the line for me. This was a collection of wooden shacks and grass-roofed shelters. The "canteen" where the food was found was one of these grass-roofed huts: inside was a long table with tureens of green and yellow stew, and Burmese, thinly clad for such a cold place, were warming themselves beside caldrons of rice bubbling over braziers. It looked like the field kitchen of some Mongolian tribe retreating after a terrible battle: the cooks were old Chinese women with black teeth, and the eaters were that mixed breed of people with a salad of genes drawn from China and Burma, whose only racial clue is their dress, sarong or trousers, parasol coolie hat or woolen cap, damp and shapeless as a mitten. The cooks ladled the stews onto large palm leaves and plopped down a fistful of rice; this the travelers ate with cups of hot weak tea. The rain beat on the roof and crackled on the mud outside, and Burmese hurried to the train with chickens bound so tightly in feather bundles they looked like a peculiar kind of native handicraft. I bought a two-cent cigar, found a stool near a brazier, and sat and smoked until the next train came.

The train I had taken to Naung-Peng didn't leave for Lashio until the "down" train from Lashio arrived. Then the escort from Maymyo and the more heavily armed escort from Lashio changed trains in order to return to the places they had set out from that morning. Each train, I noticed, had an armored van coupled just behind the engine; this was a steel box with gun sights, simplified almost to crudity, like a child's drawing of a tank, but it was empty because all the soldiers were at the end of the train, nine coaches away. How they would fight their way, under fire, eighty yards up the train during a raid, I do not know, nor did U Sit Aye supply an explanation. It was clear why the soldiers didn't travel in the iron armored van: it was a cruelly uncomfortable thing, and very dark, since the gun sights were so small.

The return to Maymyo, downhill most of the way, was

quick, and there was a continuous intake of food at small stations. U Sit Aye explained that the soldiers wired ahead for the food, and it was true, for at the smallest station a boy would rush up to the train as soon as it drew in, and with a bow this child with rain on his face would present a parcel of food at the door of the soldiers' coach. Nearer to Maymyo they wired ahead for flowers, so when we arrived each soldier stepped out with curry stains on his shirt, a plug of betel in his mouth, and a bouquet of flowers, which he clutched with greater care than his rifle.

"Can I go now?" I said to U Sit Aye. I didn't know whether I was going to be arrested for going through forbidden territory.

"You can go," he said, and smiled. "But you must not take the train to Gokteik again. If you do there will be trouble."

The Hué—Danang Passenger Train, Vietnam 1973

FROM THE AIR, THE GRAY UNREFLECTING WATER OF THE South China Sea looked ice cold, there were round Buddhist graves all through the marshes, and the royal city of Hué lay half-buried in drifts of snow. But this was wet sand, not snow, and those circular graves were bomb craters. Hué had a bizarre appearance. There had been plenty of barbed wire on the barricades but little war damage in Saigon; in Bien Hoa there were bombed-out houses; in Can Tho stories of ambushes and a hospital full of casualties. But in Hué I could see and smell the war; it was muddy roads rutted by army trucks and people running through the rain with bundles, bandaged soldiers tramping through the monsoon slime of the wrecked town or peering across their rifle barrels from the backs of overloaded trucks. The movements of the people had a distressed simultaneity. Barbed wire obstructed most streets, and houses were sloppily sandbagged. The next day, in the train, my American host, code-named Cobra One (who had come with his wife, Cobra Two, and my translator Dial for the ride) said, "Look—every house has its own bullet hole!" It was true: few houses were without a violent gouge and most had a series of ragged plugs torn out of their walls. The whole town had a dark brown look of violation, the smirches of raids among swelling puddles. It held some traces of imperial design (Vietnamese, French) but this delicacy was little more than a broken promise.

And it was very cold, with the sodden chill from the low sky and the drizzle clinging in damp rooms. I paced up and down, hugging myself to keep warm, during my lecture at the University of Hué—a colonial building, in fact, not academic at all, but rather what was once a fancy shop called Morin Brothers, which outlying planters used as a guest house and provisioner. I lectured in one of the former bedrooms, and from the windy balcony I could see the neglected courtyard, the cracked fishpond, the peeling shutters on the windows of the other rooms.

AT HUÉ STATION THE NEXT MORNING A TINY VIETNAMESE MAN in a gray gabardine suit and porkpie hat rushed forward and took my arm. "Welcome to Hué," he said. "Your carriage is ready." This was the stationmaster. He had been notified of my arrival and had shunted onto the Danang passenger train one of the director's private cars. Because Vietnam Railways has been blown to pieces, each separate section has a director's car on one of its sidings. Any other railway would have one such car, but Vietnam Railways is six separate lines, operating with laborious independence. As at Saigon, I boarded the private coach with some misgivings, knowing that my hand would tremble if I ever wrote anything ungenerous about these people. I felt loutish in my empty compartment, in my empty coach, watching Vietnamese lining up to buy tickets so that they could ride in over-crowded cars. The stationmaster had sped me away from the ticket window ("It is not necessary!"), but I had caught a glimpse of the fare: 143 piastres (twenty-five cents) to go to Danang, perhaps the cheapest seventy-five-mile ride in the world.

Dial, the translator, and Cobras One and Two boarded and joined me in the compartment. We sat in silence, peering out the window. The blocky whitewashed station building, a version of the Alamo, was riddled with bullet holes that had broken off pieces of the stucco, revealing red brickwork beneath. But the station, the same vintage as the USIS official's bay-windowed villa and Morin Brothers' shop, had been built to last—a far cry from the patch of waste ground and cement foundations just outside Hué, where the First Marine Division's collapsed barracks and splintered obstacle course lay sinking in the mud. It was as if all the apparatus of war had been timed to self-destruct the day the Americans pulled out, leaving no trace of the brutal adventure behind. In the train yard, several armored vans showed rips in their steel sides where mines had punched them apart. These vans were the homes of a number of sad-looking children. In most tropical countries adults stand, like those posed by William Blake, at the fringe of the echoing green, watching children at play. In Vietnam the children play alone, and the adults appear to have been swept away; you look for the parents among large groups of children, for the background figure of an adult. But (and this distorts the landscape) they are missing. That old woman carrying a child on her back, with the long muddy skirt and rain-drenched hair, is another child.

"Have you seen the sink in the w.c.?" asked Dial.

"No."

"You turn on the faucet and guess what comes out?"

"Rust," I said.

"Nothing," said Cobra Two.

Dial said, "Water!"

"Right," said Cobra One. "Paul, take that down. The faucets work. Running water available. What do you think of that?"

But this was the only sink in the train.

The stationmaster had said that the line to Danang had been open for four months, having been out of action for five years. So far there had been no recent disruptions. Why its reopening coincided with the American withdrawal no one could explain. My own theory was that there were now no American trucks plying back and forth along the only road that goes between Hué and Danang, Highway One, the poignantly named "Street Without Joy"; this shrinking of expensive road traffic had forced the Vietnamese into the more sensible course of opening the railway. The war had become not smaller but less mechanized, less elaborate. Money and foreign troops had complicated it, but now the Vietnamese had reverted from the corporation-style hostilities of the Americans to the colonial superstructure, slower communications, a return to farming, housing in the old buildings, and a transport system based on the railway. The American design of the war had been abandoned—the empty firebases, the skeletons of barracks, and the torn-up roads showed this to be a fact, visible from the passenger train clanking toward Danang with its cargo of Hué-grown vegetables.

The bridges on that line speak of the war; they are recent and have new rust on their girders. Others, broken, simulating gestures without motion, lay beyond them where they had been twisted and pitched into ravines by volumes of explosives. Some rivers contained masses of broken bridges, black knots of steel bunched grotesquely at the level of the water. They were not all recent. In the gorges where there were two or three, I took the oldest ones to be relics of Japanese bombing, and others to be examples of demolition from the later terrorism of the fifties and sixties, each war leaving its own unique wreck. They were impressively mangled, like outrageous metal sculptures. The Vietnamese hung their washing on them.

It was at the rivers—at these bridges—that soldiers were most in evidence. These were strategic points: a bombed bridge could put the line out of action for as long as a year. So at each side of the bridge, just above it on outcrops of rock, there were igloos of sandbags, and pillboxes and bunkers, where sentries, most of them very young, waved to the train with carbines. On their shelters were slogans flying on red and yellow banners. Dial translated them for

me. A typical one was GREET THE PEACE HAPPILY BUT DON'T
SLEEP AND FORGET THE WAR. The soldiers stood around in
their undershirts; they could be seen swinging in ham-
mocks; some swam in the rivers or were doing their washing. Some watched the train, with their rifles at their
shoulders, in those oversize uniforms, a metaphor of mis-
matching that never failed to remind me that these men—
these boys—had been dressed and armed by much larger
Americans. With the Americans gone the war looked too
big, an uncalled-for size, really, like those shirts whose
cuffs reached to the soldiers' knuckles and the helmets that
fell over their eyes.

"That's VC up there," said Cobra One. He pointed to a
series of ridges that grew, off in the distance, into hills.
"You could say eighty percent of the country is controlled
by the VC, but that doesn't mean anything because they
only have ten percent of the population."

"I was up there," said Dial. I kept forgetting that Dial
had been a Marine. "We were on patrol for about three
weeks. Christ, we were cold! But now and then we'd luck
out and get to a village. The people would see us coming
and run away, and we'd use their huts—sleep in their beds.
I remember a couple of times— it really killed me—we had
to burn all their furniture to keep warm. We couldn't find
any firewood."

The mountains had begun to rise, acquiring the shape of
amphitheaters with a prospect of the China Sea; eerie and
bare and blue, their summits smothered in mist, they trailed
smoke from slash-and-burn fires. We were on the narrow
coastal strip, moving south on the patchy shoreline that still
belonged to the Saigon government, between the mountains
and the sea. The weather had changed, or perhaps we had
finally been dragged free of the drizzle that was constant in
Hué. Now it was sunny and warm: the Vietnamese climbed
up to the roofs of the coaches and sat with their legs hanging past the eaves. We were close enough to the beach to
hear the pounding surf, and ahead in the curving inlets that
doubled up the train, fishing smacks and canoes rode the
frothy breakers to the shore, where men in parasol hats
spun circular webbed nets over the crayfish.

"God, this is such a beautiful country," said Cobra Two. She was snapping pictures out of the window, but no picture could duplicate the complexity of the beauty: over there, the sun lighted a bomb scar in the forest, and next to it smoke filled the bowl of a valley; a column of rain from one fugitive cloud slanted on another slope, and the blue gave way to black green, to rice green on the flat fields of shoots, which became, after a strip of sand, an immensity of blue ocean. The distances were enormous and the landscape was so large it had to be studied in parts, like a mural seen by a child.

"I had no idea," I said. Of all the places the railway had taken me since London, this was the loveliest.

"No one knows it," said Cobra Two. "No one in the States has the slightest idea how beautiful it is. Look at that—God, look at that!"

We were at the fringes of a bay that was green and sparkling in bright sunlight. Beyond the leaping jade plates of the sea was an overhang of cliffs and the sight of a valley so large it contained sun, smoke, rain, and cloud—all at once—independent quantities of color. I had been unprepared for this beauty; it surprised and humbled me in the same degree the emptiness had in rural India. Who has mentioned the simple fact that the heights of Vietnam are places of unimaginable grandeur? Though we can hardly blame a frightened draftee for not noticing this magnificence, we should have known all along that the French would not have colonized it, nor would the Americans have fought so long, if such ripeness did not invite the eye to take it.

"That's the Ashau Valley," said Cobra One, who until then had been doing an amusing imitation of Walter Brennan. The ridges mounted into the mist; below them, in the smoke and sun, were deep black gorges marked by waterfalls. Cobra One was shaking his head: "A lot of good men died there."

Dazzled by the scenery, I walked through the train and saw a blind man feeling his way to the door—I could hear his lungs working like a bellows; wrinkled old ladies with black teeth and black pajamas clutched wicker bales of spring onions; and soldiers—one ashen-faced in a wheel-chair, one on crutches, others with new bandages on their hands and heads, and all of them in the American uniforms that suggested travesty in its true sense. An official moved through the coaches checking the ID cards of civilian males, looking for draft evaders. This official got tangled in the piece of string held by a blind man and attached to the waist of a child leading him. There were many armed soldiers on the train, but none looked like escorts. The train was defended by concentrations of soldiers at those bridge emplacements, and this is perhaps why it is so easy to blow up the line with command-detonated mines. These mines are slipped under the rails at night; when the train goes over one of them, a hidden man—who might be a Viet Cong or a bomber hired by a trucker in Danang—explodes the charge.

Twice during that trip, at small station sidings, children were offered to me by old ladies; they were like the pale-skinned, light-haired children I had seen in Can Tho and Bien Hoa. But these were older, perhaps four or five, and it was strange to hear these American-looking children speaking Vietnamese. It was even stranger to see the small Vietnamese farmers in the vastness of a landscape whose beautiful trees and ravines and jade crags—these launched from cloud banks—hid their enemies. From the train I could turn my eyes to the mountains and almost forget the country's name, but the truth was closer and cruel: the Vietnamese had been damaged and then abandoned, almost as if, dressed in our clothes, they had been mistaken for us and shot at; as if, just when they had come to believe that we were identified with them, we had bolted. It was not that simple, but it was nearer to describing that sad history than the urgent opinions of anguished Americans who, stropping Occam's Razor, classified the war as a string of atrocities, a series of purely political errors, or a piece of interrupted heroism. The tragedy was that we had come, and, from the beginning, had not planned to stay: Danang was to be proof of that.

The train was under the gigantic Hai Van Pass ("The Pass of Clouds"), a natural division on the north side of

Danang, like a Roman wall. If the Viet Cong got past it the way would be clear to Danang, and already the Viet Cong were bivouacked on the far slopes, waiting. Like the other stretches between Huè and Danang, the most scenically dramatic mountains and valleys were—and are still—the most terrible battlefields. Beyond the Hai Van Pass we entered a long tunnel. By this time I had walked the length of the train and was standing on the front balcony of the diesel, under the bright headlights. Ahead, a large bat dislodged itself from the ceiling and flapped clumsily this way and that, winging against the walls, trying to keep ahead of the roaring engine. The bat swooped, grazing the track, then rose—more slowly now—as the end of the tunnel came into view, flying closer to the engine with every second. It was like a toy of wood and paper, its spring running down, and at last it was ten feet from my face, a brown panicky creature beating its bony wings. It tired, dropped a few feet, then in the light of the tunnel's exit—a light it could not see—its wings collapsed, it pitched forward, and quickly tumbled under the engine's wheels.

"The Street Without Joy" was above us as we raced across a treeless promontory to the Nam Ho Bridge, five dark spans secured against underwater sappers by great rusting wreaths of barbed wire. These were the outer wastes of Danang, a grim district of supply bases that has been taken over by ARVN forces and squatters; shelters—huts and lean-tos—made exclusively with war materials, sandbags, plastic sheeting, corrugated iron stamped U.S. ARMY, and food wrappers marked with the initials of charitable agencies. Danang was pushed next to the sea and all the land around it had been stripped of trees. If ever a place looked poisoned, it was Danang.

Raiding and looting were skills the war had required the Vietnamese to learn. We got out at Danang Station and after lunch drove with an American official to the south side of the city, where GIs had been housed in several large camps. Once there had been thousands of American soldiers; now there were none. But the barracks were filled to bursting with refugees; because there had been no maintenance, the camps were in a sorry condition and looked as if they had been shelled. Laundry flew from the flagpoles; windows were broken or boarded up; there were cooking fires in the roads. The less lucky refugees had set up house in wheelless trucks and the sewage stink was terrible—the camps could be smelled two hundred yards away.

"The people were waiting at the gates and over by those fences when the Americans started packing," said the American official. "Like locusts or I-don't-know-what. As soon as the last soldier left they rushed in, looted the stores, and commandeered the houses."

The refugees, using ingenuity, looted the barracks; the Vietnamese government officials, using their influence, looted the hospitals. I kept hearing stories in Danang (and, again, in the southern port of Nha Trang) of how, the day the Americans left, the hospitals were cleaned out—drugs, oxygen cylinders, blankets, beds, medical appliances, anything that could be carried. Chinese ships were anchored offshore to receive this loot, which was taken to Hong Kong and resold. But there is a just God in Heaven: a Swiss businessman told me that some of these pilfered medical supplies found their way, via Hong Kong, to Hanoi. No one knew what happened to the enriched government officials. Some of the looting stories sounded exaggerated; I believed the ones about the raided hospitals because no American official would tell me where there was a hospital receiving patients, and that's the sort of thing an American would know.

For several miles on the road south the ravaged camps swarmed with Vietnamese whose hasty adaptations could be seen in doors knocked through barracks' walls and whole barracks torn down to make ten flimsy huts. The camps themselves had been temporary—they were all plywood panels, splitting in the dampness, and peeling metal sheets, and sagging fence posts—so none of these crude shelters would last. If one felt pity for the demoralized American soldiers who had lived in these horrible camps, one felt even sorrier for the inheritors of all this junk.

The bars, with flyblown signs advertising COLD BEER, MUSIC, GIRLS, were empty and most looked bankrupt, but it was in the late afternoon that I saw the real dereliction of Danang. We drove out to the beach where, fifty feet from the crashing waves, a fairly new bungalow stood. It was a cozy beach house, built for an American general who had recently decamped. Who was this general? No one knew his name. Whose beach house was it now? No one knew that either, but Cobra One ventured, "Probably some ARVN honcho." On the porch a Vietnamese soldier idled with a carbine, and behind him a table held a collection of bottles: vodka, whisky, ginger ale, soda water, a jug of orange juice, an ice bucket. Laughter, slightly drunken and mirthless, carried from inside the house.

"I think someone's moved in," said Cobra One. "Let's have a look."

We walked past the sentry and up the stairs. The front door was open, and in the living room two Americans on sofas were tickling two busty Vietnamese girls. It was the absurd made symmetrical—both men were fat, both girls were laughing, and the sofas were side by side. If Conrad's dark reenactment of colonialism, "Outpost of Progress," were made into a comedy, it would have looked something like that.

"Hey, we got company!" said one of the men. He banged the wall behind his head with his fist, then sat up and relit his cigar.

While we introduced ourselves, a side door opened from the wall the cigar smoker had punched and a muscular black man hurried out hitching up his trousers. Then a very tiny, bat-like Vietnamese girl appeared from the room. The black said, "Howdy," and made for the front door.

"We didn't mean to interrupt your picnic," said Cobra One, but he showed no inclination to leave. He folded his arms and watched; he was a tall man with a severe gaze.

"You're not interrupting nothing," said the man with the cigar, rolling off the sofa.

"This is the head of security," said the American official who had driven us to the place. He was speaking of the fat man with the cigar.

As if in acknowledgment, the fat man set fire to his cigar once again. Then he said, "Yeah, I'm the head spook around here. You just get here?" He was at that point of drunkenness where, acutely conscious of it, he made an effort to hide it. He walked outside, away from the spilled cushions, full ashtrays, supine girls.

"You took the *what*?" asked the CIA man when we told him we had come to Danang from Hué on the train. "You're lucky you made it! Two weeks ago the VC blew it up."

"That's not what the stationmaster in Hué told us," said Cobra One.

"The stationmaster in Hué doesn't know whether to scratch his watch or wind his ass," said the CIA man. "I'm telling you they blew it up. Twelve people killed, I don't know how many wounded."

"With a mine?"

"Right. Command-detonated. It was horrible."

The CIA man, who was head of security for the entire province, was lying, but at the time I had no facts to refute the story with. The stationmaster in Hué had said there hadn't been a mining incident in months, and this was confirmed by the railway officials in Danang. But the CIA man was anxious to impress us that he had his finger on the country's pulse, the more so since his girlfriend had joined us and was draped around his neck. The other fat man was in the bungalow, talking in frantic whispers to one of the girls, and the black man was a little distance from the porch, doing chin-ups on a bar spliced between two palms. The CIA man said, "There's one thing you gotta keep in mind. The VC don't have any support in the villages—and neither do the government troops. See, that's why everything's so quiet."

The Vietnamese girl pinched his cheek and shouted to her friend at the edge of the beach who was watching the black man swing a heavy chain around his head. The man inside the bungalow came out and poured himself a whisky. He drank it worriedly, watching the CIA man rant.

"It's a funny situation," the CIA man was saying. "Like you say this village is clean and this village is all Charley, but there's one thing you gotta understand: most people aren't fighting. I don't care what you read in the papers—

these journalists are more full of shit than a Christmas turkey. I'm telling you it's quiet."

"What about the mine?"

"Yeah, the mine. You should stay off the train; that's all I can say."

"It's different at night," said the man with the whisky.

"Well, see, the country kinda changes hands after dark," said the CIA man.

"I think we'd better go," said Cobra One.

"What's the rush? Stick around," said the CIA man. "You're a writer," he said to me. "I'm a writer too—I mean, I do a little writing. I pound out articles now and then. *Boy's Life*—I do quite a bit for *Boy's Life*, and, um—"

The girls, shouting in Vietnamese and giggling, were beginning to distract him.

"—anyway, where'd you say you're going? Marble Mountain? You wanna stay away from there about this time." He looked at his watch. It was five-thirty. "There might be Charley there. I don't know. I wouldn't want to be responsible."

We left, and when we got to the car I looked back at the bungalow. The CIA man waved his cigar at us; he seemed to be unaware that a Vietnamese girl still clung to him. His friend stood on the porch with him, agitating in his hand a paper cup full of whisky and ginger ale. The black man had returned to the high bar: he was doing chin-ups; the girls were counting. The sentry sat hugging his rifle. Beyond them was the sea. The CIA man called out, but the tide was coming in and the noisy surf drowned his words. The refugees in Danang had taken over the barracks; these three had the general's beach house. In a sense they were all that remained of the American stake in the war: degenerate sentiment, boozy fears, and simplifications. For them the war was over: they were just amusing themselves, raising a little cain.

Four miles south of this, near Marble Mountain, our car stalled behind a slow ox cart. While we were waiting, a Vietnamese boy of about ten rushed over and screamed through the window.

"What did he say?" asked Cobra One.

" 'Motherfucker,' " said Dial.
"Let's get out of here."

The Trans-Siberian Express

AFTERWARD, WHENEVER I THOUGHT OF THE TRANS-
Siberian Express, I saw stainless-steel bowls of *borscht*
spilling in the dining car of the *Rossiya* as it rounded a
bend on its way to Moscow, and at the curve a clear sight
from the window of our green and black steam locomotive—from Skovorodino onward its eruptions of steamy
smoke diffused the sunlight and drifted into the forest so
that the birches smoldered and the magpies made for the
sky. I saw the gold-tipped pines at sunset and the snow lying softly around clumps of brown grass like cream poured
over the ground; the yacht-like snowplows at Zima; the
ocherous flare of the floodlit factory chimneys at Irkutsk;
the sight of Marinsk in early morning, black cranes and
black buildings and escaping figures casting long shadows
on the tracks as they ran toward the lighted station—
something terrible in that combination of cold, dark, and little people tripping over Siberian tracks; the ice chest of
frost between the cars; the protrusion of Lenin's white forehead at every stop; and the passengers imprisoned in Hard
Class: fur hats, fur leggings, blue gym suits, crying children, and such a powerful smell of sardines, body odor,
cabbage, and stale tobacco that even at the five-minute
stops the Russians jumped onto the snowy platform to risk
pneumonia for a breath of fresh air; the bad food; the stupid
economies; and the men and women ("No distinction is
made with regard to sex in assigning compartments"—
Intourist brochure), strangers to each other, who shared the
same compartment and sat on opposite bunks, mustached

male mirroring mustached female from their grubby night-caps and the blankets they wore as shawls, down to their hefty ankles stuck in crushed slippers. Most of all, I thought of it as an experience in which time had the trick distortions of a dream: the *Rossiya* ran on Moscow time, and after a lunch of cold yellow potatoes, a soup of fat lumps called *solyanka*, and a carafe of port that tasted like cough syrup, I would ask the time and be told it was four o'clock in the morning.

The *Rossiya* was not like the *Vostok*; it was new. The sleeping cars of East German make were steel syringes, in-sulated in gray plastic and heated by coal-fired boilers at-tached to furnace and samovar that gave the front end of each carriage the look of a cartoon atom smasher. The *provodnik* often forgot to stoke the furnace, and then the carriage took on a chill that somehow induced nightmares in me while at the same time denying me sleep. The other passengers in Soft were either suspicious, drunk, or un-pleasant: a Goldi and his White Russian wife and small leathery child who rode in a nest of boots and blankets, two aggrieved Canadians who ranted to the two Australian li-brarians about the insolence of the *provodnik*, an elderly Russian lady who did the whole trip wearing the same frilly nightgown, a Georgian who looked as if he had problems at the other end, and several alcoholics who played noisy games of dominoes in their pajamas. Conversation was hopeless, sleep was alarming, and the perversity of the clocks confounded my appetite. That first day I wrote in my diary, *Despair makes me hungry*.

The dining car was packed. Everyone had vegetable soup, then an omelet wrapped around a Wiener schnitzel, served by two waitresses—a very fat lady who bossed the diners incessantly, and a pretty black-haired girl who dou-bled as scullion and looked as if she might jump off the train at the next clear opportunity. I ate my lunch, and the three Russians at my table tried to bum cigarettes from me. As I had none we attempted a conversation: they were go-ing to Omsk; I was an American. Then they left. I cursed myself for not buying a Russian phrase book in Tokyo.

A man sat down with me. His hands were shaking. He

ordered. Twenty minutes later the fat lady gave him a carafe of yellow wine. He splashed it into his glass and drank it in two gulps. He had a wound on his thumb, which he gnawed as he looked worriedly around the car. The fat lady gave his shoulder a slap and he was off, moving tipsily in the direction of Hard. But the fat lady left me in peace. I stayed in the dining car, sipping the sticky wine, watching the scenery change from flat snow fields to hills—the first since Nakhodka. The drooping sun gilded them beautifully and I expected to see people in the shallow woods. I stared for an hour, but saw none.

Nor could I establish where we were. My Japanese map of the Soviet Union was not helpful, and it was only in the evening that I learned we had passed through Poshkovo, on the Chinese border. This added to my disorientation: I seldom knew where we were, I never knew the correct time, and I grew to hate the three freezers I had to pass through to get to the dining car.

The fat lady's name was Anna Feyodorovna and, though she screamed at her fellow countrymen, she was pleasant to me, and urged me to call her Annushka. I did and she rewarded me with a special dish, cold potatoes and chicken—dark sinewy meat that was like some dense textile. Annushka watched me eat. She winked over her glass of tea (she dipped bread into the tea and sucked it) and then cursed a cripple who sat down at my table. Eventually she banged a steel plate of potatoes and fatty meat in front of him.

The cripple ate slowly, lengthening the awful meal by sawing carefully at his meat. A waiter went by and there was a smash. The waiter had dropped an empty carafe onto our table, shattering the cripple's glass. The cripple went on eating with exquisite *sang-froid*, refusing to acknowledge the waiter, who was muttering apologies as he picked up pieces of broken glass from the table. Then the waiter plucked an enormous sliver of glass from the cripple's mashed potatoes. The cripple choked and pushed the plate away. The waiter got him a new meal.

"*Sprechen Sie Deutsch?*" asked the cripple.

"Yes, but very badly."

"I speak a little," he said in German. "I learned it in Berlin. Where are you from?"

I told him. He said, "What do you think of the food here?"

"Not bad, but not very good."

"I think it is very bad," he said. "What's the food like in America?"

"Wonderful," I said.

He said, "Capitalist! You are a capitalist!"

"Perhaps."

"Capitalism bad, communism good."

"Bullshit," I said in English, then in German, "You think so?"

"In America people kill each other with pistols. *Pah! Pah! Pah!* Like that."

"I don't have a pistol."

"What about the Negroes? The black people?"

"What about them?"

"You kill them."

"Who tells you these things?"

"Newspapers. I read it for myself. Also it's on the radio all the time."

"Soviet radio," I said.

"Soviet radio is good radio," he said.

The radio in the dining car was playing jazzy organ music. It was on all day, and even in the compartments—each one had a loudspeaker—it continued to mutter because it could not be turned off completely. I jerked my thumb at the loudspeaker and said, "Soviet radio is too loud."

He guffawed. Then he said, "I'm an invalid. Look here—no foot, just a leg. No foot, no foot!"

He raised his felt boot and squashed the toe with the ferrule of his cane. He said, "I was in Kiev during the war, fighting the Germans. They were shooting—*Pah! Pah!*—like that. I jumped into the water and started swimming. It was winter—cold water—very cold water! They shot my foot off, but I didn't stop swimming. Then another time my captain said to me, 'Look, more Germans—' and in the snow—very deep snow—"

That night I slept poorly on my bench-sized bunk,

dreaming of goose-stepping Germans with pitchforks, wearing helmets like the *Rossiya*'s soup bowls; they forced me into an icy river. I woke. My feet lay exposed in the draft of the cold window; the blanket had slipped off, and the blue night light of the compartment made me think of an operating theater. I took an aspirin and slept until it was light enough in the corridor to find the toilet. That day, around noon, we stopped at Skovorodino. The *provodnik*, my jailer, showed a young bearded man into my compartment. This was Vladimir. He was going to Irkutsk, which was two days away. For the rest of the afternoon Vladimir said no more. He read Russian paperbacks with patriotic pictures on their covers, and I looked out the window. Once I had thought of a train window as allowing me freedom to gape at the world; now it seemed an imprisoning thing and at times took on the opacity of a cell wall.

At one bend outside Skovorodino I saw we were being pulled by a giant steam locomotive. I diverted myself by trying (although Vladimir sucked his teeth in disapproval) to snap a picture of it as it rounded curves, shooting plumes of smoke out its side. The smoke rolled beside the train and rose slowly through the forests of birch and the Siberian cedars, where there were footprints on the ground and signs of dead fires, but not a soul to be seen. The countryside then was so changeless it might have been a picture pasted against the window. It put me to sleep. I dreamed of a particular cellar in Medford High School, then woke and saw Siberia and almost cried. Vladimir had stopped reading. He sat against the wall sketching on a pad with colored pencils, a picture of telephone poles. I crept into the corridor. One of the Canadians had his face turned to the miles of snow.

He said, "Thank God we're getting off this pretty soon. How far are you going?"

"Moscow; then the train to London."

"Tough shitsky."

"So they say."

There was a young black-haired man who swept the floor and rarely spoke to anyone. Viktor, a waiter, pointed him out to me and said, "Gitler! Gitler!"

The man ignored him, but to make his point Viktor

stamped on the floor and ground his boot as if killing a cockroach. Vassily Prokofyevich, the manager, put his forefinger under his nose to make a mustache and said, *"Heil Gitler!"* So the young man might have been an anti-Semite or, since Russian mockery is not very subtle, he might have been a Jew.

One afternoon the young man came over to me and said, "Angela Davis!"

"Gitler!" said Viktor, grinning.

"Angela Davis *karasho*," said Gitler and began to rant in Russian about the way Angela Davis had been persecuted in America. He shook his broom at me, his hair falling over his eyes, and he continued quite loudly until Vassily banged on the table.

"Politics!" said Vassily. "We don't want politics here. This is a restaurant, not a university." He spoke in Russian, but his message was plain and he was obviously very angry with Gitler.

The rest were embarrassed. They sent Gitler to the kitchen and brought another bottle of wine. Vassily said, "Gitler—*ni karasho*!" But it was Viktor who was the most conciliatory. He stood up and folded his arms, and, shushing the kitchen staff, he said in a little voice:

> *Zee fearst of My,*
> *Zee 'art of sprreng!*
> *Oh, leetle seeng,*
> *En everyseen we do,*
> *Remember always to say "pliz"*
> *En dun forget "sank you"!*

Later, Viktor took me to his compartment to show me his new fur hat. He was very proud of it, since it had cost him nearly a week's pay. The pretty waitress, Nina, was also in the compartment, which was shared by Vassily and Anna—quite a crowd for a space no bigger than an average-sized clothes closet. Nina showed me her passport and the picture of her mother and, while this was going on, Viktor disappeared. I put my arm around Nina and with my free hand took off her white scullion's cap. Her black hair fell to her shoulders. I held her tightly and kissed her, tasting the kitchen. The train was racing. But the compartment door was open, and Nina pulled away and said softly, *"Nyet, nyet, nyet."*

On the day before Christmas, in the afternoon, we arrived at Sverdlovsk. The sky was leaden and it was very cold. I hopped out the door and watched an old man being taken down the stairs to the platform. While he was being moved, the blankets had slipped down to his chest, where his hands lay rigid, two gray claws, their color matching his face. His son went over and pulled the blankets high to cover his mouth. He knelt in the ice and packed a towel around the old man's head.

Seeing me standing nearby, the son said in German, "Sverdlovsk. This is where Europe begins and Asia ends. Here are the Urals." He pointed toward the back of the train and said, "Asia," and then toward the engine, "Europe."

"How is your father?" I asked, when the stretcher bearers arrived and put on their harnesses. The stretcher was a hammock, slung between them.

"I think he's dead," he said. *"Das vedanya."*

My depression increased as we sped toward Perm in a whirling snowstorm. The logging camps and villages lay half-buried, and behind them were birches a foot thick, the ice on their branches giving them the appearance of silver filigree. I could see children crossing a frozen river in the storm, moving so slowly in the direction of some huts, they broke my heart. I lay back on my berth and took my radio, its plastic cold from standing by the window, and tried to find a station. I put up the antenna—the zombie now sharing my compartment watched me from behind his clutter of uncovered food. A lot of static, then a French station, then "Jingle Bells." The zombie smiled. I switched it off.

The next morning, Christmas, I woke and looked over at the zombie sleeping with his arms folded on his chest like a mummy's. The *provodnik* told me it was six o'clock Moscow time. My watch said eight. I put it back two hours and waited for dawn, surprised that so many people in the car had decided to do the same thing. In darkness we stood at the windows, watching our reflections. Shortly afterward I

saw why they were there. We entered the outskirts of Yaroslavl and I heard the others whispering to themselves. The
old lady in the frilly nightgown, the Goldi man and his wife
and child, the domino-playing drunks, even the zombie who
had been monkeying with my radio: they pressed their
faces against the windows as we began rattling across a
long bridge. Beneath us, half-frozen, very black, and in
places reflecting the flames of Yaroslavl's chimneys, was
the Volga.

> . . . *Royal David's city,*
> *Stood a lowly cattle shed* . . .

What was that? Sweet voices, as clear as organ tones,
drifted from my compartment. I froze and listened. The
Russians, awestruck by the sight of the Volga, had fallen silent; they were hunched, staring down at the water. But the
holy music, fragrant and slight, moved through the air,
warming it like an aroma.

> *Where a Mother laid her Baby*
> *In a manger for His bed* . . .

The hymn wavered, but the silent reverence of the Russians
and the slowness of the train allowed the soft children's
voices to perfume the corridor. My listening became a meditation of almost unbearable sadness, as if joy's highest re-
finement was borne on a needle point of pain.

> *Mary was that Mother mild,*
> *Jesus Christ her little Child* . . .

I went into the compartment and held the radio to my ear
until the broadcast ended, a program of Christmas music
from the BBC. Dawn never came that day. We traveled in
thick fog and through whorls of brown blowing mist, which
made the woods ghostly. It was not cold outside: some
snow had melted, and the roads—more frequent now—
were rutted and muddy. All morning the tree trunks, black
with dampness, were silhouettes in the fog, and the pine

groves at the very limit of visibility in the mist took on the appearance of cathedrals with dark spires. In places the trees were so dim, they were like an afterimage on the eye. I had never felt close to the country, but the fog distanced me even more, and I felt, after six thousand miles and all those days in the train, only a great remoteness; every reminder of Russia—the women in orange canvas jackets working on the line with shovels, the sight of a Lenin statue, the station signboards stuck in yellow ice, and the startled magpies croaking in Russian at the gliding train— all this annoyed me. I resented Russia's size; I wanted to be home.

The Old
Patagonian Express

Travel Is a Vanishing Act

TRAVEL IS A VANISHING ACT, A SOLITARY TRIP DOWN A pinched line of geography to oblivion.

> *What's become of Waring*
> *Since he gave us all the slip?*

But a travel book is the opposite, the loner bouncing back bigger than life to tell the story of his experiment with space. It is the simplest sort of narrative, an explanation which is its own excuse for the gathering up and the going. It is motion given order by its repetition in words. That sort of disappearance is elemental, but few come back silent. And yet the convention is to telescope travel writing, to start—as so many novels do—in the middle of things, to beach the reader in a bizarre place without having first guided him there. "The white ants had made a meal of my hammock," the book might begin; or "Down there, the Patagonian valley deepened to gray rock, wearing its eons' stripes and split by floods." Or, to choose actual first sentences at random from three books within arm's reach:

It was towards noon on March 1, 1898, that I first found myself entering the narrow and somewhat dangerous harbour of Mombasa, on the east coast of Africa. (*The Man-Eaters of Tsavo*, by Lt. Col. J. H. Patterson)

"Welcome!" says the big signboard by the side of the road as the car completes the corkscrew ascent from the heat of the South Indian plains into an almost alarming coolness. (*Ooty Preserved*, by Mollie Panter-Downes)

From the balcony of my room I had a panoramic view over Accra, capital of Ghana. (*Which Tribe Do You Belong To?* by Alberto Moravia)

My usual question, unanswered by these—by most—travel books, is: how did you get there? Even without the suggestion of a motive, a prologue is welcome, since the going is often as fascinating as the arrival. Yet, because curiosity implies delay, and delay is regarded as a luxury (but what's the hurry, anyway?), we have become used to life being a series of arrivals or departures, of triumphs and failures, with nothing noteworthy in between. Summits matter, but what of the lower slopes of Parnassus? We have not lost faith in journeys from home, but the texts are scarce. Departure is described as a moment of panic and ticket-checking in an airport lounge, or a fumbled kiss at a gangway; then silence until, "From the balcony of my room I had a panoramic view over Accra . . ."

Travel, truly, is otherwise. From the second you wake up you are headed for the foreign place, and each step (now past the cuckoo clock, now down Fulton to the Fellsway) brings you closer. *The Man-Eaters of Tsavo* is about lions devouring Indian railway laborers in Kenya at the turn of the century. But I would bet there was a subtler and just as riveting book about the sea journey from Southampton to Mombasa. For his own reasons, Colonel Patterson left it unwritten.

The literature of travel has become measly, the standard opening that farcical nose-against-the-porthole view from the plane's tilted fuselage. The joke opening, that straining for effect, is now so familiar it is nearly impossible to parody. How does it go? "Below us lay the tropical green, the flooded valley, the patchwork quilt of farms, and as we penetrated the cloud I could see dirt roads threading their way into the hills and cars so small they looked like toys. We circled the airport and, as we came in low for the landing, I saw the stately palms, the harvest, the rooftops of the shabby houses, the square fields stitched together with crude fences, the people like ants, the colorful . . ."

I have never found this sort of guesswork very convincing. When I am landing in a plane my heart is in my mouth; I wonder—doesn't everyone?—if we are going to crash. My life flashes before me, a brief selection of sordid and pathetic trivialities. Then a voice tells me to stay in my seat until the plane comes to a complete stop; and when we land the loudspeakers break into an orchestral version of "Moon River." I suppose if I had the nerve to look around I might see a travel writer scribbling, "Below us lay the tropical green—"

Meanwhile, what of the journey itself? Perhaps there is nothing to say. There is not much to say about most airplane journeys. Anything remarkable must be disastrous, so you define a good flight by negatives. You didn't get hijacked, you didn't crash, you didn't throw up, you weren't late, you weren't nauseated by the food. So you are grateful. The gratitude brings such relief your mind goes blank, which is appropriate, for the airplane passenger is a time-traveler. He crawls into a carpeted tube that is reeking of disinfectant; he is strapped in to go home, or away. Time is truncated, or in any case warped: he leaves in one time zone and emerges in another. And from the moment he steps into the tube and braces his knees on the seat in front, uncomfortably upright—from the moment he departs, his mind is focused on arrival. That is, if he has any sense at all. If he looked out of the window he would see nothing but the tundra of the cloud layer, and above is empty space. Time is brilliantly blinded: there is nothing to see. This is the reason so many people are apologetic about taking planes. They say, "What I'd really like to do is forget these plastic jumbos and get a three-masted schooner and just stand there on the poop deck with the wind in my hair."

But apologies are not necessary. An airplane flight may not be travel in any accepted sense, but it certainly is magic. Anyone with the price of a ticket can conjure up the castled crag of Drachenfels or the Lake Isle of Innisfree by simply using the right escalator at, say, Logan Airport in Boston—but it must be said that there is probably more to animate the mind, more of travel, in that one ascent on the escalator, than in the whole plane journey put together. The rest, the foreign country, what constitutes the arrival, is the ramp of an evil-smelling airport. If the passenger conceives of this species of transfer as travel and offers the public his book, the first foreigner the reader meets is either a clothes-grubbing customs man or a mustached demon at the immigration desk. Although it has become the way of the world, we still ought to lament the fact that airplanes have made us insensitive to space; we are encumbered, like lovers in suits of armor.

This is obvious. What interests me is the waking in the morning, the progress from the familiar to the slightly odd, to the rather strange, to the totally foreign, and finally to the outlandish. The journey, not the arrival, matters; the voyage, not the landing. Feeling cheated that way by other travel books, and wondering what exactly it is I have been denied, I decided to experiment by making my way to travel-book country, as far south as the trains run from Medford, Massachusetts; to end my book where travel books begin.

I had nothing better to do. I was at a stage I had grown to recognize in my writing life. I had just finished a novel, two years of indoor activity. Looking for something else to write, I found that instead of hitting nails on the head I was only striking a series of glancing blows. I hated cold weather. I wanted some sunshine. I had no job—what was the problem? I studied maps and there appeared to be a continuous track from my house in Medford to the Great Plateau of Patagonia in southern Argentina. There, in the town of Esquel, one ran out of railways. There was no line to Tierra del Fuego, but between Medford and Esquel rather a lot of them.

In this vagrant mood I boarded that first train, the one people took to work. They got off—their train trip was already over. I stayed on: mine was just beginning.

On the Frontier

It was a rainy night in Laredo—not late, and yet the place seemed deserted. A respectable frontier town, sprawling at the very end of the Amtrak line, it lay on a geometric grid of bright black streets on a dirt bluff that had the clawed and bulldozed look of a recent quarry. Below was the Rio Grande, a silent torrent slipping past Laredo in a cut as deep as a sewer; the south bank was Mexico.

The city lights were on, making the city's emptiness emphatic. In that glare I could see its character as more Mexican than Texan. The lights flashed, suggesting life, as lights do. But where were the people? There were stoplights on every corner, WALK and WAIT signs winked on and off; the two-story shop fronts were floodlit, lamps burned in the windows of one-story houses; the streetlights made the puddles bright holes in slabs of wet road. The effect of this illumination was eerie, that of a plague city brightened against looters. The stores were heavily padlocked; the churches lit up in cannonades of arc lamps; there were no bars. All that light, instead of giving an impression of warmth and activity, merely exposed its emptiness in a deadening blaze.

No traffic waited at the red lights, no pedestrians at the crosswalks. And though the city was silent, in the drizzly air was an unmistakable heart murmur, the *threep-threep* of music being played far away. I walked and walked, from my hotel to the river, from the river to a plaza, and into the maze of streets until I was almost certain I was lost. I saw nothing. And it could be frightening, seeing—four blocks away—a blinking sign I took to be a watering hole, a restaurant, an event, a sign of life, and walking to it and arriving soaked and gasping to discover that it was a shoe store or a funeral parlor, shut for the night. So, walking the streets of Laredo, I heard only my own footsteps, the false courage of their click, their faltering at alleyways, their splashes as I briskly returned to the only landmark I knew—the river.

The river itself made no sound, though it moved powerfully, eddying like a swarm of greasy snakes in the ravine from which every bush and tree had been removed in order to allow the police to patrol it. Three bridges linked the United States to Mexico here. Standing on the bluff I heard the *threep-threep* louder: it was coming from the Mexican side of the river, a just-discernible annoyance, like a neighbor's radio. Now I could see plainly the twisting river, and it struck me that a river is an appropriate frontier. Water is neutral and in its impartial winding makes the national boundary look like an act of God.

Looking south across the river, I realized that I was looking toward another continent, another country, another world. There were sounds there—music, and not only music but the pip and honk of voices and cars. The frontier was actual: people did things differently there, and looking hard I could see trees outlined by the neon beer signs, a traffic jam, the source of the music. No people, but cars and trucks were evidence of them. Beyond that, past the Mexican city of Nuevo Laredo, was a black slope—the featureless, night-haunted republics of Latin America.

A car drew up behind me. I was alarmed, then reassured when I saw it was a taxi. I gave the driver the name of my hotel and got in, but when I tried to make conversation he responded by grunting. He understood only his own language.

In Spanish I said, "It is quiet here."

That was the first time on my trip that I spoke Spanish. After this, nearly every conversation I had was in Spanish. But in the course of this narrative I shall try to avoid affecting Spanish words, and will translate all conversations into English. I have no patience with sentences that go, " '*Caramba!*' said the *campesino*, eating his *empanada* at the *estancia* . . ."

"Laredo," said the taxi driver. He shrugged.

"Where are all the people?"

"The other side."

"Nuevo Laredo?"

"Boys' Town," he said. The English took me by surprise, the phrase tickled me. He said, now in Spanish again, "There are one thousand prostitutes in the Zone."

It was a round number, but I was convinced. And that of course explained what had happened to this city. After dark, Laredo slipped into Nuevo Laredo, leaving the lights on. It was why Laredo looked respectable, even genteel, in a rainswept and mildewed way: the clubs, the bars, the brothels, were across the river. The red-light district was ten minutes away, in another country.

BUT THERE WAS MORE TO THIS MORAL SPELLED OUT IN TRANS-pontine geography than met the eye. If the Texans had the best of both worlds in decreeing that the fleshpots should remain on the Mexican side of the International Bridge— the river flowing, like the erratic progress of a tricky argument, between vice and virtue—the Mexicans had the sense of tact to keep Boys' Town camouflaged by decrepitude, on the other side of the tracks, another example of the geography of morality. Divisions everywhere: no one likes to live next door to a whorehouse. And yet both cities existed because of Boys' Town. Without the whoring and racketeering, Nuevo Laredo would not have had enough municipal funds to plant geraniums around the statue of its madly gesturing patriot in the plaza, much less advertise itself as a bazaar of wickerwork and guitar-twanging folklore—not that anyone ever went to Nuevo Laredo to be sold baskets. And Laredo required the viciousness of its sister city to keep its own churches full. Laredo had the airport and the churches, Nuevo Laredo the brothels and basket factories. Each nationality had seemed to gravitate to its own special area of competence. This was economically sound thinking; it followed to the letter the Theory of Comparative Advantage, outlined by the distinguished economist David Ricardo (1772–1823).

At first glance, this looked like the typical sort of

mushroom-and-dunghill relationship that exists at the frontiers of many unequal countries. But the longer I thought about it the more Laredo seemed like all of the United States, and Nuevo Laredo all of Latin America. This frontier was more than an example of cozy hypocrisy; it demonstrated all one needed to know about the morality of the Americas, the relationship between the puritanical efficiency north of the border, and the bumbling and passionate disorder—the anarchy of sex and hunger—south of it. It was not as simple as that, since there was obviously villainy and charity in both, and yet crossing the river (the Mexicans don't call it the Rio Grande; they call it the Rio Bravo de Norte), no more than an idle traveler making his way south with a suitcase of dirty laundry, a sheaf of railway timetables, a map, and a pair of leakproof shoes, I felt as if I was acting out a significant image. Crossing a national boundary and seeing such a difference on the other side had something to do with it: truly, every human feature there had the resonance of metaphor.

Lost Lover in Veracruz

I HAD PLANNED TO GET TO BED EARLY IN ORDER TO BE UP AT dawn to buy my ticket to Tapachula. It was when I switched the light off that I heard the music; darkness gave the sounds clarity, and it was too vibrant to be coming from a radio. It was a strong, full-throated brass band:

> *Land of Hope and Glory, Mother of the Free,*
> *How shall we extol thee, who are born of thee?*

"Pomp and Circumstance"? In Veracruz? At eleven o'clock at night?

Wider still and wider shall thy bounds be set;
God who made thee mighty, make thee mightier yet.

I dressed and went downstairs.

In the center of the plaza, near the four fountains, was the Mexican Navy Band, in white uniforms, giving Elgar the full treatment. Lights twinkled in the boughs of the laburnum trees, and there were floodlights, too—pink ones—playing on the balconies and the palms. A sizable crowd had gathered to listen—children played near the fountains, people walked their dogs, lovers held hands. The night was cool and balmy, the crowd good-humored and attentive. I think it was one of the prettiest sights I have ever seen; the Mexicans had the handsome thoughtful look, the serenity that comes of listening closely to lovely music. It was late, a soft wind moved through the trees, and the tropical harshness that had seemed to me constant in Veracruz was gone; these were gentle people, this was an attractive place.

The song ended. There was clapping. The band began playing "The Washington Post March," and I strolled around the perimeter of the plaza. There was a slight hazard in this. Because the carnival had just ended, Veracruz was full of idle prostitutes, and as I strolled I realized that most of them had not come here to the plaza to listen to the band—in fact, the greater part of the audience was composed of dark-eyed girls in slit skirts and low-cut dresses who, as I passed them, called out, "Let's go to my house," or fell into step with me and murmured, "Fuck?" This struck me as comic and rather pleasant—the military dignity of the march music, the pink light on the lush trees and balconies of the plaza, and the whispered invitations of those willing girls.

Now the band was playing Weber. I decided to sit on a bench and give it my full attention; I took an empty seat next to a couple who appeared to be chatting. They were both speaking at once. The woman was blond and was telling the man in English to go away; the man was offering her a drink and a good time in Spanish. She was insistent, he was conciliatory—he was also much younger than she. I listened with great interest, stroked my mustache, and hoped I was not noticed. The woman was saying, "My husband—understand?—my husband's meeting me here in five minutes."

In Spanish the man said, "I know a beautiful place. It is right near here."

The woman turned to me. "Do you speak English?"

I said I did.

"How do you tell these people to go away?"

I turned to the man. Now, facing him, I could see that he was no more than twenty-five. "The lady wants you to go away."

He shrugged, and then he leered at me. He did not speak, but his expression said, "You win." And he went. Two girls hurried after him.

The lady said, "I had to hit one over the head this morning with my umbrella. He wouldn't go away."

She was in her late forties, and was attractive in a brittle, meretricious way—she wore heavy makeup, eye shadow, and thick Mexican jewelry of silver and turquoise. Her hair was platinum, with hues of pink and green—perhaps it was the plaza light. Her suit was white, her handbag was white, her shoes were white. One could hardly blame the Mexican for making an attempt on her, since she bore such a close resemblance to the stereotype of the American woman who occurs so frequently in Tennessee Williams's plays and Mexican photo-comics—the vacationer with a tormented libido and a drinking problem and a symbolic name who comes to Mexico in search of a lover.

Her name was Nicky. She had been in Veracruz for nine days, and when I expressed surprise at this she said, "I may be here a month or—who knows?—maybe for a lot longer."

"You must like it here," I said.

"I do." She peered at me. "What are you doing here?"

"Growing a mustache."

She did not laugh. She said, "I'm looking for a friend."

I almost stood up and walked away. It was the way she said it.

"He's very sick. He needs help." Her voice hinted at desperation, her face was fixed. "Only I can't find him. I put him on the plane at Mazatlán. I gave him money, some new clothes, a ticket. He'd never been on a plane before. I don't know where he is. Do you read the papers?"

"All the time."

"Have you seen this?"

She showed me the local newspaper. It was folded so that a wide column showed, and under PERSONAL NOTICES there was a black-framed box with the headline in Spanish URGENT TO LOCATE. There was a snapshot with a caption. The snapshot was one of those overbright pictures that are taken of startled people in nightclubs by pestering men who say, "Peecha, peecha?" In this picture, Nicky in huge sunglasses and an evening gown—radiantly tanned and fuller faced—sat at a table (flowers, wineglasses) with a thin, mustached man. He looked a bit scared and a bit sly, and yet his arm around her suggested bravado.

I read the message: SEÑORA NICKY—WISHES URGENTLY TO GET IN TOUCH WITH HER HUSBAND SEÑOR JOSÉ——, WHO HAS BEEN LIVING IN MAZATLÁN. IT IS BELIEVED THAT HE IS NOW IN VERACRUZ. ANYONE WHO RECOGNIZES HIM FROM THIS PICTURE SHOULD IMMEDIATELY CONTACT—. There followed detailed instructions for getting in touch with Nicky, and three telephone numbers.

I said, "Has anyone called you up?"

"No," she said, and put the newspaper back into her handbag. "Today was the first day it appeared. I'm going to run it all week."

"It must be pretty expensive."

"I've got enough money," she said. "He's very sick. He's dying of TB. He said he wanted to see his mother. I put him on the plane in Mazatlán and stayed there for a few days—I had given him the number of my hotel. But when he didn't call me I got worried, so I came here. His mother's here—this is where he was headed. But I can't find him."

"Why not try his mother?"

"I can't find her either. See, he didn't know her address. He only knew that it was right near the bus station. He drew me a picture of the house. Well, I found something that looks like the house, but no one knew him there. He was going to get off the plane at Mexico City and take a bus from there—that way he'd be able to find his mother's house. It's kind of complicated."

And kind of fishy, too, I thought, but instead of speaking I made a sympathetic noise.

"But it's serious. He's sick. He only weighs about a hundred pounds now, probably less. There's a hospital in Jalapa. They could help him. I'd pay." She looked toward the bandstand. The band was playing a medley of songs from *My Fair Lady*. Nicky said, "Actually, today I went to the office of death records to see if he had died. He hasn't died at least."

"In Veracruz."

"What do you mean?"

"He might have died in Mexico City."

"He doesn't know anyone in Mexico City. He wouldn't have stayed there. He would have come straight here."

But he had boarded the plane and vanished. In nine days of searching, Nicky had not been able to find a trace of him. Perhaps it was the effect of the Dashiell Hammett novel I had just read, but I found myself examining her situation with a detective's skepticism. Nothing could have been more melodramatic, or more like a Bogart film: near midnight in Veracruz, the band playing ironical love songs, the plaza crowded with friendly whores, the woman in the white suit describing the disappearance of her Mexican husband. It is possible that this sort of movie fantasy, which is available to the solitary traveler, is one of the chief reasons for travel. She had cast herself in the role of leading lady in her search drama, and I gladly played my part. We were far from home: we could be anyone we wished. Travel offers a great occasion to the amateur actor.

And if I had not seen myself in this Bogart role, I would have commiserated with her and said what a shame it was that she could not find the man. Instead, I was detached: I wanted to know everything. I said, "Does he know you're looking for him?"

"No, he doesn't know I'm here. He thinks I'm back in Denver. The way we left it, he was just going to go home and see his mother. He hasn't been home for eight years.

See, that's what's so confusing for him. He's been living in Mazatlán. He's a poor fisherman—he can barely read."

"Interesting. You live in Denver, he lives in Mazatlán."

"That's right."

"And you're married to him?"

"No—what gave you that idea? We're not married. He's a friend."

"It says in the paper he's your husband."

"I didn't write that. I don't speak Spanish."

"That's what it says. In Spanish. He's your husband."

I was not Bogart anymore. I was Montgomery Clift playing the psychiatrist in *Suddenly Last Summer*. Katharine Hepburn hands him the death certificate of Sebastian Venable; Sebastian has been eaten alive by small boys, and the mutilation is described on the certificate. *It's in Spanish,* she says, believing the horrible secret is safe. Montgomery Clift replies coldly, *I read Spanish.*

"That's a mistake," said Nicky. "He's not my husband. He's just a beautiful human being."

She let this sink in. The band was playing a waltz.

She said, "I met him a year ago when I was in Mazatlán. I was on the verge of a nervous breakdown—my husband had left me. I didn't know which way to turn. I started walking along the beach. José saw me and got out of his boat. He put his hand out and touched me. He was smiling . . ." Her voice trailed off. She began again, "He was very kind. It was what I needed. I was in a breakdown situation. He saved me."

"What kind of boat?"

"A little boat—he's a poor fisherman," she said. She squinted. "He just put out his hand and touched me. Then I got to know him better. We went out to eat—to a restaurant. He had never had anything—he wasn't married—he didn't have a cent to his name. He had never had any good clothes, never eaten in a good restaurant, didn't know what to do. It was all new to him. 'You saved me,' I said. He just smiled. I gave him money and for the next few weeks we had a wonderful time. Then he told me he had TB."

"But he didn't speak English, right?"

"He could say a few words."

"You believed him when he said he had TB?"

"He wasn't lying, if that's what you think. I saw his doctor. The doctor told me he needed treatment. So I swore I would help him, and that's why I went to Mazatlán a month ago. To help him. He was much thinner—he couldn't go fishing. I was really worried. I asked him what he wanted. He said he wanted to see his mother. I gave him money and things and put him on the plane, and when I didn't hear from him I came here myself."

"It seems very generous of you. You could be out having a good time. Instead, you're searching Veracruz for this lost soul."

"It's what God wants me to do," she whispered.

"Yes?"

"And I'll find him, if God wants me to."

"You're going to stick at it, eh?"

"We Sagittarians are awful determined—real adventurous types! What sign are you?"

"Aries."

"Ambitious."

"That's me."

She said, "Actually, I think God's testing me."

"In what way?"

"This José business is nothing. I've just been through a very heavy divorce. And there's some other things."

"About José. If he's illiterate, then his mother's probably illiterate. In that case, she won't see your ad in the paper. So why not have a poster made—a picture, some details—and you can put it up near the bus station and where his mother's house is supposed to be."

"I think I'll try that."

I gave her more suggestions: hire a private detective, broadcast messages on the radio. Then it occurred to me that José might have gone back to Mazatlán. If he had been sick or worried he would have done that, and if he had been trying to swindle her—as I suspected he had—he would certainly have done that eventually, when he ran out of money.

She agreed that he might have gone back, but not for the reasons I said. "I'm staying here until I find him. But even if I find him tomorrow I'll stay a month. I like it here. This is a real nice town. Were you here for the carnival? No? It was a trip, I can tell you that. Everyone was down here in the plaza—"

Now the band was playing Rossini, the overture to *The Barber of Seville*.

"—drinking, dancing. Everyone was so friendly. I met so many people. I was partying every night. That's why I don't mind staying here and looking for José. And, um, I met a man."

"Local feller?"

"Mexican. He gave me good vibrations, like you're giving me. You're positive—get posters made, radio broadcasts—that's what I need."

"This new man you met—he might complicate things."

She shook her head. "He's good for me."

"What if he finds out that you're looking for José? He might get annoyed."

"He knows all about it. We discussed it. Besides," she added after a moment, "José is dying."

The concert had ended. It was so late I had become ravenously hungry. I said that I was going to a restaurant, and Nicky said, "Mind if I join you?" We had red snapper and she told me about her divorces. Her first husband had been violent, her second had been a bum. It was her word.

"A real bum?"

"A real one," she said. "He was so lazy—why, he worked for me, you know? While we were married. But he was so lazy I had to fire him."

"When you divorced him?"

"No, long before that. I fired him, but I stayed married to him. That was about five years ago. After that, he just hung around the house. When I couldn't take any more of it I divorced him. Then guess what? He goes to his lawyer and tries to get me to pay him maintenance money. *I'm* supposed to pay *him*!"

"What sort of business are you in?"

"I own slums," she said. "Fifty-seven of them—I mean, fifty-seven units. I used to own 128 units. But these fifty-seven are in eighteen different locations. God, it's a problem—people always want paint, things fixed, a new roof."

I ceased to see her as a troubled libido languishing in Mexico. She owned property; she was here living on her slum rents. She said she didn't pay any taxes because of her "depreciations" and that on paper she looked "real good." She said, "God's been good to me."

"Are you going to sell these slums of yours?"

"Probably. I'd like to live here. I'm a real Mexico freak."

"And you'll make a profit when you sell them."

"That's what it's all about."

"Then why don't you let these people live rent-free? They're doing you a favor by keeping them in repair. God would love you for that. And you'll still make a profit."

She said, "That's silly."

The bill came.

"I'll pay for myself," she said.

"Save your money," I said. "José might turn up."

She smiled at me. "You're kind of an interesting guy."

I had not said a single word about myself; she did not even know my name. Perhaps this reticence was interesting? But it wasn't reticence: she hadn't asked.

I said, "Maybe I'll see you tomorrow."

"I'm at the Diligencia."

I was at the Diligencia, too. I decided not to tell her this. I said, "I hope you find what you're looking for."

Magic Names

WE CAME TO TIERRA BLANCA. THE DESCRIPTIVE NAME DID not describe the place. Spanish names were apt only as ironies or simplifications; they seldom fit. The argument is usually stated differently, to demonstrate how dull, how literal-minded and unimaginative the Spanish explorer or cartographer was. Seeing a dark river, the witness quickly assigned a name: Rio Negro. It is a common name throughout Latin America; yet it never matched the color of the water. And the four Rio Colorados I saw bore not the slightest hint of red. Piedra Negras was marshland, not black stones; I saw no stags at Venado Tuerto, no lizards at Lagartos. None of the Laguna Verdes was green; my one La Dorada looked leaden, and Progreso in Guatemala was backward, La Libertad in El Salvador a stronghold of repression in a country where salvation seemed in short supply. La Paz was not peaceful, nor was La Democracia democratic. This was not literalness—it was whimsy. Place names called attention to beauty, freedom, piety, or strong colors; but the places themselves, so prettily named, were something else. Was it willful inaccuracy or a lack of subtlety that made the map so glorious with fine attributes and praises? Latins found it hard to live with dull facts; the enchanting name, while not exactly making their town magical, at least took the curse off it. And there was always a chance that an evocative name might evoke something to make the plain town bearable.

Earthquakes in Guatemala

GUATEMALA CITY, AN EXTREMELY HORIZONTAL PLACE, IS like a city on its back. Its ugliness, which is a threatened look (the low, morose houses have earthquake cracks in their façades; the buildings wince at you with fright lines), is ugliest on those streets where, just past the last toppling house, a blue volcano's cone bulges. I could see the volcanoes from the window of my hotel room. I was on the third floor, which was also the top floor. They were tall volcanoes and looked capable of spewing lava. Their beauty was undeniable; but it was the beauty of witches. The rumbles from their fires had heaved this city down.

The first capital had been destroyed by torrents of water. So the capital was moved three miles away to Antigua in the middle of the sixteenth century. In 1773, Antigua was flattened by an earthquake, and a more stable site—at least it was farther from the slopes of the great volcanoes—was found here, in the Valley of the Hermitage, formerly an Indian village. Churches were built—a dozen, of Spanish loveliness, with slender steeples and finely finished porches and domes. The earth shook—not much, but enough to split them. Tremors left cracks between windows, and separated, in the stained glass of those windows, the shepherd from his brittle flock, the saint from his gold staff, the martyr from his persecutors. Christs were parted from their crosses and the anatomy of chapel Virgins violated, as their enameling, the porcelain white of faces and fingers, shattered, sometimes with a report that startled the faithful in their prayers. The windows, the statues, the masonry were mended; and gold leaf was applied thickly to the splintered altars. It seemed the churches had been made whole again. But the motion of earthquakes had never really ceased. In Guatemala they were inescapable. And in 1917 the whole city was thrown into its streets—every church and house and brothel. Thousands died; that unprecedented earthquake was seen as a judgment; and more fled to the Caribbean coast, where there were only savages to contend with.

The Guatemalans, sullen at the best of times, display a scolded resignation—bordering at times on guiltiness—when the subject of earthquakes is raised. Charles Darwin is wonderful in describing the sense of dislocation and spiritual panic that earthquakes produce in people. He experienced an earthquake when the *Beagle* was anchored off the Chilean coast. "A bad earthquake," he writes, "at once destroys our oldest associations: the earth, the very emblem of solidity, has moved beneath our feet like a thin crust over a fluid;—one second of time has created in the mind a strange idea of insecurity, which hours of reflection would not have produced."

The Pretty Town of Santa Ana

THE TOWN ONLY LOOKED GODFORSAKEN; IN FACT, IT WAS comfortable. It was a nice combination of attributes. In every respect, Santa Ana, the most Central American of Central American towns, was a perfect place—perfect in its pious attitudes and pretty girls, perfect in its slumber, its coffee-scented heat, its jungly plaza, and in the dusty elegance of its old buildings whose whitewash at nightfall gave them a vivid phosphorescence. Even its volcano was in working order. My hotel, the Florida, was a labyrinthine one-story affair, with potted palms and wicker chairs and good food—fresh fish, from nearby Lake Guija, was followed by the crushed velvet of Santa Ana coffee, and Santa Ana dessert, a delicate cake of mashed beans and banana served in cream. This pleasing hotel cost four dollars a night. It was a block from the Plaza. All Santa Ana's buildings of distinction—there were three—were in the plaza: the Cathedral was neo-gothic, the town hall had the colonnaded opulence of a ducal palace, and the Santa Ana theater had once been an opera house.

In another climate, I don't think the theater would have seemed so special, but in this sleepy tropical town in the western highlands of El Salvador—and there was nothing here for the luxury-minded or ruin-hunting tourist—the theater was magnificent and strange. Its style was banana republic Graeco-Roman; it was newly whitewashed, and classical in an agreeably vulgar way, with cherubs on its façade, and trumpeting angels, and masks of comedy and tragedy, a partial sorority of Muses: a pudgy Melpomene, a pouncing Thalia, Calliope with a lyre in her lap, and—her muscles showing through her tunic as fully developed as a

101

gym teacher's—Terpsichore. There were columns, too, and a Romanesque portico, and on a shield a fuming volcano as nicely proportioned as Izalco, the one just outside town, which was probably the model for this emblem. It was a beautiful turn-of-the-century theater and not entirely neglected; once, it had provided Santa Ana with concerts and operas, but culturally Santa Ana had contracted, and catering to this shrunken condition the theater had been reduced to showing movies. That week, the offering was *New York, New York.*

I liked Santa Ana immediately; its climate was mild, its people alert and responsive, and it was small enough so that a short walk took me to its outskirts, where the hills were deep green and glossy with coffee bushes. The hard-pressed Guatemalans I had found a divided people—and the Indians in the hinterland seemed hopelessly lost; but El Salvador, on the evidence in Santa Ana, was a country of half-breeds, energetic and full of talk, practicing a kind of Catholicism based on tactile liturgy. In the Cathedral, pious Salvadoreans pinched the feet of saints and rubbed at relics, and women with infants—always remembering to insert a coin in the slot and light a candle first—seized the loose end of Christ's cincture and mopped the child's head with its tassel.

Soccer in San Salvador

I HAD READ ABOUT LATIN AMERICAN SOCCER—THE CHAOS, the riots, the passionately partisan crowds, the way political frustrations were ventilated at the stadiums. I knew for a fact that if one wished to understand the British it helped to see a soccer game; then, the British did not seem so tight-lipped and proper. Indeed, a British soccer game was an occasion for a form of gang warfare for the younger spectators. The muscular ritual of sport was always a clear demonstration of the wilder impulses in national character. The Olympic Games are interesting largely because they are a kind of world war in pantomime. "Would you mind if I went to the game with you?" I asked Alfredo, a salesman I had met on the train from Santa Ana.

Alfredo looked worried. "It will be very crowded," he said. "There may be trouble. It is better to go to the swimming pool tomorrow—for the girls."

"Do you think I came to El Salvador to pick up girls at a public swimming pool?"

"Did you come to El Salvador to see the football game?"

"Yes," I said.

Alfredo was late. He blamed the traffic. "There will be a million people at the stadium." He had brought along some friends, two boys who, he boasted, were studying English.

"How are you doing?" I asked them in English.

"Please?" said one. The other laughed. The first one said in Spanish, "We are only on the second lesson."

Because of the traffic, and the risk of car thieves at the stadium, Alfredo parked half a mile away, at a friend's house. This house was worth some study; it was a number of cubicles nailed to trees, with the leafy branches descending into the rooms. Cloth was hung from sticks to provide walls, and a strong fence surrounded it. I asked the friend how long he had lived there. He said his family had lived in the house for many years. I did not ask what happened when it rained.

But poverty in a poor country had subtle gradations. We walked down a long hill toward the stadium, and crossing a bridge I looked into a gorge expecting to see a river and saw lean-tos and cooking fires and lanterns. Who lived there? I asked Alfredo.

"Poor people," he said.

Others were walking to the stadium, too. We joined a large procession of quick-marching fans, and as we drew closer to the stadium they began yelling and shoving in anticipation. The procession swarmed over the foothills below the stadium, crashing through people's gardens and thumping the fenders of stalled cars. Here the dust was deep and the trampling feet of the fans made it rise until it became a brown fog, like a sepia print of a mob scene, with the cones of headlights bobbing in it. The mob was running now, and Alfredo and his friends were obscured by the dust cloud. Every ten feet, boys rushed forward and shook tickets at me, screaming, "Suns! Suns! Suns!"

These were the touts. They bought the cheapest tickets and sold them at a profit to people who had neither the time nor the courage to stand in a long rowdy line at a ticket window. The seat designations were those usual at a bullfight: Suns were the cheapest, bleacher seats; Shades were the more expensive ones under the canopy.

I fought my way through the touts and, having lost Alfredo, made my way uphill to the kettle-shaped stadium. It was an unearthly sight, the crowd of people emerging from darkness into luminous brown fog, the yells, the dust rising, the mountainside smoldering under a sky which, because of the dust, was starless. At that point, I considered turning back; but the mob was propelling me forward toward the stadium where the roar of the spectators inside made a sound like flames howling in a chimney.

The mob took up this cry and surged past me, stirring up the dust. There were women frying bananas and meat cakes over fires on the walkway that ran around the outside perimeter of the stadium. The smoke from these fires and the dust made each searchlight seem to burn with a smoky flame. The touts reappeared nearer the stadium. They were hysterical now. The game was about to start; they had not sold their tickets. They grabbed my arms, they pushed tickets in my face, they shouted.

One look at the lines of people near the ticket window told me that I would have no chance at all of buying a ticket legally. I was pondering this question when, through the smoke and dust, Alfredo appeared.

"Take your watch off," he said. "And your ring. Put them in your pocket. Be very careful. Most of these people are thieves. They will rob you."

I did as I was told. "What about the tickets? Shall we buy some Suns from these boys?"

"No, I will buy Shades."

"Are they expensive?"

"Of course, but this will be a great game. I could never see such a game in Santa Ana. Anyway, the Shades will be quieter." Alfredo looked around. "Hide over there by the wall. I will get the tickets."

Alfredo vanished into the conga line at a ticket window. He appeared again at the middle of the line, jumped the queue, elbowed forward, and in a very short time he had fought his way to the window. Even his friends marveled at his speed. He came toward us smiling, waving the tickets in triumph.

We were frisked at the entrance; we passed through a tunnel and emerged at the end of the stadium. From the outside it had looked like a kettle; inside, its shape was more of a salver, a tureen filled with brown, screeching faces. In the center was a pristine rectangle of green grass.

It was, those 45,000 people, a model of Salvadorean society. Not only the half of the stadium where the Suns sat (and it was jammed: not an empty seat was visible); or the better dressed and almost as crowded half of the Shades (at night, in the dry season, there was no difference in the quality of the seats: we sat on concrete steps, but ours, being more expensive than the Suns, were less crowded); there was a section that Alfredo had not mentioned: the Balconies. Above us, in five tiers of a gallery that ran around our half of the stadium, were the Balcony people. Balcony people had season tickets. Balcony people had small rooms, cupboard-sized, about as large as the average Salvadorean hut; I could see the wine bottles, the glasses, the plates of food. Balcony people had folding chairs and a good view of the field. There were not many Balcony people—two or three hundred—but at $2,000 for a season ticket in a country where the per capita income was $373 one could understand why. The Balcony people faced the screaming Suns and, beyond the stadium, a plateau. What I took to be lumpish multicolored vegetation covering the plateau was, I realized, a heap of Salvadoreans standing on top or clinging to the sides. There were thousands of them in this mass, and it was a sight more terrifying than the Suns. They were lighted by the stadium glare; there was a just-perceptible crawling movement among the bodies; it was an anthill.

National anthems were played, amplified songs from scratched records, and then the game began. It was apparent from the outset who would win. Mexico was bigger and faster, and seemed to follow a definite strategy; El Salvador had two ball hoggers, and the team was tiny and erratic. The crowd hissed the Mexicans and cheered El Salvador. One of the Salvadorean ball hoggers went jinking down the field, shot, and missed. The ball went to the Mexicans, who tormented the Salvadoreans by passing it from man to man and then, fifteen minutes into the game, the Mexicans scored. The stadium was silent as the Mexican players kissed one another.

Some minutes later the ball was kicked into the Shades section. It was thrown back into the field and the game was resumed. Then it was kicked into the Suns' section. The Suns fought for it; one man gained possession, but he was pounced upon and the ball shot up and ten Suns went tumbling after it. A Sun tried to run down the steps with it. He was caught and the ball wrestled from him. A fight began, and now there were scores of Suns punching their way to the ball. The Suns higher up in the section threw bottles and cans and wadded paper on the Suns who were fighting, and the shower of objects—meat pies, bananas, hankies—continued to fall. The Shades, the Balconies, the Anthill watched this struggle.

And the players watched, too. The game had stopped. The Mexican players kicked the turf, the Salvadorean team shouted at the Suns.

Please return the ball. It was the announcer. He was hoarse. *If the ball is not returned, the game will not continue.*

This brought a greater shower of objects from the upper seats—cups, cushions, more bottles. The bottles broke with a splashing sound on the concrete seats. The Suns lower down began throwing things back at their persecutors, and it was impossible to say where the ball had gone.

The ball was not returned. The announcer repeated his threat.

The players sat down on the field and did limbering-up exercises until, ten minutes after the ball had disappeared from the field, a new ball was thrown in. The spectators cheered but, just as quickly, fell silent. Mexico had scored another goal.

Soon, a bad kick landed the ball into the Shades. This ball was fought for and not thrown back, and one could see the ball progressing through the section. The ball was seldom visible, but one could tell from the free-for-alls—now here, now there—where it was. The Balconies poured water on the Shades, but the ball was not surrendered. And now it was the Suns' turn to see the slightly better-off Salvadoreans in the Shades section behaving like swine. The announcer made his threat: the game would not resume until the ball was thrown back. The threat was ignored, and after a long time the ref walked onto the field with a new ball.

In all, five balls were lost this way. The fourth landed not far from where I sat, and I could see that real punches were being thrown, real blood spurting from Salvadorean noses, and the broken bottles and the struggle for the ball made it a contest all its own, more savage than the one on the field, played out with the kind of mindless ferocity you read about in books on gory medieval sports. The announcer's warning was merely ritual threat; the police did not intervene—they stayed on the field and let the spectators settle their own scores. The players grew bored: they ran in place, they did push-ups. When play resumed and Mexico gained possession of the ball it deftly moved down the field and invariably made a goal. But this play, these goals—they were no more than interludes in a much bloodier sport which, toward midnight (and the game was still not over!), was varied by Suns throwing firecrackers at one another and onto the field.

The last time play was abandoned and fights broke out among the Suns—the ball bobbing from one ragged Sun to another—balloons were released from the upper seats. But they were not balloons. They were white, blimpy, and had a nipple on the end; first one, then dozens. This caused great laughter, and they were batted from section to section. They were of course contraceptives, and they caused Alfredo no end of embarrassment. "That is very bad," he said, gasping in shame. He had apologized for the interruptions; for the fights; the delayed play. Now this—dozens of airborne rubbers. The game was a shambles; it ended in confusion, fights, litter. But it shed light on the recreations of Salvadoreans, and as for the other thing—the inflated contraceptives—I later discovered that the Agency for International Development's largest Central American family planning program is in El Salvador. I doubt whether the birth rate has been affected, but children's birthday parties in rural El Salvador must be a great deal of fun, what with the free balloons.

Mexico won the game, six to one. Alfredo said that El Salvador's goal was the best one of the game, a header from thirty yards. So he managed to rescue a shred of pride. But people had been leaving all through the second half, and the rest hardly seemed to notice or to care that the game had ended. Just before we left the stadium I looked up at the anthill. It was a hill once again; there were no people on it, and depopulated, it seemed very small.

Outside, on the stadium slopes, the scene was like one of those lurid murals of Hell you see in Latin American churches. The color was infernal, yellow dust sifted and whirled among crater-like pits, small cars with demonic headlights moved slowly from hole to hole like mechanical devils. And where, on the mural, you see the sins printed and dramatized, the gold lettering saying LUST, ANGER, AVARICE, DRUNKENNESS, GLUTTONY, THEFT, PRIDE, JEALOUSY, USURY, GAMBLING, and so on, here after midnight were groups of boys lewdly snatching at girls, and knots of people fighting, counting the money they had won, staggering and swigging from bottles, shrieking obscenities against Mexico, thumping the hoods of cars or dueling with the branches they had yanked from trees and the radio aerials they had twisted from cars. They trampled the dust and howled. The car horns were like harsh moos of pain—and one car was being overturned, by a gang of shirtless, sweating youths. Many people were running to get free of the mob, holding handkerchiefs over their faces. But there were tens of thousands of people here, and animals, too, maimed dogs snarling and cowering as in a classic vision of Hell. And it was hot: dark, grimy air that was hard to breathe, and freighted with the stinks of sweat; it was so thick it muted the light. It tasted of stale fire and ashes. The mob did not disperse; it was too angry to go home, too insulted by defeat to ignore its hurt. It was loud and it moved as if thwarted and pushed; it danced madly in what seemed a deep hole.

Alfredo knew a shortcut to the road. He led the way through the parking lot and a ravaged grove of trees behind some huts. I saw people lying on the ground, but whether they were wounded or sleeping or dead I could not tell.

I asked him about the mob.

"What did I tell you?" he said. "You are sorry you came, right?"

"No," I said, and I meant it. Now I was satisfied. Travel is pointless without certain risks. I had spent the whole evening scrutinizing what I saw, trying to memorize details, and I knew I would never go to another soccer game in Latin America.

Holy Mass in San Vicente

ELEVEN OLD LADIES WERE KNEELING IN THE FRONT PEWS and praying. The church was cool, so I took a pew at the rear and tried to spot the statue of Saint Joseph. From the eleven black-shawled heads came the steady murmur of prayer; it was a simmer of incantation, low voices like thick

Salvadorean soup mumbling in a pot, the same bubbling rhythm of formula prayers. They were like specters, the row of crones draped in black, uttering muffled prayers in the shadowy church; the sunbeams breaking through the holes in the stained-glass windows made logs of light that seemed to prop up the walls; there was a smell of burned wax, and the candle flames fluttered in a continuous tremble, like the voices of those old ladies. Inside El Pilar the year might have been 1831, and these the wives and mothers of Spanish soldiers praying for deliverance from the onslaught of frantic Indians.

A tinkling bell rang from the sacristy. I sat primly and piously, straightening my back, in an instinctive reflex. It was habitual: I could not enter a church without genuflecting and dipping my fingers in the holy water font. A priest scuffed to the altar rail, flanked by two acolytes. The priest raised his arms, and that gesture—but perhaps it was his good looks, the well-combed curate rather stuck on his clerical smoothness—was the stagey flourish of a nightclub master of ceremonies. He was praying, but his prayers were mannered, Spanish, not Latin, and then he extended one arm toward a corner of the church that was hidden from me. He performed a little wrist play, a wave of his hand, and the music began.

It was not solemn music. It was two electric guitars, a clarinet, maracas, and a full set of drums—as soon as it had started to blurt I shifted my seat for a look at the musicians. It was the harsh wail of tuneless pop music that I had been avoiding for weeks, the squawk and crash that I had first heard issuing from Mexico as I stood on the high riverbank at Laredo. I had, since then, only rarely been out of earshot of it. How to describe it? With the guitar whine was an irregular beat, and each beat like a set of crockery dropped on the floor; a girl and boy shook maracas and sang—this was a cat's-yowl attempt at harmonizing, but off-key it did not even have the melodiousness of a set of madly scraping locusts.

They were of course singing a hymn. In a place where Jesus Christ was depicted as a muscular tough, a blue-eyed Latin with slicked-down hair, a deeply handsome young fellow, religion was a kind of love affair. In some Catholicism, and frequently in Spanish America, prayer has become a romancing with Jesus. He is not a terrible God, not a destroyer, not a cold and vindictive ascetic; he is princely and with it the ultimate macho figure. The hymn was a love song, but very much a Spanish-American one, crowing with lugubrious passion, the word *heart* repeated in every verse. And it was extremely loud. This was worship, but there was no substantial difference between what was going on here in this old church and what one could hear in the jukebox down the street in El Bar Americano. The church had been brought to the people; it had not made the people more pious—they had merely used this as an opportunity to entertain themselves and take the boredom out of the service. A mass or these evening prayers was an occasion to concentrate the mind in prayer; this music turned it into a distraction.

Music of this special deafening kind seemed important in Spanish America, because it prevented any thought whatsoever. The goon with the transistor in the train, the village boys gathered around their yakketing box, the man in Santa Ana who brought his cassette machine to breakfast and stared at its groaning amplifier, all the knee jerks and finger snapping and tooth sucking seemed to have one purpose—a self induced stupor for people who lived in a place where alcohol was expensive and drugs illegal. It was deafness and amnesia; it celebrated nothing but lost beauty and broken hearts; it had no memorable melody; it was splinters of glass ceaselessly flushed down a toilet, the thud of drums and the grunts of singers. People I met on my trip were constantly telling me they loved music. Not pop music from the United States, but this music. I knew what they meant.

Meanwhile, the priest had sat down beside the altar, looking pleased with himself. Well he might: the music had its effect. As soon as it had started, people had begun to pour into the church: schoolchildren with satchels and wearing uniforms, young children—barefoot urchins, kids with twisted nitty hair who had been frolicking in the plaza; mumbling old men with machetes, and two farm boys clutching straw hats to their chests, and a lady with a tin wash basin and a gang of boys, and a bewildered dog. The dog sat in the center aisle and beat its stub of tail against the tiles. The music was loud enough to have reached the market up the street, for here were three ladies in full skirts carrying empty baskets and leather purses. Some sat, some waited at the back of the church. They watched the band, not the tabernacle, and they were smiling. Oh, yes, this is what religion is all about—rejoice, smile, be happy, the Lord is with you; snap your fingers, He has redeemed the world. There were two shattering clashes of cymbals.

The music stopped. The priest stood up. The prayers began.

And the people who had come into the church during the song pushed to the rear door. The eleven old ladies in the front pews did not move, and only they remained to say the Confiteor. The priest paced back and forth at the altar rail. He gave a short sermon: God loves you, he said; you must learn how to love Him. It was not easy in the modern world to find time for God: there were temptations, and the evidence of sin was everywhere. It was necessary to work hard and dedicate each labor to the glory of God. Amen.

Again, a wave of the hand, and the music started. This time it was much louder, and it attracted a greater number of people from the plaza to hear it. It was a similar song: yowl, thump, *heart, heart*, yowl, crash, dooby-doo, thump, crash, crash. There was no hesitation among the onlookers when it ended. At the final crash, they fled. But not for long. Ten minutes later (two prayers, a minute of meditation, some business with an incense burner, another pep talk) the band again began to play and the people returned. This routine continued for a full hour, and it was still going on when I took myself away—during a song, not a sermon or prayer; I had a train to catch.

The sky was purple and pink, the volcano black; lurid chutes of orange dust filled the valleys, and the lake was fiery, like a pool of molten lava.

To Limón with Mr. Thornberry

"T HIS SCENERY," SAID MR. THORNBERRY, "IT BLOWS MY mind." Mr. Thornberry had a curious way of speaking, he squinted until his eyes were not more than slits; his face tightened into a grimace and his mouth went square, mimicking a grin, and then without moving his lips he spoke through his teeth. It was the way people talked when they were heaving ash barrels, sort of screwing their faces up and groaning their words.

Lots of things blew Mr. Thornberry's mind: the way the river thundered, the grandeur of the valley, the little huts, the big boulders, and the climate blew his mind most of all—he had figured on something more tropical. It was an odd phrase from a man of his age, but after all Mr. Thornberry was a painter. I wondered why he had not brought his sketchbook. He repeated that he had left the hotel on the spur of the moment. He was, he said, traveling light. "Where's your bag?"

I pointed to my suitcase on the luggage rack.

"It's pretty big."

"That's everything I have. I might meet a beautiful woman in Limón and decide to spend the rest of my life there."

"I did that once."

"I was joking," I said.

But Mr. Thornberry was still grimacing. "It was a disaster in my case."

Out of the corner of my eye I saw that the river was seething, and men were standing in the shallows—I could not make out what they were doing—and pink and blue flowers grew beside the track.

113

Mr. Thornberry told me about his painting. You couldn't be a painter during the Depression; couldn't make a living at it. He had worked in Detroit and New York City. He had had a miserable time of it. Three children, but his wife had died when the third was still an infant—tuberculosis, and he had not been able to afford a good doctor. So she died and he had to raise the kids himself. They had grown up and married and he had gone to New Hampshire to take up painting, what he had always wanted to do. It was a nice place, northern New Hampshire; in fact, he said, it looked a hell of a lot like this part of Costa Rica.

"I thought it looked like Vermont. Bellows Falls."

"Not really."

There were logs in the water, huge dark ones tumbling against one another and jamming on the rocks. Why logs? I did not want to ask Mr. Thornberry why they were here. He had not been in Costa Rica longer than me. How could he know why this river, on which there were now no houses, carried logs in its current as long as telegraph poles and twice as thick? I would concentrate on what I saw: I would discover the answer. I concentrated. I discovered nothing.

"Sawmill," said Mr. Thornberry. "See those dark things in the water?" He squinted; his mouth went square. "Logs."

Damn, I thought, and saw the sawmill. So that's why the logs were there. They had been cut upriver. They must have—

"They must have floated those logs down to be cut into lumber," said Mr. Thornberry.

"They do that back home," I said.

"They do that back home," said Mr. Thornberry.

He was silent for some minutes. He brought a camera out of his shoulder bag and snapped pictures out the window. It was not easy for him to shoot past me, but I was damned if I would yield my corner seat. We were in another cool valley, with rock columns all around us. I saw a pool of water.

"Pool of water," said Mr. Thornberry.

"Very nice," I said. Was that what I was supposed to say?

Mr. Thornberry said, "What?"

"Very nice pool of water."

Mr. Thornberry hitched forward. He said, "Cocoa."

"I saw some back there."

"But there's much more of it here. Mature trees."

Did he think I was blind?

"Anyway," I said, "there's some coffee mixed in with it."

"Berries," said Mr. Thornberry, squinting. He heaved himself across my lap and snapped a picture. No, I would not give him my seat.

I had not seen the coffee berries; how had he? I did not want to see them.

"The red ones are ripe. We'll probably see some people picking them soon. God, I hate this train." He fixed that straining expression on his face. "Blows my mind."

Surely a serious artist would have brought a sketch pad and a few pencils and be doodling in a concentrated way, with his mouth shut. All Mr. Thornberry did was fool with his camera and talk; he named the things he saw, no more than that. I wanted to believe that he had lied to me about being a painter. No painter would gab so aimlessly.

"Am I glad I met you!" said Mr. Thornberry. "I was going crazy in that seat over there."

I said nothing. I looked out the window.

"Kind of a pipeline," said Mr. Thornberry.

There was a rusty tube near the track, running parallel in the swamp that had displaced the river. I had not seen the river go. There were palm trees and that rusty tube: kind of a pipeline, as he had said. Some rocky cliffs rose behind the palms; we ascended the cliffs and beneath us were streams—

"Streams," said Mr. Thornberry.

—and now some huts, rather interesting ones, like sharecroppers' cottages, made of wood, but quite solidly built, upraised on poles above the soggy land. We stopped at the village of Swampmouth: more of those huts.

"Poverty," said Mr. Thornberry.

The houses in style were perhaps West Indian. They were certainly the sort I had seen in the rural South, in the farming villages of Mississippi and Alabama, but they were trimmer and better maintained. There was a banana grove in each mushy yard and in each village a general store, nearly always with a Chinese name on the store sign; and most of the stores were connected to another building, which served as a bar and a pool room. There was an air of friendliness about these villages, and though many of the households were pure black, there were mixed ones as well; Mr. Thornberry pointed this out. "Black boy, white girl," he said. "They seem to get along fine. Pipeline again."

Thereafter, each time the pipeline appeared—and it did about twenty times from here to the coast—Mr. Thornberry obligingly indicated it for me.

We were deep in the tropics. The heat was heavy with the odor of moist vegetation and swamp water and the cloying scent of jungle flowers. The birds had long beaks and stick-like legs and they nosedived and spread their wings, becoming kite-shaped to break their fall. Some cows stood knee-deep in swamp, mooing. The palms were like fountains, or bunches of ragged feathers, thirty feet high—no trunk that I could see, but only these feathery leaves springing straight out of the swamp.

Mr. Thornberry said, "I was just looking at those palm trees."

"They're like giant feathers," I said.

"Funny green fountains," he said. "Look, more houses." Another village.

Mr. Thornberry said, "Flower gardens—look at those bougainvilleas. They blow my mind. Mama in the kitchen, kids on the porch. That one's just been painted. Look at all the vegetables!"

It was as he said. The village passed by and we were again in swampy jungle. It was humid and now overcast. My eyelids were heavy. Note taking would have woken me up, but there wasn't room for me to write, with Mr. Thornberry darting to the window to take a picture every five minutes. And he would have asked why I was writing. His talking made me want to be secretive. In the damp greenish light the woodsmoke of the cooking fires clouded the air further. Some of the people cooked under the houses, in that open space under the upraised floor.

"Like you say, they're industrious," said Mr. Thornberry. When had I said that? "Every damn one of those houses back there was selling something."

No, I thought, this couldn't be true. I hadn't seen anyone selling anything.

"Bananas," said Mr. Thornberry. "It makes me mad when I think that they sell them for twenty-five cents a pound. They used to sell them by the hand."

"In Costa Rica?" He had told me his father was Costa Rican.

"New Hampshire."

He was silent a moment, then he said, "Buffalo."

He was reading a station sign. Not a station—a shed.

"But it doesn't remind me of New York." Some miles earlier we had come to the village of Bataan. Mr. Thornberry reminded me that there was a place in the Philippines called Bataan. The March of Bataan. Funny, the two places having the same name, especially a name like Bataan. We came to the village of Liverpool. I braced myself.

"Liverpool," said Mr. Thornberry. "Funny."

It was stream-of-consciousness, Mr. Thornberry a less allusive Leopold Bloom, I a reluctant Stephen Dedalus. Mr. Thornberry was seventy-one. He lived alone, he said; he did his own cooking. He painted. Perhaps this explained everything. Such a solitary existence encouraged the habit of talking to himself: he spoke his thoughts. And he had been alone for years. His wife had died at the age of twenty-five. But hadn't he mentioned a marital disaster? Surely it was not the tragic death of his wife.

I asked him about this, to take his attention from the passing villages, which, he repeated, were blowing his mind. I said, "So you never remarried?"

"I got sick," he said. "There was this nurse in the hospital, about fifty or so, a bit fat, but very nice. At least, I thought so. But you don't know people unless you live with them. She had never been married. There's our pipeline. I wanted to go to bed with her right away—I suppose it was me being sick and her being my nurse. It happens a lot. But she said, 'Not till we're married.' " He winced and continued. "It was a quiet ceremony. Afterward, we went to Hawaii. Not Honolulu, but one of the little islands. It was beautiful—jungle, beaches, flowers. She hated it. 'It's too quiet,' she said. Born and raised in a little town in New Hampshire, a one-horse town—you've seen them—and she goes to Hawaii and says it's too quiet. She wanted to go to nightclubs. There weren't any nightclubs. She had enormous breasts, but she wouldn't let me touch them. 'You make them hurt.' I was going crazy. And she had a thing about cleanliness. Every day of our honeymoon we went down to the launderette and I sat outside and read the paper while she did the wash. She washed the sheets every day. Maybe they do that in hospitals, but in everyday life that's not normal. I guess I was kind of disappointed." His voice trailed off. He said, "Telegraph poles . . . pig . . . pipeline again," and then, "It was a real disaster. When we got back from the honeymoon I said, 'Looks like it's not going to work.' She agreed with me and that day she moved out of the house. Well, she had never really moved in. Next thing I know she's suing me for divorce. She wants alimony, maintenance, the whole thing. She's going to take me to court."

"Let me get this straight," I said. "All you did was go on honeymoon, right?"

"Ten days," said Mr. Thornberry. "It was supposed to be two weeks, but she couldn't take the silence. Too quiet for her."

"And then she wanted alimony?"

"She knew my sister had left me a lot of money. So she went ahead and sued me."

"What did you do?"

Mr. Thornberry grinned. It was the first real smile I had seen on his face the whole afternoon. He said, "What did I do? I countersued her. For fraud. She, she had a friend—a man. He had called her up when we were in Hawaii. She told me it was her brother. Sure."

He was still looking out the window, but his thoughts were elsewhere. He was chuckling. "I didn't have to do a thing after that. She gets on the witness stand. The judge asks her, 'Why did you marry this man?' She says, 'He told me he had a lot of money!' He told me he had a lot of money! Incriminated herself, see? She was laughed out of court. I gave her five grand and was glad to get rid of her." Almost without pausing he said: "Palm trees," then, "Pig," "Fence," "Lumber," "More morning glories—Capri's full of them." "Black as the ace of spades," "American car."

The hours passed; Mr. Thornberry spoke without letup. "Pool table," "Must be on welfare," "Bicycle," "Pretty girl," "Lanterns."

I had wanted to push him off the train, but after what he had told me I pitied him. Maybe the nurse had sat beside him like this; maybe she had thought, *If he says that one more time I'll scream.*

I said, "When was this abortive honeymoon?"

"Last year."

I saw a three-story house, with a veranda on each story. It was gray and wooden and toppling, and it reminded me of the Railway Hotel I had seen in Zacapa. But this one looked haunted. Every window was broken and an old steam locomotive was rusting in the weedy front yard. It might have been the house of a plantation owner—there were masses of banana trees nearby. The house was rotting and uninhabited, but from the remainder of the broken fence and the yard, the verandas and the barn, which could have been a coach house, it was possible to see that long ago it had been a great place, the sort of dwelling lived in by tyrannical banana tycoons in the novels of Asturias. In the darkening jungle and the heat, the decayed house looked fantastic, like an old ragged spider's web, with some of its symmetry still apparent.

Mr. Thornberry said, "That house. Costa Rican gothic."

I thought: *I saw it first.*

"Brahma bull," said Mr. Thornberry. "Ducks." "Greek." "Kids playing." Finally, "Breakers."

In the Zone

IT WAS SAVE OUR CANAL DAY. TWO UNITED STATES CON-
gressmen had brought the news to the Canal Zone that New
Hampshire was solidly behind them in their struggle to
keep the Zone in American hands (reminding me of the
self-mocking West Indian joke, "Go ahead, England, Bar-
bados is behind you!"). The New Hampshire governor had
declared a holiday in his state, to signify his support. One
congressman, speaking at a noisy rally of Americans in
Balboa, reported that 75 percent of the United States was
against the Panama Canal Treaty. But all this was academic; and the noise—there was a demonstration, too—
little more than the ventilation of jingoistic yawps. Within
very few months the treaty would be ratified. I told this to
a Zonian lady. She said she didn't care. She had enjoyed
the rally: "We've been feeling left out, as if everyone were
against us."

The Zonians, three thousand workers for the Panama Canal Company and their families, saw the treaty as a sellout;
why should the canal be turned over to these undeserving
Panamanian louts in twenty years? Why not, they argued
simply, continue to run it as it had been for the past sixty-
three years? At a certain point in every conversation I had
with these doomed residents of Panama, the Zonian would
bat the air with his arms and yell, *It's our canal!*

"Want to know the trouble with these people?" said an
American political officer at the embassy. "They can't decide whether the canal is a government department or a
company or an independent state."

Whatever it was it was certainly a lost cause; but it was
no less interesting for that. Few places in the world can

match the Canal Zone in its complex origins, its unique geographical status, or in the cloudiness of its future. The canal itself is a marvel: into its making went all the energies of America, all her genius, and all her deceits. The Zone, too, is a paradox: it is a wonderful place, but a racket. The Panamanians hardly figure in the canal debate—they want the canal for nationalistic reasons; but Panama scarcely existed before the canal was dug. If justice were to be done, the whole isthmus should be handed back to the Colombians, from whom it was squeezed in 1903. The debate is between the Ratifiers and the Zonians, and though they sound (and behave) like people whom Gulliver might have encountered in Glubdubdrib, they are both Americans: they sail under the same flag. The Zonians, however—when they become especially frenzied—often burn their Stars and Stripes, and their children cut classes at Balboa High School to trample on its ashes. The Ratifiers, loud in their denunciation of Zonians when they are among friends, shrink from declaring themselves when they are in the Zone. A Ratifier from the embassy, who accompanied me to a lecture I was to give at Balboa High, flatly refused to introduce me to the Zonian students for fear that if he revealed himself they would riot and overturn his car. Two nights previously, vengeful Zonians had driven nails into the locks of the school gates in order to shut the place down. When a pestilential little squabble, I thought; and felt more than ever like Lemuel Gulliver.

It is, by common consent, a company town. There is little in the way of personal freedom in the Zone. I am not talking about the liberal guarantees of freedom of speech or assembly, which are soothing abstractions but seldom used; I mean, the Zonian has to ask permission before he may paint his house another color or even shellac the baseboard in his bathroom. If he wishes to asphalt his driveway he must apply in writing to the Company; but he will be turned down: only pebbles are permitted. The Zonian is living in a Company house; he drives on Company roads, sends his children to Company schools, banks at the Company bank, borrows money from the Company credit union, shops at the Company store (where the low prices are pegged to those in New Orleans), sails at the Company club, sees movies at the Company theater, and if he eats out, takes his family to the Company cafeteria in the middle of Balboa and eats Company steaks and Company ice cream. If a plumber or an electrician is needed, the Company will supply one. The system is maddening, but if the Zonian is driven crazy, there is a Company psychiatrist. The community is entirely self-contained. Children are born in the Company hospital; people are married in Company churches—there are many denominations, but Baptists predominate. And when the Zonian dies he is embalmed in the Company mortuary—a free casket and burial are part of every Company contract.

The society is haunted by two contending ghosts, that of Lenin and that of General Bullmoose. There are no Company signs, no billboards or advertising at all; only a military starkness in the appearance of the Company buildings. The Zone seems like an enormous army base—the tawny houses, all right angles and tiled roofs, the severe landscaping, the stenciled warnings on chain-link fences, the sentry posts, the dispirited wives and stern fattish men. There are military bases in the Zone, but these are indistinguishable from the suburbs. This surprised me. Much of the canal hysteria in the States was whipped up by the news that the Zonians were living the life of Riley, with servants and princely salaries and subsidized pleasures. It would have been more accurate if the Zonian were depicted as an army man, soldiering obediently in the tropics. His restrictions and rules have killed his imagination and deafened him to any subtleties of political speech; he is a Christian; he is proud of the canal and has a dim, unphrased distrust of the Company; his salary is about the same as that of his counterpart in the United States—after all, the fellow is a mechanic or welder: why shouldn't he get sixteen dollars an hour? He knows some welders who get much more in Oklahoma. And yet the majority of the Zonians live modestly: the bungalow, the single car, the outings to the cafeteria and movie house. The high Company officials live like viceroys, but they are the exception. There is a pecking order, as in all colonies; it is in miniature like the East India Company and even reflects the social organization of that colonial enterprise: the Zonian suffers a notoriously outdated lack of social mobility. He is known by his salary, his club, and the nature of his job. The Company mechanic does not rub shoulders with the Company administrators who work in what is known all over the Zone as The Building—the seat of power in Balboa Heights. The Company is uncompromising in its notion of class; consequently, the Zonian—in spite of his pride in the canal—often feels burdened by the degree of regimentation.

"Now I know what socialism is," said a Zonian to me at Miraflores.

Shadowing an Indian

WITH THE SIGHT OF MY FIRST INDIAN IN BOGOTÁ, MY SPANish images quickly faded from mind. There are 365 Indian tribes in Colombia; some climb to Bogotá, seeking work; some were there to meet the Spanish and never left. I saw an Indian woman and decided to follow her. She wore a felt hat, the sort detectives and newspapermen wear in Hollywood movies. She had a black shawl, a full skirt, and sandals, and, at the end of her rope, two donkeys. The donkeys were heavily laden with metal containers and bales of rags. But that was not the most unusual feature of this Indian woman with her two donkeys in Bogotá. Because the traffic was so bad they were traveling down the pavement, past the smartly dressed ladies and the beggars, past the art galleries displaying rubbishy graphics (South America must lead the world in the production of third-rate abstract art, undoubtedly the result of having a vulgar moneyed class and the rise of the interior decorator—you can go to an opening nearly every night even in a dump like

Barranquilla); the Indian woman did not spare a glance for the paintings, but continued past the Bank of Bogotá, the plaza (Bolívar, his sword implanted at his feet), past the curio shops with leather goods and junk carvings, and jewelers showing trays of emeralds to tourists. She starts across the street, the donkeys plodding under their loads, and the cars honk and swerve and the people make way for her. This could be a wonderful documentary film, the poor woman and her animals in the stern city of four million; she is a reproach to everything in view, though few people see her and no one turns. If this was filmed, with no more elaborate scenario than she was walking from one side of Bogotá to the other, it would win a prize; if she was a detail in a painting it would be a masterpiece (but no one in South America paints the human figure with any conviction). It is as if 450 years have not happened. The woman is not walking in a city: she is walking across a mountainside with sure-footed animals. She is in the Andes, she is home; everyone else is in Spain.

She walked, without looking up, past a man selling posters, past the beggars near an old church. And, glancing at the posters, examining the beggars, I lost her. I paused, looked aside, and then she was gone.

High Plains Drifter

NEARER VILLAZÓN THE TRAIN HAD SPEEDED UP AND SENT grazing burros scampering away. We came to the station: the altitude was given—we were as high here as we had been at La Paz. The Argentine sleeping car was shunted onto a siding, and the rest of the train rolled down a hill and out of sight. There were five of us in this sleeping car, but no one knew when we would be taken across the border. I found the conductor, who was swatting flies in the corridor; and I asked him.

"We will be here a long time," he said. He made it sound like years.

The town was not a town. It was a few buildings necessitated by the frontier post. It was one street, unpaved, of low hut-like stores. They were all shut. Near the small railway station, about twenty women had set up square homemade umbrellas and were selling fruit and bread and shoelaces. On arriving at the station, the mob of Indians had descended from the train, and there had been something like excitement; but the people were now gone, the train was gone. The market women had no customers and nothing moved but the flies above the mud puddles. It made me gasp to walk the length of the platform, but perhaps I had walked too fast—at the far end an old crazy Indian woman was screaming and crying beside a tree stump. No one took any notice of her. I bought half a pound of peanuts and sat on a station bench, shelling them. "Are you in that sleeping car?" asked a man hurrying toward me. He was shabbily dressed and indignant.

I told him I was.

"What time is it leaving?"

I said, "I wish I knew."

He went into the station and rapped on a door. From within the building a voice roared, "Go away!"

The man came out of the station. He said, "These people are all whores." He walked through the puddles back to the sleeping car.

The Indian woman was still screaming, but after an hour or two I grew accustomed to it, and the screams were like part of the silence of Villazón. The sleeping car looked very silly stranded on the track. And there was no train in sight, no other coach or railway car. We were on a bluff. A mile south, across a bridge and up another hill was the Argentine town of La Quiaca. It too was nowhere, but it was there that we were headed, somehow, sometime.

A pig came over and sucked at the puddle near my feet and sniffed at the peanut shells. The clouds built up, massing over Villazón, and a heavy truck rattled by, blowing its horn for no reason, raising dust, and heading into Bolivia. Still the Indian woman screamed. The market women packed their boxes and left. It was dusk, and the place seemed deader than ever.

Night fell. I went to the sleeping car. It lay in darkness: no electricity, no lights. The corridor was thick with flies. The conductor beat a towel at them.

"What time are we going?"

"I do not know," he said.

I wanted to go home.

But it was pointless to be impatient. I had to admit that this was unavoidable emptiness, a hollow zone which lay between the more graspable experience of travel. What good would it do to lose my temper or seek to shorten this time? I would have to stick it out. But time passes slowly in the darkness. The Indian woman screamed; the conductor cursed the flies.

I left the sleeping car and walked toward a low lighted building, which I guessed might be a bar. There were no trees here, and little moonlight: the distances were deceptive. It took me half an hour to reach the building. And I was right: it was a coffee shop. I ordered a coffee and sat in the empty room waiting for it to come. Then I heard a train whistle.

A frail barefoot Indian girl put the coffee cup down.

"What train is that?"

"It is the train to La Quiaca."

"Shit!" I put some money down and without touching the coffee ran all the way back to the sleeping car. When I arrived, the engine was being coupled to the coach, and my throat burned from the effort of running at such a high altitude. My heart was pounding. I threw myself onto my bed and panted.

Outside, a signalman was speaking to one of the passengers.

"The tracks up to Tucumán are in bad shape," he said. "You might not get there for days."

Damn this trip, I thought.

We were taken across the border to the Argentine station over the hill. Then the sleeping car was detached and we were again left on a siding. Three hours passed. There was no food at the station, but I found an Indian woman who was watching a teapot boil over a fire. She was surprised that I should ask her to sell me a cup, and she took the money with elaborate grace. It was past midnight, and at the station there were people huddled in blankets and sitting on their luggage and holding children in their arms. Now it started to rain, but just as I began to be exasperated I remembered that these people were the Second Class passengers, and it was their cruel fate to have to sit at the dead center of this continent waiting for the train to arrive. I was much luckier than they. I had a berth and a First Class ticket. And there was nothing to be done about the delay.

So I did what any sensible person would do, stuck on the Bolivia-Argentina frontier on a rainy night. I went to my compartment and washed my face; I put on my pajamas and went to bed.

Buenos Aires

Buenos Aires is at first glance, and for days afterward, a most civilized anthill. It has all the elegance of the Old World in its buildings and streets; and in its people, all the vulgarity and frank good health of the New World. All the newsstands and bookstores—what a literate place, one thinks; what wealth, what good looks. The women in Buenos Aires were well dressed, studiously chic, in a way that has been abandoned in Europe. I had expected a fairly prosperous place, cattle and gauchos, and a merciless dictatorship; I had not counted on its being charming, on the seductions of its architecture, or the vigor of its appeal. It was a wonderful city for walking, and while walking I decided it would be a pleasant city to live in. I had been prepared for Panama and Cuzco, but Buenos Aires was not what I had expected. In the story "Eveline" in James Joyce's *Dubliners*, the eponymous heroine reflects on her tedious life and her chance to leave Dublin with Frank: *He had fallen on his feet in Buenos Aires, he said, and had come over to the old country just for a holiday.* Frank is an adventurer in the New World and is full of stories (*he told her stories of the terrible Patagonians*); soon, he proposes marriage, and he urges her to make her escape from Dublin. She is determined to leave, but at the last moment—*All the seas of the world tumbled about her heart*—her nerve fails her. Frank boards the boat train, and she remains in Dublin, *like a helpless animal*.

The stories in *Dubliners* are sad—there are few sadder in literature—but "Eveline" did not seem to me such a chronicle of thwarted opportunity until I saw the city she missed. There had seemed to me to be no great tragedy in failing to get to Buenos Aires; I assumed that Joyce used the city for its name, to leave the stinks of Dublin for the "good airs" of South America. But the first girl I met in Buenos Aires was Irish, a rancher, and she spoke Spanish with a brogue. She had come in from Mendoza to compete in the World Hockey Championships, and she asked me—though I would have thought the answer obvious—whether I, too, was a hockey player. In America, the Irish became priests, politicians, policemen—they looked for conventional status and took jobs that would guarantee them a degree of respect. In Argentina, the Irish became farmers and left the Italians to direct traffic. Clearly, Eveline had missed the boat.

In the immigrant free-for-all in Buenos Aires, in which a full third of Argentina's population lives, I looked in vain for what I considered to be seizable South American characteristics. I had become used to the burial ground features of ruined cities, the beggars' culture, the hacienda economy, and complacent and well-heeled families disenfranchising Indians, government by nepotism, the pig on the railway platform. The primary colors of such crudities had made my eye unsubtle and had spoiled my sense of discrimination. After the starving children of Colombia and the decrepitude of Peru, which were observable facts, it was hard to become exercised about press censorship in Argentina, which was ambiguous and arguable and mainly an idea. I had been dealing with enlarged visual simplicities; I found theory rarefied and, here, in a city that seemed to work, was less certain of my ground. And yet, taking the measure of it by walking its streets, restoring my circulation—I had not really walked much since I had left Cuzco—it did not seem so very strange to me that this place had produced a dozen world-class concert violinists and Fanny Foxe, the stripper; Che Guevara, Jorge Luis Borges, and Adolf Eichmann had all felt equally at home here.

There was a hint of this cultural overlay in the composition of the city. The pink flowered "drunken branch" trees of the pampas grew in the parks, but the parks were English and Italian, and this told in their names, Britannia Park, Palermo Park. The downtown section was architecturally French, the industrial parts German, the harbor Italian. Only the scale of the city was American; its dimensions, its sense of space, gave it a familiarity. It was a clean city. No one slept in its doorways or parks—this, in a South American context, is almost shocking to behold. I found the city safe to walk in at all hours, and at three o'clock in the morning there were still crowds in the streets. Because of the daytime humidity, groups of boys played football in the floodlit parks until well after midnight. It was a city without a significant Indian population—few, it seemed, strayed south of Tucumán, and what Indians existed came from Paraguay, or just across the Rio de la Plata in Uruguay. They worked as domestics, they lived in outlying slums, they were given little encouragement to stay.

It was a divided culture, but it was also a divided country. The Argentines I met said it was two countries—the uplands of the north, full of folklore and mountains and semibarbarous settlers; and the "humid pampas" of the south, with its cattle ranches and its emptiness, a great deal of it still virgin territory (pampas derives from an Aymara word meaning "space"). You have to travel a thousand miles for this division to be apparent, and Argentines—in spite of what they claim is their adventurous spirit—only travel along selected routes. They know Chile. Some know

Brazil. They spend weekends in the Patagonian oasis of Bariloche. But they do not travel much in the north of Argentina, and they don't know, or even care very much, about the rest of South America. Mention Quito and they will tell you it is hellish, small, poor, and primitive. A trip to Bolivia is unthinkable. Their connections tend to be with Europe. They fancy themselves Frenchified and have been told so often that their capital is like Paris that they feel no need to verify it with a visit to France. They prefer to maintain their ancestral links with Europe; many go to Spain, but almost a quarter of a million visit Italy every year. The more enterprising are Anglophiles. They are unsure of the United States, and their uncertainty makes them scorn it.

"But what do you know about Argentina?" they asked me, and by way of forestalling their lectures—they seemed deeply embarrassed about their political record—I said things like, "Well, when I was in Jujuy . . . ," or "Now, Humahuaca's awfully nice . . . ," or "What struck me about La Quiaca . . ." No one I met had been to La Quiaca or taken the train across the border. The person in Buenos Aires who wishes to speak of the squalor of the distant provinces tells you about the size of the cockroaches in nearby Rosario.

Borges

THE BRASS PLAQUE ON THE LANDING OF THE SIXTH FLOOR said *Borges*. I rang the bell and was admitted by a child of about seven. When he saw me he sucked his finger in embarrassment. He was the maid's child. The maid was Paraguayan, a well-fleshed Indian, who invited me in, then left me in the foyer with a large white cat. There was one dim light burning in the foyer, but the rest of the apartment was dark. The darkness reminded me that Borges was blind.

Curiosity and unease led me into a small parlor. Though the curtains were drawn and the shutters closed, I could make out a candelabra, the family silver Borges mentions in one of his stories, some paintings, old photographs, and books. There was little furniture—a sofa and two chairs by the window, a dining table pushed against one wall, and a wall and a half of bookcases. Something brushed my legs. I switched on a lamp; the cat had followed me here.

There was no carpet on the floor to trip the blind man, no intrusive furniture he could barge into. The parquet floor gleamed; there was not a speck of dust anywhere. The paintings were amorphous, but the three steel engravings were precise. I recognized them as Piranesi's *Views of Rome*. The most Borges-like one was *The Pyramid of Cestius* and could have been an illustration from Borges's own *Ficciones*. Piranesi's biographer, Bianconi, called him "the Rembrandt of the ruins." "I need to produce great ideas," said Piranesi. "I believe that were I given the planning of a new universe I would be mad enough to undertake it." It was something Borges himself might have said.

The books were a mixed lot. One corner was mostly Everyman editions, the classics in English translation—Homer, Dante, Virgil. There were shelves of poetry in no particular order—Tennyson and e. e. cummings, Byron, Poe, Wordsworth, Hardy. There were reference books, Harvey's *English Literature*, *The Oxford Book of Quotations*, various dictionaries—including Doctor Johnson's—and an old leatherbound encyclopedia. They were not fine editions; the spines were worn, the cloth had faded; but they had the look of having been read. They were well thumbed, they sprouted paper page markers. Reading alters the appearance of a book. Once it has been read, it never looks the same again, and people leave their individual imprint on a book they have read. One of the pleasures of reading is seeing this alteration of the pages, and the way, by reading it, you have made the book yours.

There was a sound of scuffing in the corridor, and a distinct grunt. Borges emerged from the dimly lighted foyer, feeling his way along the wall. He was dressed formally, in a dark blue suit and dark tie; his black shoes were loosely tied, and a watch chain depended from his pocket. He was taller than I had expected, and there was an English cast to his face, a pale seriousness in his jaw and forehead. His eyes were swollen, staring, and sightless. But for his faltering, and the slight tremble in his hands, he was in excellent health. He had the fussy precision of a chemist. His skin was clear—there were no age blotches on his hands—and there was a firmness in his face. People had told me he was "about eighty." He was then in his seventy-ninth year, but he looked ten years younger. "When you get to my age," he tells his double in the story "The Other," "you will have lost your eyesight almost completely. You'll still make out the color yellow and lights and shadows. Don't worry. Gradual blindness is not a tragedy. It's like a slow summer dusk."

"Yes," he said, groping for my hand. Squeezing it, he guided me to a chair. "Please sit down. There's a chair here somewhere. Please make yourself at home."

He spoke so rapidly that I was not aware of an accent until he had finished speaking. He seemed breathless. He spoke in bursts, but without hesitation, except when starting a new subject. Then, stuttering, he raised his trembling hands and seemed to claw the subject out of the air and shake ideas from it as he went on.

"You're from New England," he said. "That's wonderful. That's the best place to be from. It all began there— Emerson, Thoreau, Melville, Hawthorne, Longfellow. They started it. If it weren't for them there would be nothing. I was there—it was beautiful."

"I've read your poem about it," I said. Borges's "New England 1967" begins, *They have changed the shapes of my dream* . . .

"Yes, yes," he said. He moved his hands impatiently, like a man shaking dice. He would not talk about his work; he was almost dismissive. "I was lecturing at Harvard. I hate lecturing—I love teaching. I enjoyed the States—New England. And Texas is something special. I was there with my mother. She was old, over eighty. We went to see the Alamo." Borges's mother had died not long before, at the great age of ninety-nine. Her room is as she left it in death. "Do you know Austin?"

I said I had taken the train from Boston to Fort Worth and that I had not thought much of Fort Worth.

"You should have gone to Austin," said Borges. "The rest of it is nothing to me—the Midwest, Ohio, Chicago. Sandburg is the poet of Chicago, but what is he? He's just noisy—he got it all from Whitman. Whitman was great, Sandburg is nothing. And the rest of it," he said, shaking his fingers at an imaginary map of North America. "Canada? Tell me, what has Canada produced? Nothing. But the South is interesting. What a pity they lost the Civil War don't you think it is a pity, eh?"

I said I thought defeat had been inevitable for the South. They had been backward-looking and complacent, and now they were the only people in the States who ever talked about the Civil War. People in the North never spoke of it. If the South had won, we might have been spared some of these Confederate reminiscences.

"Of course they talk about it," said Borges. "It was a terrible defeat for them. Yet they had to lose. They were agrarian. But I wonder—is defeat so bad? In *The Seven Pillars of Wisdom*, doesn't Lawrence say something about 'the shamefulness of victory'? The Southerners were courageous, but perhaps a man of courage does not make a good soldier. What do you think?"

Courage alone could not make you a good soldier, I said, not any more than patience alone could make you a good fisherman. Courage might make a man blind to risk, and an excess of courage, without caution, could be fatal.

"But people respect soldiers," said Borges. "That's why no one really thinks much of the Americans. If America were a military power instead of a commercial empire, people would look up to it. Who respects businessmen? No one. People look at America and all they see are traveling salesmen. So they laugh."

He fluttered his hands, snatched with them, and changed the subject. "How did you come to Argentina?"

"After Texas, I took the train to Mexico."

"What do you think of Mexico?"

"Ramshackle, but pleasant."

Borges said, "I dislike Mexico and the Mexicans. They are so nationalistic. And they hate the Spanish. What can happen to them if they feel that way? And they have nothing. They are just playing—at being nationalistic. But what they like especially is playing at being Red Indians. They like to play. They have nothing at all. And they can't fight, eh? They are very poor soldiers—they always lose. Look what a few American soldiers could do in Mexico! No, I don't like Mexico at all."

He paused and leaned forward. His eyes bulged. He found my knee and tapped it for emphasis.

"I don't have this complex," he said. "I don't hate the Spanish. Although I much prefer the English. After I lost my sight in 1955 I decided to do something altogether new. So I learned Anglo-Saxon. Listen . . ."

He recited the entire Lord's Prayer in Anglo-Saxon.

"That was the Lord's Prayer. Now this—do you know this?"

He recited the opening lines of *The Seafarer*.

"*The Seafarer*," he said. "Isn't it beautiful? I am partly English. My grandmother came from Northumberland, and there are other relatives from Staffordshire. 'Saxon and Celt and Dane'—isn't that how it goes? We always spoke English at home. My father spoke to me in English. Perhaps I'm partly Norwegian—the Vikings were in Northumberland. And York—York is a beautiful city, eh? My ancestors were there, too."

"Robinson Crusoe was from York," I said.

"Was he?"

" 'I was born in the year something-something, in the city of York, of a good family . . .' "

"Yes, yes, I had forgotten that."

I said there were Norse names all over the north of England, and gave as an example the name Thorpe. It was a place name and a surname.

Borges said, "Like the German *Dorf*."

"Or Dutch *dorp*."

"This is strange. I will tell you something. I am writing a story in which the main character's name is Thorpe."

"That's your Northumberland ancestry stirring."

"Perhaps. The English are wonderful people. But timid. They didn't want an empire. It was forced upon them by the French and the Spanish. And so they had their empire. It was a great thing, eh? They left so much behind. Look what they gave India—Kipling! One of the greatest writers."

I said that sometimes a Kipling story was only a plot, or an exercise in Irish dialect, or a howling gaffe, like the climax of "At the End of the Passage," where a man photographs the bogeyman on a dead man's retina and then burns the pictures because they are so frightening. But how did the bogeyman get there?

"It doesn't matter—he's always good. My favorite is 'The Church that Was at Antioch.' What a marvelous story that is. And what a great poet. I know you agree with me—I read your piece in the *New York Times*. What I want you to do is read me some of Kipling's poems. Come with me," he said, getting to his feet and leading me to a bookshelf. "On that shelf—you see all the Kipling books? Now on the left is the *Collected Poems*. It's a big book."

He was conjuring with his hands as I ran my eye across the Elephant Head Edition of Kipling. I found the book and carried it back to the sofa.

Borges said, "Read me 'The Harp Song of the Dane Women.' " I did as I was told.

> What is a woman that you forsake her,
> And the hearth-fire and the home-acre,
> To go with the old grey Widow-maker?

" 'The old grey Widow-maker,' " he said. "That is so good. You can't say things like that in Spanish. But I'm interrupting—go on."

I began again, but at the third stanza he stopped me. " '. . . the ten-times-fingering weed to hold you'—how beautiful!" I went on reading this reproach to a traveler—just the reading of it made me feel homesick—and every few stanzas Borges exclaimed how perfect a particular phrase was. He was quite in awe of these English compounds. Such locutions were impossible in Spanish. A simple poetic phrase such as "world-weary flesh" must be rendered in Spanish as "this flesh made weary by the world." The ambiguity and delicacy is lost in Spanish, and Borges was infuriated that he could not attempt lines like Kipling's.

Borges said, "Now for my next favorite, 'The Ballad of East and West.' "

There proved to be even more interruption fodder in this ballad than there had been in "The Harp Song," but though it had never been one of my favorites, Borges drew my attention to the good lines, chimed in on several couplets, and continued to say, "You can't do that in Spanish."

"Read me another one," he said.

"How about 'The Way Through the Woods'?" I said, and read it and got goose pimples.

Borges said, "It's like Hardy. Hardy was a great poet, but I can't read his novels. He should have stuck to poetry."

"He did, in the end. He gave up writing novels."

"He should never have started," said Borges. "Want to see something interesting?" He took me back to the shelves and showed me his *Encyclopaedia Britannica*. It was the rare eleventh edition, not a book of facts but a work of literature. He told me to look at "India" and to examine the signature on the illustrated plates. It was that of Lockwood Kipling. "Rudyard Kipling's father—you see?"

We went on a tour through his bookshelves. He was especially proud of his copy of Johnson's *Dictionary* ("It was sent to me from Sing-Sing Prison, by an anonymous person"), his *Moby-Dick*, his translation by Sir Richard Burton of *The Thousand and One Nights*. He scrabbled at the shelves and pulled out more books; he led me to his study and showed me his set of Thomas De Quincey, his *Beowulf*—touching it, he began to quote—and his Icelandic sagas.

"This is the best collection of Anglo-Saxon books in Buenos Aires," he said.

"If not in South America."

"Yes, I suppose so."

We went back to the parlor library. He had forgotten to show me his edition of Poe. I said that I had recently read *The Narrative of Arthur Gordon Pym*.

"I was talking about *Pym* just last night to Bioy Casares," said Borges. Bioy Casares had been a collaborator on a sequence of stories. "The ending of that book is so strange—the dark and the light."

"And the ship with the corpses on it."

"Yes," said Borges a bit uncertainly. "I read it so long ago, before I lost my sight. It is Poe's greatest book."

"I'd be glad to read it to you."

"Come tomorrow night," said Borges. "Come at seven-thirty. You can read me some chapters of *Pym* and then we'll have dinner."

I got my jacket from the chair. The white cat had been chewing the sleeve. The sleeve was wet, but now the cat was asleep. It slept on its back, as if it wanted its belly scratched. Its eyes were tightly shut.

IT WAS GOOD FRIDAY. ALL OVER LATIN AMERICA THERE WERE somber processions, people carrying images of Christ, lugging crosses up volcanic mountains, wearing black shrouds, flagellating themselves, saying the Stations of the Cross on their knees, parading with skulls. But in Buenos Aires there was little of this penitential activity to be seen. Devotion, in this secular city, took the form of moviegoing. *Julia*, which had won a number of Oscars, opened on Good Friday, but the theater was empty. Across the street, at the Electric, *The Ten Commandments*—the fifties Bible epic—was showing. The box-office line was two blocks long. And there was such a crowd at Zeffirelli's *Jesus of Nazareth* that theatergoers, five hundred or more, were standing piously in the rain.

I had spent the day transcribing the notes I had made on my lap the night before. Borges's blindness had enabled me to write unselfconsciously as he spoke. Again I boarded the Buenos Aires Subterranean to keep our appointment.

This time, the lights in Borges's apartment were on. His loose shuffling shoes announced him and he appeared, as overdressed in the humid night heat as he had been the previous evening.

"Time for Poe," he said. "Please take a seat."

The Poe volume was on the seat of a nearby chair. I picked it up and found *Pym*, but before I could begin, Borges said, "I've been thinking about *The Seven Pillars of Wisdom*. Every page of it is very fine, and yet it is a dull book. I wonder why."

"He wanted to write a great book. George Bernard Shaw told him to use a lot of semicolons. Lawrence set out to be exhaustive, believing that if it was monumentally ponderous it would be regarded as great. But it's dull, and there's no humor in it. How can a book on the Arabs not be funny?"

"*Huckleberry Finn* is a great book," said Borges. "And funny. But the ending is no good. Tom Sawyer appears and it becomes bad. And there's Nigger Jim"—Borges had begun to search the air with his hands—"yes, we had a slave market here at Retiro. My family wasn't very wealthy. We had only five or six slaves. But some families had thirty or forty."

I had read that a quarter of Argentina's population had once been black. There were no blacks in Argentina now. I asked Borges why this was so.

"It is a mystery. But I remember seeing many of them." Borges looked so youthful that it was easy to forget that he was as old as the century. I could not vouch for his reliability, but he was the most articulate witness I had met on my trip. "They were cooks, gardeners, handymen," he said. "I don't know what happened to them."

"People say they died of TB."

"Why didn't they die of TB in Montevideo? It's just over there, eh? There is another story, equally silly, that they fought the Indians, and the Indians and the Negroes killed each other. That would have been in 1850 or so, but it isn't true. In 1914, there were still many Negroes in Buenos Aires—they were very common. Perhaps I should say 1910, to be sure." He laughed suddenly. "They didn't work very hard. It was considered wonderful to have Indian blood, but black blood is not so good a thing, eh? There are some prominent families in Buenos Aires that have it—a touch of the tar brush, eh? My uncle used to tell me, 'Jorge, you're as lazy as a nigger after lunch.' You see, they didn't do much work in the afternoon. I don't know why there are so few here, but in Uruguay or Brazil—in Brazil you might run into a white man now and then, eh? If you're lucky, eh? Ha!"

Borges was laughing in a pitying, self-amused way. His face lit up.

"They thought they were natives! I overheard a black woman saying to an Argentine woman, 'Well, at least we didn't come here on a ship!' She meant that she considered the Spanish to be immigrants. 'At least we didn't come here on a ship!' "

"When did you hear this?"

"So many years ago," said Borges. "But the Negroes were good soldiers. They fought in the War of Independence."

"So they did in the United States," I said. "But a lot were on the British side. The British promised them their freedom for serving in the British infantry. One southern regiment was all black—Lord Dunmore's Ethiopians, it was called. They ended up in Canada."

"Our blacks won the Battle of Cerrito. They fought in the war against Brazil. They were very good infantrymen. The gauchos fought on horseback, the Negroes didn't ride. There was a regiment—the Sixth. They called it, not the regiment of Mulattos and Blacks, but in Spanish 'the Regiment of Brownies and Darkies.' So as not to offend them. In *Martin Fierro*, they are called 'men of humble color.' . . . Well, enough, enough. Let's read *Arthur Gordon Pym*."

"Which chapter? How about the one where the ship approaches full of corpses and birds?"

"No, I want the last one. About the dark and the light."

I read the last chapter, where the canoe drifts into the Antarctic, the water growing warmer and then very hot, the white fall of ashes, the vapor, the appearance of the white giant. Borges interrupted from time to time, saying in Spanish, "That is enchanting"; "That is lovely"; and "How beautiful!"

When I finished, he said, "Read the last chapter but one."

I read Chapter 24: Pym's escape from the island, the pursuit of the maddened savages, the vivid description of vertigo. That long terrifying passage delighted Borges, and he clapped his hands at the end.

Borges said, "Now how about some Kipling? Shall we puzzle out 'Mrs. Bathurst' and try to see if it is a good story?"

I said, "I must tell you that I don't like 'Mrs. Bathurst' at all."

"Fine. It must be bad. *Plain Tales from the Hills* then. Read 'Beyond the Pale.'"

I read "Beyond the Pale," and when I got to the part where Bisesa sings a love song to Trejago, her English lover, Borges interrupted, reciting,

> Alone upon the housetops, to the North
> 　I turn and watch the lightning in the sky,—
> The glamour of thy footsteps in the North,
> 　Come back to me, Beloved, or I die!

"My father used to recite that one," said Borges. When I had finished the story, he said, "Now you choose one."

I read him the opium smoker's story, "The Gate of the Hundred Sorrows."

"How sad that is," said Borges. "It is terrible. The man can do nothing. But notice how Kipling repeats the same lines. It has no plot at all, but it is lovely." He touched his suit jacket. "What time is it?" He drew out his pocket watch and touched the hands. "Nine-thirty—we should eat."

As I was putting the Kipling book back into its place— Borges insisted that the books must be returned to their exact place—I said, "Do you ever reread your own work?"

"Never. I am not happy with my work. The critics have greatly exaggerated its importance. I would rather read"—he lunged at the bookshelves and made a gathering motion with his hands—"*real* writers. Ha!" He turned to me and said, "Do you reread my work?"

"Yes. 'Pierre Menard' . . ."

"That was the first story I ever wrote. I was thirty-six or thirty-seven at the time. My father said, 'Read a lot, write a lot, and don't rush into print'—those were his exact words. The best story I ever wrote was 'The Intruder' and 'South' is also good. It's only a few pages. I'm lazy—a few pages and I'm finished. But 'Pierre Menard' is a joke, not a story."

"I used to give my Chinese students 'The Wall and the Books' to read."

"Chinese students? I suppose they thought it was full of howlers. I think it is. It is an unimportant piece, hardly worth reading. Let's eat."

He got his cane from the sofa in the parlor and we went out, down in the narrow elevator, and through the wrought-iron gates. The restaurant was around the corner—I could not see it, but Borges knew the way. So the blind man led me. Walking down this Buenos Aires street with Borges was like being led through Alexandria by Cavafy, or through Lahore by Kipling. The city belonged to him, and he had had a hand in inventing it.

The restaurant was full this Good Friday night, and it was extremely noisy. But as soon as Borges entered, tapping his cane, feeling his way through the tables he obviously knew well, a hush fell upon the diners. Borges was recognized, and at his entrance all talking and eating ceased. It was both a reverential and curious silence, and it was maintained until Borges took his seat and gave the waiter our order.

We had hearts of palm, and fish, and grapes. I drank wine, Borges stuck to water. He cocked his head sideways to eat, trying to spear the sections of palm with his fork. He tried a spoon next, and then despairingly used his fingers.

"Do you know the big mistake that people make when they try to film *Doctor Jekyll and Mister Hyde*?" he said. "They use the same actor for both men. They should use two different actors. That is what Stevenson intended. Jekyll was two men. And you don't find out until the end that it is the same man. You should get that hammer stroke at the end. Another thing. Why do directors always make Hyde a womanizer? He was actually very cruel."

I said, "Hyde tramples on a child and Stevenson describes the sound of the bones breaking."

"Yes, Stevenson hated cruelty, but he had nothing against physical passion."

"Do you read modern authors?"

"I never cease to read them. Anthony Burgess is good—a very generous man, by the way. We are the same—Borges, Burgess. It's the same name."

"Any others?"

"Robert Browning," said Borges, and I wondered if he was pulling my leg. "Now, he should have been a short story writer. If he had, he would have been greater than Henry James, and people would still read him." Borges had started on his grapes. "The food is good in Buenos Aires, don't you think?"

"In most ways, it seems a civilized place."

He looked up. "That may be so, but there are bombs every day."

"They don't mention them in the paper."

"They're afraid to print the news."

"How do you know there are bombs?"

"Easy. I hear them," he said.

Indeed, three days later there was a fire that destroyed much of the new color television studio that had been built for the World Cup broadcasts. This was called "an electrical fault." Five days later two trains were bombed in Lomas de Zamora and Bernal. A week later a government minister was murdered; his corpse was found in a Buenos Aires street, and pinned to it was a note reading, *A gift from the Montoneros.*

"But the government is not so bad," said Borges. "Videla is a well-meaning military man." Borges smiled and said slowly, "He is not very bright, but at least he is a gentleman."

"What about Perón?"

"Perón was a scoundrel. My mother was in prison under Perón. My sister was in prison. My cousin. Perón was a bad leader and, also, I suspect, a coward. He looted the country. His wife was a prostitute."

"Evita?"

"A common prostitute."

We had coffee. Borges called the waiter and said in Spanish, "Help me to the toilet." He said to me, "I have to go and shake the bishop's hand. Ha!"

Walking back through the streets, he stopped at a hotel entrance and gave the metal awning posts two whacks with his cane. Perhaps he was not as blind as he pretended, perhaps it was a familiar landmark. He had not swung timidly. He said, "That's for luck."

As we turned the corner into Maipú, he said, "My father used to say, 'What a rubbish story the Jesus story is. That this man was dying for the sins of the world. Who could believe that?' Is it nonsense, isn't it?"

I said, "That's a timely thought for Good Friday."

"I hadn't thought of that! Oh, yes!" He laughed so hard he startled two passersby.

As he fished out his door key, I asked him about Patagonia.

"I have been there," he said. "But I don't know it well. I'll tell you this, though. It's a dreary place. A very dreary place."

"I was planning to take the train tomorrow."

"Don't go tomorrow. Come and see me. I like your reading."

"I suppose I can go to Patagonia next week."

"It's dreary," said Borges. He had got the door open, and now he shuffled to the elevator and pulled open the metal gates. "The gate of the hundred sorrows," he said, and entered chuckling.

In Patagonia

IT HAD BEEN MY INTENTION TO ARRIVE IN ESQUEL ON HOLY Saturday and to wake on Easter Sunday and watch the sunrise. But Easter had passed. This was no special date, and I had overslept. I got up and went outside. It was a sunny breezy day—the sort of weather that occurs every day of the year in that part of Patagonia.

I walked to the station. The engine that had taken me to Esquel looked derelict on the siding, as if it would never run again. But it had a hundred more years in it, I was sure. I walked beyond it, past the one-story houses to the one-roomed huts, to where the road turned into a dusty track. There was a rocky slope, some sheep, the rest bushes and weeds. If you looked closely you could see small pink and yellow flowers on these bushes. The wind stirred them. I went closer. They shook. But they were pretty. Behind my head was a great desert.

The Patagonian paradox was this: to be here, it helped to be a miniaturist, or else interested in enormous empty spaces. There was no intermediate zone of study. Either the vastness of the desert space, or the sight of a tiny flower. You had to choose between the tiny or the vast.

The paradox diverted me. My arrival did not matter. It was the journey that counted. And I would follow Johnson's advice. Early in his career he had translated the book of a Portuguese traveler in Abyssinia. In his preface, Johnson wrote, "He has amused the reader with no romantick absurdity, or incredible fictions; whatever he relates, whether true or not, is at least probable, and he who tells nothing exceeding the bounds of probability, has a right to

144

demand that they should believe him who cannot contradict him."

The sheep saw me. The younger ones kicked their heels. When I looked again, they were gone, and I was an ant on a foreign anthill. It was impossible to verify the size of anything in this space. There was no path through the bushes, but I could look over them, over this ocean of thorns which looked so mild at a distance, so cruel nearby, so like misshapen nosegays close up. It was perfectly quiet and odorless.

I knew I was nowhere, but the most surprising thing of all was that I was still in the world after all this time, on a dot at the lower part of the map. The landscape had a gaunt expression, but I could not deny that it had readable features and that I existed in it. This was a discovery—the look of it. I thought: *Nowhere is a place.*

Down there the Patagonian valley deepened to gray rock, wearing its eons' stripes and split by floods. Ahead, there was a succession of hills, whittled and fissured by the wind, which now sang in the bushes. The bushes shook with this song. They stiffened again and were silent. The sky was clear blue. A puff of cloud, white as a quince flower, carried a small shadow from town, or from the South Pole. I saw it approach. It rippled across the bushes and passed over me, a brief chill, and then went rucking east. There were no voices here. There was this, what I saw; and, though beyond it were mountains and glaciers and albatrosses and Indians, there was nothing here to speak of, nothing here to delay me further. Only the Patagonian paradox: the vast space, the very tiny blossoms of the sagebrush's cousin. The nothingness itself, a beginning for some intrepid traveler, was an ending for me. I had arrived in Patagonia, and I laughed when I remembered I had come here from Boston, on the subway train that people took to work.

The Kingdom
by the Sea

English Traits

O NCE, FROM BEHIND A CLOSED DOOR, I HEARD AN Englishwoman exclaim with real pleasure, "They are *funny*,
the Yanks!" And I crept away and laughed to think that an
English person was saying such a thing. And I thought:
*They wallpaper their ceilings! They put little knitted bobble
hats on their soft-boiled eggs to keep them warm! They
don't give you bags in supermarkets! They say sorry when
you step on their toes! Their government makes them get a
hundred-dollar license every year for watching television!
They issue drivers' licenses that are valid for thirty or forty
years—mine expires in the year 2011! They charge you for
matches when you buy cigarettes! They smoke on buses!
They drive on the left! They spy for the Russians! They say
"nigger" and "Jewboy" without flinching! They call their
houses Holmleigh and Sparrow View! They sunbathe in
their underwear! They don't say "You're welcome"! They
still have milk bottles and milkmen, and junk dealers with
horse-drawn wagons! They love candy and Lucozade and
leftovers called bubble-and-squeak! They live in Barking
and Dorking and Shellow Bowells! They have amazing
names, like Mr. Eatwell and Lady Inkpen and Major Twad-
dle and Miss Tosh! And they think* we're *funny?*

The longer I lived in London, the more I came to see
how much of Englishness was bluff and what wet blankets
they could be. You told an Englishman you were planning
a trip around Britain and he said, "It sounds about as much
fun as chasing a mouse around a pisspot." They could be
deeply dismissive and self-critical. "We're awful," they
said. "This country is hopeless. We're never prepared for
anything. Nothing works properly." But being self-critical

in this way was also a tactic for remaining ineffectual. It was surrender.

And when an English person said "we," he did not mean himself—he meant the classes above and below him, the people he thought should be making decisions, and the people who should be following. "We" meant everyone else.

"Mustn't grumble" was the most English of expressions. English patience was mingled inertia and despair. What was the use? But Americans did nothing but grumble! Americans also boasted. "I do some pretty incredible things" was not an English expression. "I'm fairly keen" was not American. Americans were show-offs—it was part of our innocence—we often fell on our faces; the English seldom showed off, so they seldom looked like fools. The English liked especially to mock the qualities in other people they admitted they didn't have themselves. And sometimes they found us truly maddening. In America you were admired for getting ahead, elbowing forward, rising, pushing in. In England this behavior was hated—it was the way "wops" acted, it was "Chinese fire drill," it was disorder. But making a quick buck was also a form of queue jumping, and getting ahead was a form of rudeness: A "bounder" was a person who had moved out of his class. It was not a question of forgiving such things; it was, simply, that they were never forgotten. The English had long, merciless memories.

Rambler

As soon as I had left Deal I saw a low, flat cloud, iron-gray and then blue, across the Channel, like a stubborn fogbank. The closer I got to Dover, the more clearly it was defined, now like a long battleship and now like a flotilla and now like an offshore island. I walked on and saw it was a series of headlands. It was France, looking like Brewster across Cape Cod Bay.

Ahead on the path a person was coming toward me, down a hill four hundred yards away; but whether it was a man or a woman I could not tell. Some minutes later I saw her scarf and her skirt, and for more minutes on those long slopes we strode toward each other under the big sky. We were the only people visible in the landscape—there was no one behind either of us. She was a real walker—arms swinging, flat shoes, no dog, no map. It was lovely, too: blue sky above, the sun in the southeast, and a cloudburst hanging like a broken bag in the west. I watched this woman, this fairly old woman, in her warm scarf and heavy coat, a bunch of flowers in her hand—I watched her come on, and I thought, *I am not going to say hello until she does.*

She did not look at me. She drew level and didn't notice me. There was no other human being in sight on the coast, only a fishing boat out there like a black flatiron. Hetta Poumphrey—I imagined that was the woman's name—was striding, lifting the hem of her coat with her knees. Now she was a fraction past me, and still stony-faced.

"Morning!" I said.

"Oh." She twisted her head at me. "Good morning!"

She gave me a good smile, because I had spoken first. But if I hadn't, we would have passed each other, Hetta and I, in that clifftop meadow—not another soul around—five feet apart, in the vibrant silence that was taken for safety here without a word.

Falklands News

THE HOTEL WAS NOT FULL—A DOZEN MEN, ALL OF THEM middle-aged and hearty and full of chat, making a remark and then laughing at it too loudly. They had been beating up and down the coast with cases of samples, and business was terrible. You mentioned a town, any town—Dover—and they always said, "Dover's shocking." They had the harsh, kidding manner of traveling salesmen, a clumsy carelessness with the waitresses, a way of making the poor girls nervous, bullying them because they had had no luck with their own wives and daughters.

Mr. Figham, motor spares and car accessories, down from Maidstone, said the whole of Kent was his "parish"—his territory, shocking place. He was balding and a little boastful and salesman-skittish; he asked for the sweets trolley, and as the pretty waitress stopped, he looked at the way her uniform tightened against her thigh and said, "That chocolate cake tickles my fancy—"

The waitress removed the cake dish.

"—and it's about the only thing that does, at my age."

Mr. Figham was not much more than fifty, and the three other men at his table, about the same age, laughed in a sad agreeing way, acknowledging that they were impotent and being a little wry about their sorry cocks not working properly. To eavesdrop on middle-aged Englishmen was often to hear them commenting on their lack of sexual drive.

I sat with all the salesmen later that night watching the hotel's television, the Falklands news. There was some anticipation. "I was listening to my car radio as I came down the M-Twenty. . . . One of my people said . . . A chap's supply in Ashford had heard . . ." But no one was definite—no one dared. ". . . something about British casualties . . ."

It was the sinking of the *Sheffield*. The news was announced on television. It silenced the room: the first British casualties, a brand-new ship. Many men were dead and the ship was still burning.

As long as the Falklands War had been without British deaths, it was an ingenious campaign, clever footwork, an adventure. That was admired here: a nimble reply, no blood, no deaths. But this was dreadful and incriminating, and it had to be answered. It committed Britain to a struggle that no one really seemed to want.

One of the salesmen said, "That'll take the wind out of our sails."

There was a Chinese man in the room. He began to speak—the others had been watching him, and when he spoke they looked sharply at him, as if expecting him to say something in Chinese. But he spoke in English.

He said, "That's a serious blow for us."

Everyone murmured, *Yes, that was a serious blow for us,* and *What next?* But I didn't open my mouth, because already I felt like an enemy agent. I agreed with what the Argentine writer Jorge Luis Borges had said about this Falklands War: "It is like two bald men fighting over a comb."

John Bratby

A MAN IN HASTINGS SAID TO ME, "WHY DID I COME HERE to live? That's easy. Because it is one of the three cheapest places in England." He told me the other two, but in my enthusiasm to know more about Hastings I forgot to write the others down. This man was the painter John Bratby. He did the paintings for the movie *The Horse's Mouth*, and his own life somewhat resembled that of Gulley Jimson, the painter hero of the Joyce Cary novel on which the movie was based.

Mr. Bratby was speaking in a room full of paintings, some of them still wet. He said, "I could never buy a house this large in London or anywhere else. I'd have a poky flat if I didn't live in Hastings."

His house was called the Cupola and Tower of the Winds and it matched its name. It was tall and crumbling, and it creaked when the wind blew, and there were stacks of paintings leaning against every wall. Mr. Bratby was thick-set and had the listening expression of a forgetful man. He said he painted quickly. He sometimes referred to his famous riotous past—so riotous, it had nearly killed him. He had been a so-called kitchen sink painter with a taste for drawing rooms. Now he lived in a quiet way. He said he believed that Western society was doomed, but he said this as he looked out of his Cupola window at the rooftops and the sea of Hastings, a pleasant view.

"Our society is changing from one based on the concept of the individual and freedom," Mr. Bratby said, "to one where the individual is nonexistent—lost in a collectivist state."

I said I didn't think it would be a collectivist state so much as a wilderness in which most people lived hand to mouth, and the rich would live like princes—better than the rich had ever lived, except that their lives would constantly be in danger from the hungry, predatory poor. All the technology would serve the rich, but they would need it for their own protection and to ensure their continued prosperity. The poor would live like dogs. They would be dangerous and pitiful, and the rich would probably hunt them for sport.

This vision of mine did not rouse Mr. Bratby, who was at that moment painting my portrait—"There is no commercial consideration to this at all." He had said of my painting, "This is for posterity to see, when our society has completely changed." He did not reject my description of the future. He scratched his head and went on dreading a police state where everyone wore baggy blue suits and called each other "Comrade"—the Orwell nightmare, which was a warning rather than a reasonable prediction. Anyway, it was almost 1984, and here was J. Bratby in a delightful wreck of a house, painting his heart out in Hastings, the bargain paradise of the south coast!

It seemed to me that his fear of the future was actually a hatred of the present, and yet he was an otherwise cheery soul and full of projects ("Guess what it is—the long one. It's all the Canterbury pilgrims. Chaucer, you see."). He said he never traveled but that his wife was very keen on it—had always wanted to go to New Orleans, for some reason. Now, his wife, Pam, was very attentive. She wore red leather trousers and made me a bacon sandwich. Bratby said that he had met her through a lonely hearts column, one of those classified ads that say LONELY GENT, 54, STOUT BUT NOT FAT, A PAINTER BY PROFESSION, SOUTH COAST, WISHES TO MEET . . . In this way they had met and had hit it off and got married.

Shallys

Hove, LIKE MANY OTHER PLACES ON THE ENGLISH COAST, had chalets. The name was misleading. They were huts, and *chalet* was mispronounced to suit them: "shally," the English said, an appropriate word made out of shanty and alley. There were hundreds of them shoulder to shoulder along the Front. They had evolved from bathing machines, I guessed. The English were prudish about nakedness (and swimming for the Victorians had been regarded as the opposite of a sport—it was a sort of immersion cure, a cross between colonic irrigation and baptism). The bathing machine—a shed on a pair of wheels—had been turned into a stationary changing room, and then arranged in rows on the beachfront, and at last had become a miniature house—a shally.

Hove's shallys were the size of English garden sheds. I looked into them, fully expecting to see rusty lawnmowers and rakes and watering cans. Sometimes they held bicycles, but more often these one-room shallys were furnished like dollhouses or toy bungalows. You could see what the English considered essential to their comfort for a day at the beach. They were painted, they had framed prints (cats, horses, sailboats) on the wall and plastic roses in jam-jar vases. All had folding deck chairs inside and a shelf at the rear on which there was a hotplate and a dented kettle and some china cups. They were fitted out for tea and naps—many had camp cots, plastic cushions, and blankets; some had fishing tackle; a few held toys. It was not unusual to see half a fruitcake, an umbrella, and an Agatha Christie inside; and most held an old person, looking flustered.

All the shallys had numbers, some very high numbers, testifying to their multitude. But the numbers did not distinguish them, for they all had names: Seaview, the Waves, Sunny Hours, Bide-a-Wee, picked out on their doors or else lettered on plaques. They had double doors; some looked more like horse boxes than cottages. They had curtains. They had folding panels to keep out the wind. Many had a transistor radio buzzing, but the shally people were old-fashioned—they actually were the inheritors of the bathing-machine mentality—and they called their radios "the wireless" or even "my steam radio."

They were rented by the year, or leased for several years, or owned outright—again, like bathing machines. But they were thoroughly colonized. They had small framed photographs of children and grandchildren. When it rained, their occupiers sat inside with their knees together, one person reading, the other knitting or snoozing, always bumping elbows. In better weather they did these things just outside, a foot or so from the front door. I never saw a can of beer or a bottle of whisky in a shally. The shally people had lived through the war. They had no money but plenty of time. They read newspapers, and that day everyone looked as if he were boning up for an exam on the Falklands campaign. It was becoming a very popular war.

The shallys were very close together, but paradoxically they were very private. In England, proximity creates invisible barriers. Each shally seemed to stand alone, no one taking any notice of the activity next door. Seaview was having tea while the Waves pondered the *Daily Express*; Sunny Hours was taking a siesta, and the pair at Bide-a-Wee were brooding over their mail. All conversation was in whispers. The shallys were not a community. Each shally was separate and isolated, nothing neighborly about it. Each had its own English atmosphere of hectic calm. A bylaw

stipulated that no one was allowed to spend a night in a
shally, so the shally was a daylight refuge, and it was used
with the intense preoccupation and the sort of all-excluding
privacy that the English bring to anything they own—not
creating any disturbance or encroaching on anyone else's
shally, and not sharing. Anyone who wished to know how
the English lived would get a good idea by walking past the
miles of these shallys, for while the average English home
was closed to strangers—and was closed to friends, too:
nothing personal, it just isn't done—the shally was completely open to the stranger's gaze, like the dollhouses they
somewhat resembled that had one wall missing. It was easy
to look inside. That's why no one ever did.

Bognor

I STAYED IN BOGNOR LONGER THAN I HAD PLANNED. I GREW
to like Miss Pottage at Camelot. The beach was fine in the
sunshine, and there was always an old man selling huge,
horrible whelks out of a wooden box on the Front. He said
he caught them himself. It was sunny, but the shops were
closed and the Front was deserted. The season hadn't
started, people said.

I began to think that Bognor had been misrepresented.
The oral tradition of travel in Britain was a shared experience of received opinion. Britain seemed small enough and
discussed enough to be known at second hand. Dickens was
known that way: it was an English trait to know about
Dickens and Dickens's characters without ever having read
him. Places were known in this same way. That was why
Brighton had a great reputation and why Margate was
avoided. Dover, people said, the white cliffs of Dover. And
Eastbourne's lovely. And the Sink Ports, they're lovely, too.

It was Dickens all over again, and with the same sort of distortions, the same prejudices, and some places they had all wrong.

"I don't know as much as I should about Dungeness," a man said to me, who didn't know anything about it at all. I went away laughing.

Broadstairs was serious, but Bognor was a joke. I was told, "It's like Edward the Seventh said"—it was George the Fifth—"his last words before he died. 'Bugger Bognor!' That's what I say." Bognor had an unfortunate name. Any English place name with *bog* or *bottom* in it was doomed. ("The bowdlerization of English place names has been a steady development since the late eighteenth century. In Northamptonshire alone, Buttocks Booth became Booth-ville, Pisford became Pitsford, and Shitlanger was turned into Shutlanger.") Camber Sands had a nice rhythmical lilt and was seen as idyllic—but it wasn't; Bognor contained a lavatorial echo, so it was seen as scruffy—but it wasn't. All English people had opinions on which seaside places in England were pleasant and which were a waste of time. This was in the oral tradition. The English seldom traveled at random. They took well-organized vacations and held very strong views on places to which they had never been.

Sad Captain

I WALKED ALONG WEST CLIFF AND DOWN A ZIGZAG PATH TO the promenade. I was not quite sure where I was headed, but this was the right direction—west; I had been going west for weeks. I walked past Alum Chine, where Stevenson wrote "Dr. Jekyll" (Bournemouth was the most literary place, with the ghosts of Henry James, Paul Verlaine, Tess Durbeyfield, Mary Shelley, and a half a dozen others haunting its chines) and then, looking west, and seeing the two standing rocks on the headland across the bay, called Old Harry and Old Harry's Wife, I decided to walk to Swanage, about fourteen miles along the coast.

My map showed a ferry at a place called Sandbanks, the entrance to Poole Harbour. I wondered whether it was running—the season had not started—so, not wishing to waste my time, I asked a man on the Promenade.

"I don't know about any ferry," he said.

He was an old man and had gray skin and he looked fire-proof. His name was Desmond Bowles, and I expected him to be deaf. But his hearing was very good. He wore a black overcoat.

"What are those boys doing?" he demanded.

They were windsurfing, I explained.

"All they do is fall down," he said.

One of the pleasures of the coast was watching windsurfers teetering and falling into the cold water, and trying to climb back and falling again. This sport was all useless struggle.

"I've just walked from Pokesdown—"

That was seven miles away.

"—and I'm eighty-six years old," Mr. Bowles said.

"What time did you leave Pokesdown?"

"I don't know."

"Will you walk it again?"

"No," Mr. Bowles said. But he kept walking. He walked stiffly, without pleasure. His feet were huge, he wore old, shiny, bulging shoes, and his hat was crushed in his hand. He swung the hat for balance and faced forward, panting at the Promenade. "You can walk faster than me—go on, don't let me hold you up."

But I wanted to talk to him: eighty-six and he had just walked from Pokesdown! I asked him why.

"I was a stationmaster there, you see. Pokesdown and Boscombe—those were my stations. I was sitting in my house—I've got a bungalow over there"—he pointed to the cliff—"and I said to myself, 'I want to see them again.' I took the train to Pokesdown and when I saw it was go-ing to be sunny I reckoned I'd walk back. I retired from

the railways twenty-five years ago. My father was in the
railways. He was transferred from London to Portsmouth
and of course I went with him. I was just a boy. It was
1902."

"Where were you born?"

"London," he said.

"Where, in London?"

Mr. Bowles stopped walking. He was a big man. He
peered at me and said, "I don't know where. But I used to
know."

"How do you like Bournemouth?"

"I don't like towns," he said. He started to walk again.
He said, "I like this."

"What do you mean?"

He motioned with his crumpled hat, swinging it outward.
He said, "The open sea."

It was early in my trip, but already I was curious about
English people in their cars staring seaward, and elderly
people in deck chairs all over the south coast watching
waves, and now Mr. Bowles, the old railwayman, saying, "I
like this . . . the open sea." What was going on here? There
was an answer in Elias Canetti's *Crowds and Power*, an unusual and brilliant—some critics have said eccentric—
analysis of the world of men in terms of crowds. There are
crowd symbols in nature, Canetti says—fire is one, and rain
is another, and the sea is a distinct one. "The sea is multi-
ple, it moves, and it is dense and cohesive"—like a
crowd—"Its multiplicity lies in its waves"—the waves are
like men. The sea is strong, it has a voice, it is constant, it
never sleeps, "it can soothe or threaten or break out in
storms. But it is always there." Its mystery lies in what it
covers: "Its sublimity is enhanced by the thought of what
it contains, the multitudes of plants and animals hidden
within it." It is universal and all-embracing; "it is an image
of stilled humanity; all life flows into it and it contains all
life."

Later in his book, when he is dealing with nations,
Canetti describes the crowd symbol of the English. It is the
sea: all the triumphs and disasters of English history are
bound up with the sea, and the sea has offered the English-

man transformation and danger. "His life at home is complementary to life at sea: security and monotony are its essential characteristics."

"The Englishman sees himself as a captain," Canetti says: this is how his individualism relates to the sea.

So I came to see Mr. Bowles, and all those old south coast folk staring seaward, as sad captains fixing their attention upon the waves. The sea murmured back at them. The sea was a solace. It contained all life, of course, but it was also the way out of England—and it was the way to the grave, seaward, out there, offshore. The sea had the voice and embrace of a crowd, but for this peculiar nation it was not only a comfort, representing vigor and comfort. It was an end, too. Those people were looking in the direction of death.

Mr. Bowles was still slogging along beside me. I asked him if he had fought in the First World War.

"First and Second," he said. "Both times in France." He slowed down, remembering. He said, "The Great War was awful . . . it was terrible. But I wasn't wounded. I was in it for four years."

"But you must have had leave," I said.

"A fortnight," he said, "in the middle."

Mr. Bowles left me at Canford Cliffs, and I walked on to Sandbanks.

(1) B & B: Victory Guest House

"**Y**OU'RE ALONE?" MRS. STARLING SAID AT THE VICTORY Guest House, glancing at my knapsack, my leather jacket, my oily shoes.

"So far," I said.

"I'll show you to your room," she said, a little rattled by my reply.

I was often warmed by a small thrill in following the younger landladies up four flights to the tiny room at the top of the house. We would enter, breathless from the climb, and stand next to the bed somewhat flustered, until she remembered to ask for the £5 in advance—but even that was ambiguous and erotic.

Most of them said, *You're alone?* or *Just a single, then?* I never explained why. I said I was in publishing. I said I had a week off. I did not say that I had no choice but to travel alone, because I was taking notes and stopping everywhere to write them. I could think clearly only when I was alone, and then my imagination began to work as my mind wandered. They might have asked: How can you bear your own company? I would have had to reply: Because I talk to myself—talking to myself has always been part of my writing and, by the way, I've been walking along the seawall from Dawlish in the rain muttering, "Wombwell . . . warmwell . . . nutwell . . . cathole . . ."

(2) B & B: The Puttocks

ABOUT A HALF HOUR AFTER ARRIVING IN NEWQUAY I WAS sitting in a parlor, a dog chewing my shoe, and having a cup of tea with Florence Puttock ("I said leave that shoe alone!"), who was telling me about the operation on her knee. It was my mention of walking that brought up the subject of the feet, legs, knees, and her operation. And the television was on—there was a kind of disrespect these days in not turning it on for Falklands news. And Queenie, the other Peke, had a tummy upset. And Mrs. Puttock's cousin Bill hadn't rung all day—he usually rang just after lunch. And Donald Puttock, who lisped and was sixty-one—he had taken early retirement because of his back—Donald was watching the moving arrows on the Falklands map and listening to Florence talking about ligaments, and he said, "I spent me 'ole life in 'ornchurch."

Somehow, I was home

But it was not my home. I had burrowed easily into this cozy privacy, and I could leave any time I wished. I had made the choice, for the alternatives in most seaside towns were a hotel, or a guest house, or a bed-and-breakfast place. This last alternative always tempted me, but I had to feel strong to do it right. A bed-and-breakfast place was a bungalow, usually on a suburban street some distance from the Front and the Promenade and the hotels. It was impossible to enter such a house and not feel you were interrupting a domestic routine—something about Florence's sewing and Donald's absurd slippers. The house always smelled of cooking and disinfectant, but most of all it smelled of in-laws.

It was like every other bungalow on the street, except for one thing. This one had a sign in the window saying VA-CANCIES. I had the impression that this was the only expense in starting such an establishment. You went over to Maynards and bought a VACANCIES sign, and then it was simply a matter of airing out the spare bedroom. Soon, an odd man would show up—knapsack, leather jacket, oily hiker's shoes—and spend an evening listening to the householders' stories of the high cost of living, or the greatness of Bing Crosby, or a particularly painful operation. The English, the most obsessively secretive people in their day-to-day living, would admit you to the privacy of their homes, and sometimes even unburden themselves, for just £5. "I've got an awful lot on my plate at the moment," Mrs. Spackle would say. "There's Bert's teeth, the Hoover's packed up, and my Enid thinks she's in the family way. . . ." When it was late, and everyone else in bed, the woman you knew as Mrs. Garlick would pour you a schooner of cream sherry, say, "Call me Ida," and begin to tell you about her amazing birthmark.

Bed and breakfast was always vaguely amateur, the

woman of the house saying she did it because she liked to cook, and could use a little extra cash ("money for jam"), and she liked company, and their children were all grown up, and the house was rather empty and echoey. The whole enterprise of bed and breakfast was carried on by the woman, but done with a will, because she was actually getting paid for doing her normal household chores. No special arrangements were required. At its best it was like a perfect marriage; at its worst it was like a night with terrible in-laws. Usually I was treated with a mixture of shyness and suspicion; but that was traditional English hospitality—wary curiosity and frugal kindness.

The English required guests to be uncomplaining, and most of the lower-middle-class people who ran bed-and-breakfast places were intolerant of a guest's moaning, and they thought—with some justification—that they had in their lives suffered more than that guest. "During the war," they always began, and I knew I was about to lose the argument in the face of some evidence of terrible hardship. During the war, Donald Puttock was buzz-bombed by the Germans as he crouched under his small staircase in Hornchurch, and, as he often said, he was lucky to be alive.

I told him I was traveling around the coast.

"Just what we did!" Mr. Puttock said. He and Florence had driven from Kent to Cornwall in search of a good place to live. They had stopped in all the likely places. Newquay was the best. They would stay here until they died. If they moved at all (Florence wanted fewer bedrooms), it would be down the road.

"Course, the local people 'ere 'ate us," Mr. Puttock said, cheerfully.

"Donald got his nose bitten off the other day by a Cornishman," Mrs. Puttock said. "Still hasn't got over it."

"I don't give a monkey's," Mr. Puttock said.

Later, Mrs. Puttock said that she had always wanted to do bed and breakfast. She wasn't like some of them, she said, who made their guests leave the house after breakfast and stay away all day—some of these people you saw in the bus shelter, they weren't waiting for the number fifteen; they were bed-and-breakfast people, killing time. It was bed-and-breakfast etiquette to stay quietly out of the house all day, even if it was raining.

Mrs. Puttock gave me a card she had had printed. It listed the attractions of her house.

- TV Lounge
- Access to rooms at all times
- Interior-sprung mattresses
- Free parking space on premises
- Free shower available
- Separate tables

The lounge was the Puttocks' parlor, the parking space was their driveway, the shower was a shower, and the tables tables. This described their house, which was identical with every other bungalow in Newquay.

I was grateful for the bed-and-breakfast places. At ten-thirty, after the Falklands news (and now every night there was "Falklands Special"), while we were all a bit dazed by the violence and the speculation and Mr. Puttock was saying, "The Falklands look like bloody Bodmin Moor, but I suppose we have to do something," Mrs. Puttock would say to me, "Care for a hot drink?" When she was in the kitchen making Ovaltine, Mr. Puttock and I were talking baloney about the state of the world. I was grateful, because to me this was virgin territory—a whole house open to my prying eyes: books, pictures, postcard messages, souvenirs, and opinions. I especially relished looking at family photographs. "That's us at the Fancy Dress Ball in Romford just after the war. . . . That's our cat, Monty. . . . That's me in a bathing costume. . . ." My intentions were honorable but my instincts were nosy, and I went sniffing from bungalow to bungalow to discover how these people lived.

(3) B & B: The Bull

Mr. Deedy at the Bull said, "See, no one wants to make plans ahead. They go on working. It's not only the money. They don't like to go away, because they don't know whether they'll have jobs to go back to."

Then "Falklands Special" was on television, and we dutifully trooped toward Mrs. Deedy's shout of "It's the news!" The news was very bad: more deaths, more ships sunk. But there was always great bewilderment among people watching the news, because there was never enough of it and it was sometimes contradictory. Why were there so few photographs of fighting? Usually it was reporters speaking of disasters over crackly telephones. The English seemed—in private—ashamed and confused, and regarded Argentina as pathetic, ramshackle, and unlucky, with a conscript army of very young boys. They hated discussing it, but they could talk all night on the subject of how business was bad.

"You just reminded me," Mrs. Deedy said. "The Smiths have canceled. They had that September booking. Mr. Smith rang this morning."

"Knickers," Mr. Deedy said.

"His wife died," Mrs. Deedy said.

"Oh?" Mr. Deedy was doubtful—sorry he had said knickers.

"She wasn't poorly," Mrs. Deedy said. "It was a heart attack."

Mr. Deedy relaxed at the news of the heart attack. It was no one's fault, really—not like a sickness or a crime. This was more a kind of removal.

"That's another returned deposit," Mrs. Deedy said. She was cross.

"That makes two so far," Mr. Deedy said. "Let's hope there aren't any more."

The next day I heard two tattling ladies talking about the Falklands. It was being said that the British had become jingoistic because of the war, and that a certain swagger was now evident. It was true of the writing in many newspapers, but it was seldom true of the talk I heard. Most people were like Mrs. Mullion and Miss Custis at the Britannia in Combe Martin, who, after some decent platitudes, wandered from talk of the Falklands to extensive reminiscing about the Second World War.

"After all, the Germans were occupying France, but life went on as normal," Mrs. Mullion said.

"Well, this is just it," Miss Custis said. "You've got to carry on. No sense packing up."

"We were in Taunton then."

"Were you? We were Cullompton," Miss Custis said. "Mutterton, actually."

"Rationing seemed to go on for ages!" Mrs. Mullion said.

"I still remember when chocolate went off the ration. And then people bought it all. And then it went on the ration again!"

They had begun to cheer themselves up in this way.

"More tea?" Mrs. Mullion said.

"Lovely," Miss Custis said.

(4) B & B: Allerford

Porlock, the home of the man who interrupted the writing of "Kubla Khan," was one street of small cottages, with a continuous line of cars trailing through it. Below it, on the west side of the bay, was Porlock Weir, and there were hills on all sides that were partly wooded.

A hundred and seventy years ago a man came to Porlock and found it quiet. But he did not find fault. He wrote: "There are periods of comparative stagnation, when we say, even in London, that there is nothing stirring; it is therefore not surprising that there should be some seasons of the year when things are rather quiet in West Porlock."

I walked toward Allerford, and on the way fell into conversation with a woman feeding birds in her garden. She told me the way to Minehead—not the shortest way, but the prettiest way, she said. She had light hair and dark eyes. I said her house was beautiful. She said it was a guest house; then she laughed. "Why don't you stay tonight?" She meant it and seemed eager, and then I was not sure what she was offering. I stood there and smiled back at her. The sun was shining gold on the grass and the birds were taking the crumbs in a frenzied way. It was not even one o'clock, and I had never stopped at a place this early in the day.

I said, "Maybe I'll come back some time."

"I'll still be here," she said, laughing a bit sadly.

There was an ancient bridge at Allerford. I bypassed it and cut into the woods, climbing toward the hill called Selworthy Beacon. The woods were full of singing birds, warblers and thrushes; and then I heard the unmistakable sound of a cuckoo, which was as clear as a clock, striking fifteen. The sun was strong, the gradient was easy, the bees were buzzing, there was a soft breeze; and I thought: *This was what I was looking for when I set out this morning— though I had no idea I would find it here.*

All travelers are optimists, I thought. Travel itself was a sort of optimism in action. I always went along thinking: *I'll be all right, I'll be interested, I'll discover something, I won't break a leg or get robbed, and at the end of the day I'll find a nice old place to sleep. Everything is going to be fine, and even if it isn't, it will be worthy of note—worth leaving home for.* Sometimes the weather, even the thin rain of Devon, made it worth it. Or else the birdsong in sunlight, or the sound of my shoe soles on the pebbles of the downward path—here, for example, walking down North Hill through glades full of azaleas, which were bright purple. I continued over the humpy hills to Minehead.

Holiday Camp

To THE EAST, BEYOND THE GRAY, PUDDLY FORESHORE—THE tide was out half a mile—I saw the bright flags of Butlin's, Minehead, and vowed to make a visit. Ever since Bognor I had wanted to snoop inside a coastal holiday camp, but I had passed the fences and gates without going in. It was not possible to make a casual visit. Holiday camps were surrounded by prison fences, with coils of barbed wire at the top. There were dog patrols and BEWARE signs stenciled with skulls. The main entrances were guarded and had turnstiles and a striped barrier that was raised to let certain vehicles through. Butlin's guests had to show passes in order to enter. The whole affair reminded me a little of Jonestown.

And these elaborate security measures fueled my curiosity. What exactly was going on in there? It was no use my peering through the chain-link fence—all I could see at this Butlin's were the Boating Lake and the reception area and some snorers on deck chairs. Clearly, it was very large. Later I discovered that the camp was designed to accommodate fourteen thousand people. That was almost twice the population of Minehead! They called it "Butlinland" and they said it had everything.

I registered as a Day Visitor. I paid a fee. I was given a brochure and a booklet and *Your Holiday Programme*, with a list of the day's events. The security staff seemed wary of me. I had ditched my knapsack in a boardinghouse, but I was still wearing my leather jacket and oily hiking shoes.

My knees were muddy. So as not to alarm the gatekeepers, I had pocketed my binoculars. Most of the Butlin's guests wore sandals and short sleeves, and some wore funny hats—holiday high spirits. The weather was overcast and cold and windy. The flags out front were as big as bed-sheets and made a continual cracking. I was the only person at Butlin's dressed for this foul weather. I felt like a com-mando. It made some people there suspicious.

With its barracks-like buildings and its forbidding fences, it had the prison look of the Butlin's at Bognor. A prison look was also an army-camp look, and just as depressing. This one was the more scary for being brightly painted. It had been tacked together out of plywood and tin panels in primary colors. I had not seen flimsier buildings in En-gland. They were so ugly, they were not pictured anywhere in the Butlin's brochure, but instead shown as simplified floor plans in blue diagrams. They were called "flatlets" and "suites." The acres of barracks were called the Accom-modation Area.

It really was like Jonestown! The Accommodation Area with the barracks was divided into camps—Green, Yellow, Blue, and Red Camp. There was a central dining room and a Nursery Center. There was a Camp Chapel. There was also a miniature railway and a chairlift and a monorail—all of them useful: it was a large area to cover on foot. It was just the sort of place the insane preacher must have imag-ined when he brought his desperate people to Guyana. It was self-contained and self-sufficient. With a fence that high, it had to be.

The Jonestown image was powerful, but Butlin's also had the features of a tinselly New Jerusalem. This, I felt, would be the English coastal town of the future, if most English people had their way. It was already an English town of a sort—glamorized and less substantial than the real thing, but all the same recognizably an English town, with the usual landmarks, a cricket pitch, a football field, a launderette, a supermarket, a bank, a betting shop, and a number of take-away food joints. Of course, it was better organized and had more amenities than most English towns the same size—that was why it was popular. It was also a permanent funfair. One of Butlin's boasts was "No dirty dishes to wash!" Another was "There is absolutely no need to queue!" No dishwashing, no standing in line—it came near to parody, like a vacation in a Polish joke. But these promises were a sort of timid hype; England was a country of modest expectations, and no dishes and no lines were part of the English dream.

It was not expensive—£178 ($313) a week for a family of four, and that included two meals a day. It was mostly families—young parents with small children. They slept in a numbered cubicle in the barracks at one of the four camps, and they ate at a numbered table in one of the dining rooms, and they spent the day amusing themselves.

The Windsor Sports Ground (most of the names had regal echoes, an attempt at respectability) and the Angling Lake were not being used by anyone the day I was there. But the two snooker and table tennis rooms were very busy; each room was about half the size of a football field and held scores of tables. No waiting! There was bingo in the Regency Building, in a massive room with a glass wall, which was the bottom half of the indoor swimming pool— fluttering legs and skinny feet in water the color of chicken bouillon. There was no one on the Boating Lake, and no one in the outdoor pool, and the chapel was empty. The Crazy Golf was not popular. So much for the free amusements.

"Yes, it *is* true, nearly everything at Butlin's is free!" the brochure said.

But what most of the people were doing was not free. They were feeding coins into fruit machines and one-armed bandits in the Fun Room. They were playing pinball. They were also shopping for stuffed toys and curios, or buying furs in the Fur Shop, or getting their hair done at the Hairdressing Salon. They were eating. The place had four fish-and-chip shops. There were tea shops, coffee bars, and candy stores. They cost money, but people seemed to be spending fairly briskly. They were also drinking. There were about half a dozen bars. The Embassy Bar (Greek statues, fake chandeliers, red wallpaper) was quite full, although it was the size of a barn. The Exmoor Bar had 157 tables and probably held a thousand drinkers. It was the scale of the place that was impressive—the scale and the shabbiness.

It was not Disneyland. Disneyland was a blend of technology and farce. It was mostly fantasy, a tame kind of surrealism, a comfortable cartoon in three dimensions. But the more I saw of Butlin's, the more it resembled English life; it was very close to reality in its narrowness, its privacies, and its pleasures. It was England without work—leisure had been overtaken by fatigue and dull-wittedness: electronic games were easier than sports, and eating junk food had become another recreation. No one seemed to notice how plain the buildings were, how tussocky the grass was, or that everywhere there was a pervasive sizzle and smell of food frying in hot fat.

In that sense, too, it was like a real town. People walked around believing that it was all free; but most pastimes there cost money, and some were very expensive—like a ticket to the cabaret show that night, Freddie and the Dreamers, a group of middle-aged musicians who were a warmed-over version of their sixties' selves.

If it had a futuristic feel, it was the deadened imagination and the zombie-like attitude of the strolling people, condemned to a week or two of fun under cloudy skies. And it was also the arrangements for children. The kids were taken care of—they could be turned loose in Butlin's in perfect safety. They couldn't get hurt or lost. There was a high fence around the camp. There was a Nursery Chalet Patrol and a Child Listening Service and a large Children's Playground. In the planned cities of the future, provisions like this would be made for children.

Most of the events were for children, apart from whist and bingo. As a Day Visitor, I had my choice of the Corona Junior Fancy Dress Competition, a Kids' Quiz Show, the Trampoline Test, the Donkey Derby, or the Beaver and Junior Talent Contest Auditions. The Donkey Derby was being held in a high wind on Gaiety Green—screaming children and plodding animals. I went to the talent show auditions in the Gaiety Revue Theatre. A girl of eight did a suggestive dance to a lewd pop song; two sisters sang a song about Jesus; Amanda and Kelly sang "Daisy"; and Miranda recited a poem much too fast. Most of the parents were elsewhere—playing the one-armed bandits and drinking beer.

I wandered into the Camp Chapel ("A Padre is available in the Centre at all times"). There was a notice stuck to the chapel door. *At all three services prayers are being said for our Forces in the Southern Atlantic.* I scrutinized the Visitors' Book. It asked for nationality, and people had listed "Welsh" or "Cornish" or "English" or "Scottish" next to their names. There was a scattering of Irish. But after the middle of April people had started to put "British" for nationality—that was after the Falklands War had begun.

I found three ladies having tea in the Regency Building: Daphne Bunsen, from Bradford, said, "We don't talk about this Falklands business here, 'cause we're on holiday. It's a right depressing soobject."

"Anyway," Mavis Hattery said, "there's only one thing to say."

What was that?

"I say, 'Get it over with! Stop playing cat and mouse!' "

Mrs. Bunsen said they loved Butlin's. They had been here before and would certainly come back. Their sadness was they could not stay longer. "And Mavis's room is right posh!"

"I paid a bit extra," Mrs. Hattery said. "I have a fitted carpet in my shally."

It was easy to mock Butlin's for its dreariness and its brainless pleasures. It was an inadequate answer to leisure, but there were scores of similar camps all around the coast, so there was no denying its popularity. It combined the security and equality of prison with the vulgarity of an amusement park. I asked children what their parents were doing. Usually the father was playing billiards and the mother was shopping, but many said their parents were sleeping—having a kip. Sleeping until noon, not having to cook or mind children, and being a few steps away from the fish-and-chip shop, the bar, and the betting shop—it was a sleazy paradise in which people were treated more or less like animals in a zoo. In time to come, there would be more holiday camps on the British coast—"Cheap and cheerful," Daphne Bunsen said.

Butlin's was staffed by "Redcoats"—young men and women who wore red blazers. It was a Redcoat named Rod Firsby who told me that the camp could accommodate fourteen thousand people ("but nine thousand is about average"). Where did the people come from? I asked. He said they came from all over. It was when I asked him what sorts of jobs they did that he laughed.

"Are you joking, sunshine?" he said.

I said no, I wasn't.

He said, "Half the men here are unemployed. That's the beauty of Butlin's—you can pay for it with your dole money."

Happy Little Llanelli

LLANELLI HAD LOOKED PROMISING ON THE MAP. IT WAS IN the southwest corner of Dyfed, on the estuary of the Loughor River. I walked from the station to the docks. The town was musty-smelling and dull and made of decayed bricks. My map had misled me. I wanted to leave, but first I wanted to buy a guidebook to Wales in order to avoid such mistakes in the future.

I passed a store with textbooks in the window. Dead flies lay on their sides on the book covers; they had not been swatted, but had simply starved; they seemed asleep. There were shelves in this bookstore, but not many books. There was no salesperson. A husky voice came from behind a beaded curtain.

"In here."

I went in. A man was whispering into a telephone. He paid no attention to me. There were plenty of books in

here. On the covers were pictures of naked people. The
room smelled of cheap paper and ink. The magazines were
in cellophane wrappers. They showed breasts and rubber
underwear, and there were children on some of them—the
titles suggested that the naked tots were violated inside. No
guidebooks here, but as this pornography shop was Welsh,
the door had a bell that went *bing-bong!* in a cheery way
as I left.

Welsh politeness was softhearted and smiling. Even
Llanelli's Skinheads were well behaved, and the youths
with swastikas on their leather jackets and bleached hair
and earrings or green hair and T-shirts saying ANARCHY!—
even they seemed sweet-natured. And how amazing that the
millions of Welsh, who shared about a dozen surnames,
were the opposite of anonymous. They were conspicuous
individuals and at a personal level tried hard to please.
"You're a gentleman!" one man would cry to another,
greeting him on the street.

At Jenkins the Bakers ("Every bite—pure delight") I saw
a strawberry tart with clotted cream on top. Were they fresh
strawberries?

"Oh, yes, fresh this morning," Mrs. Jenkins said.

I asked for one.

"But they're thirty pence, darling," Mrs. Jenkins said,
warning me and not moving. She expected me to tell her to
forget it. She was on my side in the most humane way, and
gave a commiserating smile, as if to say, It's a shocking
amount of money for a strawberry tart!

When I bought two, she seemed surprised. It must have
been my knapsack and my vagabond demeanor. I went
around the corner and stuffed them into my mouth.

"Good morning—I mean, good evening!" Mr. Maddocks
the stationmaster said at Llanelli Station. "I knew I'd get it
right in the end. It's patience you want!"

The rest of the people on the platform were speaking
Welsh, but on seeing the train draw in—perhaps it was the
excitement—they lapsed into English.

Tenby

THE ELEGANT HOUSES OF TENBY STANDING TALL ON THE cliff reminded me of beautifully bound books on a high shelf—their bay windows had the curvature of book spines. The town was elevated on a promontory, so the sea on three sides gave its light a penetrating purity that reached the market square and fortified the air with the tang of ocean-washed rocks. It was odd that a place so pretty should also be so restful, and yet that was the case. But Tenby was more than pretty. It was so picturesque, it looked like a watercolor of itself.

It had not been preserved by the fastidious tyrants who so often took over British villages—the new class who moved in and gutted the houses, and then, after restoring the thatched roofs and mullioned windows, hid a chromium kitchen in the inglenook, which ran on microchips. Such people could make a place so picturesque that it was uninhabitable. Tenby had been maintained, and it had mellowed; it was still sturdy, and I was glad I had found it. But it was the sort of place that denied a sense of triumph to the person who secretly felt he had discovered it—because its gracefulness was well known; it had been painted and praised; it was old even in Tudor times; and it had produced Augustus John (who wrote about Tenby in his autobiography, *Chiaroscuro*), as well as the inventor of the equal sign (=) in mathematics, Robert Recorde. But, then, there were no secret places in Britain that I had seen; there were only forgotten places, and places that were being buried or changed by our harsh century.

Tenby had been spared, and it was the more pleasing for being rather quiet and empty. I walked around dreamily.

For the first time since I had set out on this trip I felt that a watering place was fulfilling its purpose—calming me, soothing me, making me want to snore over a book on a veranda with a sea view.

Naked Lady

Mᵧ STRANGE ENCOUNTER TOOK PLACE AT THE HOTEL Harlech, a dismal semiruin not far from the silted-up river in Cardigan. It had been closed for years, and it smelled that way—of mice and unwashed clothes. The smell of rags is like the smell of dead men anyway, but this was compounded with the smells of dirt and wood smoke and the slow river. I knew as soon as I checked in that it was a mistake. I was shown to my room by a sulking girl of fifteen, who had a fat pouty face and a potbelly.

"It seems a little quiet," I said.

Gwen said, "You're the only guest."

"In the whole hotel?"

"In the whole hotel."

My bed smelled, too, as though it had been slept in—just slept in recently, someone having crawled out a little while ago, leaving it warm and disgusting.

The owner of the Harlech was a winking woman with a husky laugh, named Reeny. She kept a purse in the cleavage between her breasts; she smoked while she was eating; she talked about her boyfriend—"My boyfriend's been all around the world on ships." Reeny's boyfriend was a pale unshaven man of fifty who limped through the hotel, his shirttails out, groaning because he could never find his hairbrush. His name was Lloyd, and he was balding. Lloyd seldom spoke to me, but Reeny was irrepressible, always urging me to come down to the bar for a drink.

The bar was a darkened room with torn curtains and a simple table in the center. There were usually two tattooed youths and two old men at the table, drinking beer with Lloyd. Reeny acted as barmaid, using a tin tray. And it was she who changed the records: the music was loud and terrible, but the men had no conversation, and they looked haggard and even rather ill.

The unexpected thing was that Reeny was very cheerful and hospitable. The hotel was dirty and her food unspeakable and the dining room smelled of urine, but Reeny was kind, and she loved to talk, and she spoke of improving the hotel, and she knew that Lloyd was a complaining old fake. Relax, enjoy yourself, have another helping, Reeny said. She had the right spirit, but the hotel was a mess. "This is Paul—he's from America," Reeny said, and winked at me. She was proud of me. That thought made me very gloomy.

One night she introduced me to Ellie. She was red-eyed and very fat and had a gravelly voice; she was somewhat toothless and freckled; she came from Swansea. "Aye," she said. "Swansea's a bloody bog." Ellie was drunk—and she was deaf in the way drunks often are. Reeny was talking about America, but Ellie was still mumbling about Swansea.

"At least we're not tight," Ellie said. "Aye, we're careful, but the Cardies are tight."

"That's us," Reeny said. "Cardies, from Cardigan. Aye, we're tighter than the Scots."

Ellie screwed up her face to show how tight the Cardies were, and then she demanded to know why I was not drunk—and she appealed to the silent, haggard men, who stared back at her with dull damp eyes. Ellie was wearing a baggy gray sweater. She finished her pint of beer and then wiped her hands on her sweater.

"What do you think of the Cardies?" she said.

"Delightful," I said. But I thought, *Savages*.

At midnight they were still drinking.

"I'm going upstairs," I said.

"None of the rooms have locks," Reeny said. "That's why there are no keys. See?"

Ellie said, "Aarrgh, it's a quiet place, Reen!"

"Too bloody quiet, I say," Reeny said. "We have to drive to Saundersfoot for a little nightlife."

Saundersfoot was thirty-three miles away.

"What is it, Lloyd?" Reeny said.

Lloyd had been grinning.

He said, "He looks worried," meaning me.

"I'm not worried," I said.

This always sounds to me a worried man's protest. I stood there, trying to smile. The four local men at the table merely stared back with their haggard faces.

"There's no locks in this place," Lloyd said, with pleasure.

Then Reeny screeched, "We won't rob you or rape you!"

She said it so loudly that it was a few seconds before I could take it in. She was vivacious but ugly.

I recovered and said, "What a shame. I was looking forward to one or the other."

Reeny howled at this.

In the sour bed, I could hear rock music coming from the bar, and sometimes shouts. But I was so tired, I dropped off to sleep, and I dreamed of Cape Cod. I was with my cousin and saying to her, "Why do people go home so early? This is the only good place in the world. I suppose they're worried about traffic. I'd never leave—"

Then something tore. It was a ripping sound in the room. I sat up and saw a tousled head. I thought it was a man. It was a man's rough face, a squashed nose, a crooked mouth. I recognized the freckles and the red eyes. It was Ellie.

I said, "What are you doing?"

She was crouching so near to the bed that I could not see her body. The ripping sound came again—a zipper on my knapsack. Ellie was slightly turned away from me. She did not move. When I saw that it was Ellie and not a man, I relaxed—and I knew that my wallet and money were in my leather jacket, hanging on a hook across the room.

She said, "Where am I?"

"You're in my room."

She said, turning to me, "What are you doing here?"

"This is my room!"

Her questions had been drowsy in a theatrical way. She

was still crouching near my knapsack. She was breathing hard.

I said, "Leave that thing alone."

"Aarrgh," she groaned, and plumped her knees against the floor.

I wanted her to go away.

I said, "I'm trying to sleep." Why was I being so polite?

She groaned again, a more convincing groan than the last one, and she said, "Where have I left me clothes?"

And she stood up. She was a big woman with big jolting breasts and freckles on them. She was, I saw, completely naked.

"Close your eyes," she said, and stepped closer.

I said, "It's five in the morning, for God's sake."

The sun had just struck the curtains.

"Aarrgh, I'm sick," she said. "Move over."

I said, "You don't have any clothes on."

"You can close your eyes," she said.

I said, "What were you doing to my knapsack?"

"Looking for me clothes," she said.

I said in a pleading way, "Give me a break, will you?"

"Don't look at me nakedness," she said.

"I'm going to close my eyes," I said, "and when I open them I don't want to see you in this room."

Her naked flesh went flap-flap like a rubber raincoat as she tramped across the hard floor. I heard her go—she pulled the door shut—and then I checked to see that my money was safe and my knapsack unviolated. The zippers were open, but nothing was gone. I remembered what Reeny had screamed at me: *We won't rob you or rape you!*

At breakfast, Reeny said, "I've not been up at this hour for ten year! Look, it's almost half-eight!"

Reeny had a miserable cough and her eyes were sooty with mascara. Her Welsh accent was stronger this morning, too.

I told her about Ellie.

She said, "Aye, is that so? I'll pull her leg about that! Aye, that is funny."

An old woman came to the door. She was unsteady, she

peered in. Reeny asked her what she wanted. She said she wanted a pint of beer.

"It's half-eight in the morning!" Reeny said.

"A half a pint, then," the old woman said.

"And it's Sunday!" Reeny said. She turned to me and said, "We're dry on a Sunday around here. That's why it's so quiet. But you can get a drink at St. Dogmaels."

The woman looked pathetic. She said that in the coming referendum she would certainly vote for a change in the licensing law. She was not angry, but had that aged, beaten look that passes for patience.

"Oh, heavens!" Reeny said. "What shall I do, Paul? You tell me."

I said to the old woman, "Have a cup of tea."

"The police have been after me," Reeny said. "They're always looking in." Reeny walked to the cupboard. "I could lose my license." She took out a bottle of beer and poured it. "These coppers have no bloody mercy." The glass was full. "Forty-five pence," she said.

The woman drank that and then bought two more bottles. She paid and left, without another word. She had taken no pleasure in the drink and there was no satisfaction in having wheedled the beer out of Reeny on a dry day in Cardigan—in fact, she had not wheedled, but had merely stood there gaping in a paralyzed way.

I said, "It's a hell of a breakfast—a beer."

"She's an alcoholic," Reeny said. "She's thirty-seven. Doesn't look it, does she? Take me, I'm thirty-three and no one believes it. My boyfriend says I've got the figure of a girl of twenty. You're not going, are you?"

Jan Morris

EIGHT MORE MILES ON THIS SUNNY DAY AND WE DREW INTO Criccieth, where I hopped out of the train. I owned a guide-book that said, "*Criccieth*: For several years this small town was the home of James (now Jan) Morris, probably the finest living travel writer." The "James (now Jan)" needed no explanation, since the story of how she changed from a man to a woman in a clinic in Casablanca was told in her book *Conundrum*, 1974. She still lived near Criccieth, outside the village of Llanystumdwy, in what was formerly the stables of the manor house, looking northward to the mountains of Eryri and southward to Cardigan Bay.

I seldom looked people up in foreign countries—I could never believe they really wanted to see me; I had an uncomfortable sense that I was interrupting something intimate—but I did look up Jan Morris. She had written a great deal about Wales, and I was here, and I knew her vaguely. Her house was built like an Inca fort, of large black rocks and heavy beams. She had written, "It is built in the old Welsh way, with rough gigantic stones, piled one upon the other in an almost natural mass, with a white wooden cupola on top. Its architecture is of the variety known these days as 'vernacular,' meaning that no professional architect has ever had a hand in it."

She was wearing a straw calypso hat tipped back on her bushy hair, and a knit jersey, and white slacks. It was a very hot day and she was dressed for it. There is a certain educated English voice that is both correct and malicious. Jan Morris has such a voice. It was not deep but it was languid, and the maleness that still trembled in it made it sultry and attractive. There was nothing ponderous about her. She shrugged easily and was a good listener, and she laughed as a cat might—full-throated and with a little hiss of pleasure, stiffening her body. She was kind, reckless, and intelligent.

Her house was very neat and full of books and pictures. "I have filled it with *Cymreictod*—Welshness." Yes, solid country artifacts and beamed ceilings and a NO SMOKING sign in Welsh—she did not allow smoking in her house. Her library was forty-two feet long and the corresponding room upstairs was her study, with a desk and a stereo.

Music mattered to her in an unusual way. She once wrote, "Animists believe that the divine is to be found in every living thing, but I go one further; I am an inanimist, holding that even lifeless objects can contain immortal yearnings. . . . I maintain, for instance, that music can permanently influence a building, so I often leave the record player on when I am out of the house, allowing its themes and melodies to soak themselves into the fabric."

Perhaps she was serious. Inanimate objects can seem to possess something resembling vitality, or a mood that answers your own. But melodies soaking into wood and stone? "My kitchen adores Mozart," the wise guy might say, or, "The parlor's into Gladys Knight and the Pips." But I did not say anything; I just listened approvingly.

"I suppose it's very selfish, only one bedroom," she said.

But it was the sort of house everyone wanted, on its own, at the edge of a meadow, solid as could be, well-lighted, pretty, painted, cozy, with an enormous library and study and a four-poster: perfect for a solitary person and one cat. Hers was called Solomon.

Then she said, "Want to see my grave?"

I said of course and we went down to a cool shaded wood by a riverside. Jan Morris was a nimble walker: she had climbed to twenty thousand feet with the first successful Everest expedition in 1953. Welsh woods were full of small twisted oaks and tangled boughs and moist soil and dark ferny corners. We entered a boggier area of straight green trees and speckled shade.

"I always think this is very Japanese," she said.

It did look that way, the idealized bushy landscape of the woodblock print, the little riverside grotto.

She pointed across the river and said, "That's my grave—right there, that little island."

It was like a beaver's dam of tree trunks padded all around with moss, and more ferns, and the river slurping and gurgling among boulders.

"There's where I'm going to be buried—or rather scattered. It's nice, don't you think? Elizabeth's ashes are going to be scattered there, too." Jan Morris was married to Elizabeth before the sex change.

It seemed odd that someone so young should be thinking of death. She was fifty-six, and the hormones she took made her look a great deal younger—early forties, perhaps. But it was a very Welsh thought, this plan for ashes and a grave site. It was a nation habituated to ghostliness and sighing and mourning. I was traveling on the Celtic fringe, where they still believed in giants.

What did I think of her grave? she asked.

I said the island looked as though it would wash away in a torrent and that her ashes would end up in Cardigan Bay. She laughed and said it did not matter.

At our first meeting about a year before, in London, she had said suddenly, "I am thinking of taking up a life of crime," and she had mentioned wanting to steal something from Woolworth's. It had not seemed so criminal to me, but over lunch I asked her whether she had done anything about it.

"If I had taken up a life of crime I would be hardly likely to tell you, Paul!"

"I was just curious," I said.

She said, "These knives and forks. I stole them from Pan American Airways. I told the stewardess I was stealing them. She said she didn't care."

They were the sort of knives and forks you get on an airplane with your little plastic tray of soggy meat and gravy.

Talk of crime led us to talk of arson by Welsh nationalists. I asked why only cottages were burned, when there were many tin caravans—as the English called mobile homes—on the coast that would make a useful blaze. She said her son was very pro-Welsh and patriotic and would probably consider that.

I said that the Welsh seemed like one family.

"Oh, yes, that's what my son says. He thinks as long as he is in Wales he's safe. He'll always be taken care of. He can go to any house and he will be taken in and fed and given a place to sleep."

"Like the travelers in Arabia who walk up to a Bedouin's tent and say, 'I am a guest of God,' in order to get hospitality. *Ana dheef Allah.*"

"Yes," she said. "It's probably true—it is like a family here in Wales."

And like all families, I said, sentimental and suspicious and quarrelsome and secretive. But Welsh nationalism was at times like a certain kind of feminism, very monotonous and one-sided.

She said, "I suppose it does look that way, if you're a man."

I could have said: Didn't it look that way to you when you were a man?

She said, "As for the caravans and tents, yes, they look awful. But the Welsh don't notice them particularly. They are not noted for their visual sense. And those people, the tourists, are seeing Wales. I'm glad they're here, in a way, so they can see this beautiful country and understand the Welsh."

Given the horror of the caravans, it was a very generous thought, and it certainly was not my sentiment. I always thought of Edmund Gosse saying, "No one will see again on the shore of England what I saw in my early childhood." The shore was fragile and breakable and easily poisoned.

Jan Morris was still speaking of the Welsh. "Some people say that Welsh nationalism is a narrow movement, cutting Wales off from the world. But it is possible to see it as liberating Wales and giving it an importance—of bringing it into the world."

We finished lunch and went outside. She said, "If only you could see the mountains. I know it's boring when people say that—but they really are spectacular. What do you want to do?"

I said that I had had a glimpse of Portmeirion from the train and wanted a closer look, if there was time.

We drove there in her car and parked under the pines. She had known the architect Clough Williams-Ellis very well. "He was a wonderful man," she said. "On his death-bed he was still chirping away merrily. But he was very worried about what people would say about him. Funny man! He wrote his own obituary! He had it there with him as he lay dying. When I visited him, he asked me to read it. Of course, there was nothing unflattering in it. I asked him why he had gone to all the trouble of writing his own obituary.

"He said, 'Because I don't know what *The Times* will write in the obituary they do of me.'"

We walked through the gateway and down the stairs to the little Italian fantasy town on this Welsh hillside.

"He was obsessed that they would get something wrong or be critical. He had tried every way he could of getting hold of his *Times* obituary—but failed, of course. They're always secret."

She laughed. It was that hearty malicious laugh.

"The funny thing was, I was the one who had written his obituary for *The Times*. They're all written carefully before-hand, you know."

I said, "And you didn't tell him?"

"No." Her face was blank. Was she smiling behind it? "Do you think I should have?"

I said, "But he was on his deathbed."

She laughed again. She said, "It doesn't matter."

There was a carved bust of Williams-Ellis in a niche, and resting crookedly on its dome was a hand-scrawled sign saying, THE BAR UPSTAIRS IS OPEN.

Jan said, "He would have liked that."

We walked through the place, under arches, through gateways, past Siamese statuary and Greek columns and gardens and pillars and colonnades; we walked around the piazza.

"The trouble with him was that he didn't know when to stop."

It was a sunny day. We lingered at the blue Parthenon,

the Chantry, the Hercules statue, the town hall. You think, *What is it doing here?* More cottages.

"Once, when we lost a child, we stayed up there in that white cottage." She meant herself and Elizabeth, when they were husband and wife.

There was more. Another triumphal arch, the Prior's Lodge, pink and green walls.

Jan said, "It's supposed to make you laugh."

But instead, it was making me very serious, for this folly had taken over forty years to put together, and yet it still had the look of a faded movie set.

"He even designed the cracks and planned where the mossy parts should be. He was very meticulous and very flamboyant, too, always in one of these big, wide-brimmed antediluvian hats and yellow socks."

I was relieved to get out of Portmeirion; I had been feeling guilty, with the uncomfortable suspicion that I had been sight-seeing—something I had vowed I would not do.

Jan said, "Want to see my gravestone?"

It was the same sudden, proud, provocative, mirthful way that she had said, *Want to see my grave?*

I said of course.

The stone was propped against the wall of her library. I had missed it before. The lettering was very well done, as graceful as the engraving on a bank note. It was inscribed *Jan & Elizabeth Morris*. In Welsh and English, above and below the names, it said,

Here Are Two Friends
At the End of One Life

I said it was as touching as Emily Dickinson's gravestone in Amherst, Massachusetts, which said nothing more than *Called Back*.

When I left, and we stood at the railway station at Porthmadog, Jan said, "If only these people knew who was getting on the train!"

I said, "Why should they care?"

She grinned. She said, "That knapsack—is that all you have?"

I said yes. We talked about traveling light. I said the great thing was to have no more than you could carry comfortably and never to carry formal clothes—suits, ties, shiny shoes, extra sweaters: what sort of travel was that?

Jan Morris said, "I just carry a few frocks. I squash them into a ball—they don't weigh anything. It's much easier for a woman to travel light than a man."

There was no question that she knew what she was talking about, for she had been both a man and a woman. She smiled at me, and I felt a queer thrill when I kissed her good-bye.

Railway Buff

"I LOVE STEAM, DON'T YOU?" STAN WIGBETH SAID TO ME ON the Ffestiniog Railway, and then he leaned out of the window. He was not interested in my answer, which was, "Up to a point." Mr. Wigbeth smiled and ground his teeth in pleasure when the whistle blew. He said there was nothing to him more beautiful than a steam "loco." He told me they were efficient and brilliantly made; but engine drivers had described to me how uncomfortable they could be, and how horrible on winter nights, because it was impossible to drive most steam engines without sticking your face out the side window every few minutes.

I wanted Mr. Wigbeth to admit that they were outdated and ox-like, dramatic-looking but hell to drive; they were the choo-choo fantasies of lonely children; they were fun but filthy. Our train was pulled through the Welsh mountains by a Fairlie, known to the buffs as a "double engine"—two boilers—"the most uncomfortable engine I've ever driven," a railwayman once told me. It was very hot for the driver because of the position of the boilers. The footplate of the Fairlie was like an Oriental oven for poaching ducks in their own sweat. Mr. Wigbeth did not agree with any of this. Like many other railway buffs, he detested our century.

This had originally been a tram line, he told me; all the way from Porthmadog to Blaenau Ffestiniog—horse trams, hauling slate from the mountain quarries. Then it was named the Narrow Gauge Railway and opened to passengers in 1869. It was closed in 1946 and eventually reopened in stages. The line was now—this month—completely open.

"We're lucky to be here," Mr. Wigbeth said, and checked his watch—a pocket watch, of course: the railway buff's timepiece. He was delighted by what he saw. "Right on time!"

It was a beautiful trip to Blaenau, on the hairpin curves of the steep Snowdonia hills and through the thick evening green of the Dwyryd Valley. To the southeast, amid the lovely mountains, was the Trawsfynydd Nuclear Power Station, three or four gigantic gray slabs. An English architect, noted for his restrained taste, had been hired in 1959 to make it prettier, or at least bearable, but he had failed. Perhaps he should have planted vines. Yet this monstrosity emphasized the glory of these valleys. I found the ride restful, even with the talkative Mr. Wigbeth beside me. Then he was silenced by a mile-long tunnel. The light at the end of the tunnel was Blaenau Ffestiniog, at the head of the valley.

"Where are you off to, then?" Mr. Wigbeth asked.

"I'm catching the next train to Llandudno Junction."

"It's a diesel," he said, and made a sour face.

"So what?"

"I don't call that a train," he said. "I call that a tin box!"

He was disgusted and angry. He put on his engine driver's cap and his jacket with the railway lapel pins, and after a last look at his conductor-type pocket watch, he got into his little Ford Cortina and drove twenty-seven stop-and-go miles back to Bangor.

Llandudno

I WAS NOT FRIGHTENED AT THE HOTEL IN LLANDUDNO UNTIL I was taken upstairs by the pockmarked clerk, and then I sat in the dusty room alone and listened. The only sound was my breathing, from having climbed the four flights of stairs. The room was small; there were no lights in the passageway; the wallpaper had rust stains that could have been spatters of blood. The ceiling was high, the room narrow: it was like sitting at the bottom of a well. I went downstairs.

The clerk was watching television in the lounge—he called it a lounge. He did not speak to me. He was watching "Hill Street Blues," a car chase, some shouting. I looked at the register and saw what I had missed before—that I was the only guest in this big, dark forty-room hotel. I went outside and wondered how to escape. Of course I could have marched in and said, "I'm not happy here—I'm checking out," but the clerk might have made trouble and charged me. Anyway, I wanted to punish him for running such a scary place.

I walked inside and upstairs, grabbed my knapsack, and hurried to the lounge, rehearsing a story that began, "This is my bird-watching gear. I'll be right back—" The clerk was still watching television. As I passed him (he did not look up), the hotel seemed to me the most sinister building I had ever been in. On my way downstairs I had had a moment of panic when, faced by three closed doors in a hallway, I imagined myself in one of those corridor labyrinths of the hotel in a nightmare, endlessly tramping torn carpets and opening doors to discover again and again that I was trapped.

I ran down the Promenade to the bandstand and stood panting while the band played "If You Were the Only Girl in the World." I wondered if I had been followed by the clerk. I paid twenty pence for a deck chair, but feeling that I was being watched (perhaps it was my knapsack and oily shoes?), I abandoned the chair and continued down the Promenade. Later, I checked into the Queens Hotel, which looked vulgar enough to be safe.

Llandudno was the sort of place that inspired old-fashioned fears of seaside crime. It made me think of poisoning and suffocation, screams behind varnished doors, creatures scratching at the wainscoting. I imagined constantly that I was hearing the gasps of adulterers from the dark windows of those stuccoed terraces that served as guest houses—naked people saying gloatingly, "We shouldn't be doing this!" In all ways, Llandudno was a perfectly preserved Victorian town. It was so splendid-looking that it took me several days to find out that it was in fact very dull.

It had begun as a fashionable watering place and developed into a railway resort. It was still a railway resort, full of people strolling on the Promenade and under the glass-and-iron canopies of the shop fronts on Mostyn Street. It had a very old steamer ("Excursions to the Isle of Man") moored at its pier head, and very old hotels, and a choice of very old entertainments—*Old Mother Riley* at the Pavilion, the Welsh National Opera at the Astra Theatre doing *Tosca*, or Yorkshire comedians in vast saloon bars telling very old jokes. "We're going to have a loovely boom competition," a toothy comedian was telling his drunken audience in a public house near Happy Valley. A man was blindfolded and five girls selected, and the man had to judge—by touching them—which one's bum was the shapeliest. It caused hilarity and howls of laughter; the girls were shy—one simply walked offstage; and at one point some men were substituted and the blindfolded man crouched and began searching the men's bums as everyone jeered. And then the girl with the best bum was selected as the winner and awarded a bottle of carbonated cider called Pomagne.

I overheard two elderly ladies outside at the rail, looking above Llandudno Bay. They were Miss Maltby and Miss Thorn, from Glossop, near Manchester.

"It's a nice moon," Miss Maltby said.

"Aye," Miss Thorn said. "It is."

"But that's not what we saw earlier this evening."

"No. That was the sun."

Miss Maltby said, "You told me it was the moon."

"It was all that mist, you see," Miss Thorn said. "But I know now it was the sun."

Looking Seaward

Now I saw British people lying stiffly on the beach like dead insects, or huddled against the canvas windbreaks they hammered into the sand with rented mallets, or standing on cliffs and kicking stones roly-poly into the sea—and I thought: *They are symbolically leaving the country.*

Going to the coast was as far as they could comfortably go. It was the poor person's way of going abroad—standing at the seaside and staring at the ocean. It took a little imagination. I believed that these people were fantasizing that they were over there on the watery horizon, at sea. Most people on the Promenade walked with their faces averted from the land. Perhaps another of their coastal pleasures was being able to turn their backs on Britain. I seldom saw anyone with his back turned to the sea (it was the rarest posture on the coast). Most people looked seaward with anxious hopeful faces, as if they had just left their native land.

Insulted England

THE REST OF THE COAST, FROM THE WINDOW OF THE TRAIN, was low and disfigured. There were small bleak towns like Parton and Harrington, and huge horrible ones like Workington, with its steelworks—another insolvent industry. And Maryport was just sad; it had once been an important coal and iron port, and great sailing ships had been built there in Victorian times. Now it was forgotten. Today there was so little shipbuilding on the British coast it could be said not to exist at all. But that was not so odd as the fact that I saw very few vessels in these harbors and ports—a rusty freighter, a battered trawler, some plastic sailboats—there was not much more, where once there had been hundreds of seagoing vessels.

I watched for more. What I saw was ugly and interesting, but before I knew what was happening, the line cut inland, passing bramble hedges and crows in fields of silage and small huddled-together farm buildings and church steeples in distant villages. We had left the violated coast, and now the mild countryside reasserted itself. It was green farms all the way to Carlisle—pretty and extremely dull.

KESWICK PUNKS, a scrawl said in Carlisle, blending Coleridge and Wordsworth with Johnny Rotten. But that was not so surprising. It was always in the fine old provincial towns and county seats that one saw the wildest-looking youths, the pink-haired boys and the girls in leopard-skin tights, the nose jewels and tattooed earlobes. I had seen green hair and swastikas in little Llanelli. I no longer felt that place names like Taunton or Exeter or Bristol were evocative of anything but graffiti-covered walls, like those of noble Carlisle, crowned with a castle and with

enough battlements and city walls to satisfy the most ener-
getic vandal. VIOLENT REVOLUTION, it said, and THE EX-
PLOITED and ANARCHY and SOCIAL SCUM. Perhaps they were
pop groups? THE REJECTS, THE DEFECTS, THE OUTCASTS, THE
DAMNED, and some bright new swastikas and THE BARMY
ARMY. And on the ancient walls, SKINHEADS RULE!

Some of it was hyperbole, I supposed, but it was worth
spending a day or so to examine it. It fascinated me as
much as did the motorcycle gangs, who raced out of the
oak forests and country lanes to terrorize villagers or simply to sit in a thatch-roofed pub, averting their sullen dirty
faces. I did not take it personally when they refused to talk
to me. They would not talk to anyone. They were English,
they were country folk, they were shy. They were dangerous only by the dozen; individually they were rather sweet
and seemed embarrassed to be walking down the High
Street of dear old Haltwhistle in leather jackets inscribed
HELL'S ANGELS or THE DAMNED.

The graffiti suggested that England—perhaps the whole
of Britain—was changing into a poorer, more violent place.
And it was easier to see this deterioration on the coast and
in the provincial towns than in a large city. The messages
were intended to be shocking, but England was practically
unshockable, so the graffiti seemed merely a nuisance, an
insult. And that was how I began to think of the whole
country; if I had only one word to describe the expression
of England's face I would have said: insulted.

Mrs. Wheeney, Landlady

I EXPECTED FORMALITIES—CUSTOMS AND IMMIGRATION—
Larne was so foreign-seeming, so dark and dripping, but
there was not even a security check; just a gangway and the

wet town beyond it. I wandered the streets for an hour, feeling like Billy Bones, and then rang the bell at a heavy-looking house displaying a window card saying VACANCIES. I had counted ten others, but this one I could tell had big rooms and big armchairs.

"Just off the ferry?" It was Mrs. Fraser Wheeney, plucking at her dress, hair in a bun, face like a seal pup—pouty mouth, soulful eyes, sixty-five years old; she had been sitting under her own pokerwork, REJOICE IN THE LORD ALWAYS, waiting for the doorbell to ring. "Twenty-one-fifteen it came in—been looking around town?"

Mrs. Wheeney knew everything, and her guest house was of the in-law sort—oppression and comfort blended, like being smothered with a pillow. But business was terrible; only one other room was taken. Why, she could remember when, just after the ferry came in, she would have been turning people away! That was before the recent troubles, and what a lot of harm they'd done! But Mrs. Wheeney was dead tired and had things on her mind—the wild storm last night.

"Thonder!" she thundered. "It opened up me hud!"

We were walking upstairs under a large motto—FOR GOD SO LOVED THE WORLD, and so forth.

"It gave me huddicks!"

The house was full of furniture, and how many floors? Four or five anyway, and pianos on some of them, and there was an ottoman, and a wing chair, and pokerwork scenes from the Old Testament, Noah possibly, and was that Abraham and Isaac? The whole house was dark and varnished and gleaming—the smell of varnish still powerful, with the sizzle of a coal fire. It was June in Northern Ireland, so only one room had a fire trembling in the grate.

"And it went through me neighbor's roof," she said, still talking about the storm, the thunder and lightning.

Another flight of stairs, heavy carpet, more Bible mottoes, an armchair on the landing.

"Just one more," Mrs. Wheeney said. "This is how I get me exercise. Oh, it was turrible. One of me people was crying—"

Mirrors and antlers and more mottoes and wood paneling, and now I noticed that Mrs. Wheeney had a mustache. She was talking about the *reeyun*—how hard it was; about breakfast at *eeyut*—but she would be up at *sux*; and what a dangerous *suttee* Belfast was.

CHRIST JESUS CAME INTO THE WORLD TO SAVE SINNERS was the motto over my bedstead, in this enormous drafty room, and the bed was a great slumping trampoline. Mrs. Wheeney was saying that she had not slept a wink all the previous night. It was the thunder and the poor soul in number eight, who was scared to death.

"It's funny how tired you get when you miss a night's sleep." she said. "Now me, I'm looking forward to going to bed. Don't worry about the money. You can give me the five pounds tomorrow."

The rain had started again and was hitting the window with a swish like sleet. It was like being among the Jumblies, on a dark and rainy coast. They were glad to see aliens here, and I was happy among these strangers.

Belfast

I KNEW AT ONCE THAT BELFAST WAS AN AWFUL CITY. IT HAD A bad face—moldering buildings, tough-looking people, a visible smell, too many fences. Every building that was worth blowing up was guarded by a man with a metal detector who frisked people entering and checked their bags. It happened everywhere, even at dingy entrances, at buildings that were not worth blowing up, and, again and again, at the bus station, the railway station. Like the bombs themselves, the routine was frightening, then fascinating, then maddening, and then a bore—but it went on and became a part of the great waste motion of Ulster life. And security looked like parody, because the whole place was already scorched and broken with bomb blasts.

It was so awful I wanted to stay. It was a city that was so demented and sick that some aliens mistook its desperate frenzy for a sign of health, never knowing it was a death agony. It had always been a hated city. "There is no aristocracy—no culture—no grace—no leisure worthy of the name," Sean O'Faolain wrote in his *Irish Journey*. "It all boils down to mixed grills, double whiskies, dividends, movies, and these strolling, homeless, hate-driven poor." But if what people said was true, that it really was one of the nastiest cities in the world, surely then it was worth spending some time in, for horror interest?

I lingered a few days, marveling at its decrepitude, and then vowed to come back the following week. I had never seen anything like it. There was a high steel fence around the city center, and that part of Belfast was intact, because to enter it, one had to pass through a checkpoint—a turnstile for people, a barrier for cars and buses. More metal detectors, bag searches, and questions: lines of people waited to be examined so that they could shop, play bingo, or go to a movie.

Giant's Causeway

I BEGAN TO DEVELOP A HABIT OF ASKING DIRECTIONS, FOR THE pleasure of listening to them.

"Just a munnut," a man in Bushmills said. His name was Emmett; he was about sixty-odd and wore an old coat. He had a pound of bacon in his hand, and pressing the bacon to the side of his head in a reflective way, he went on.

"Der's a wee wudden brudge under the car park. And der's a bug one farder on—a brudge for trums. Aw, der used to be trums up and down! Aw, but they is sore on money and unded it. Lussun, ye kyan poss along da strond if the tide is dine. But walk on da odder side whar der's graws." He moved the bacon to his cheek. "But it might be weyat!"

"What might be wet?"

"Da graws," Mr. Emmett said.

"Long grass?"

"In its notral styat."

This baffled me for a while—*notral styat*—and then I thought: *Of course, in its natural state!*

Kicking through bracken, I pushed on and decided to head for the Giant's Causeway.

BOSWELL: Is not the Giant's Causeway worth seeing?

JOHNSON: Worth seeing? Yes; but not worth going to see.

I stayed on the coastal cliffs and then took a shortcut behind a coastal cottage, where I was startled by a big square-faced dog. The hairy thing growled at me and I leaped to get away, but I tripped and fell forward into a bed of nettles. My hands stung for six hours.

The Giant's Causeway was a spectacular set of headlands made of petrified boilings and natural columns and upright pipe-shaped rocks. Every crack and boulder and contour had a fanciful name. This massive coastal oddity had been caused by the cooling of lava when this part of Ireland had oozed during a period of vulcanism. I walked along it, to and from Dunseverick Castle—"once the home of a man who saw the Crucifixion" (supposed to be Conal Cearnach, a roving Irish wrestler who happened to be in a wrestling match in Jerusalem the day Christ was crucified).

The basalt cliffs were covered with black slugs and jackdaws, and at seven in the evening the sun broke through the clouds as powerfully as a sunrise, striping the sea in pink. It was very quiet. The wind had dropped. No insects, no cars, no planes—only a flock of sheep baaing in a meadow on a nearby hilltop. The coves and bays were crowded with diving gulls and fulmars, but the cliffs were so deep, they contained the birds' squawks. The sun gleamed on the still sea, and in the west above Inishowen Head I could spy the blue heights of Crocknasmug. Yes, the Giant's Causeway was worth going to see.

It had been a tourist attraction for hundreds of years. Every traveler to Britain had come here to size it up. There had been tram lines out to it, as Mr. Emmett had told me in Bushmills. But the troubles had put an end to this, and now the coast had regained a rough primeval look—just one stall selling postcards, where there had been throngs of noisy shops.

This landscape had shaped the Irish mind and influenced Irish beliefs. It was easy to see these headlands and believe in giants. And now with people too afraid to travel much, the landscape had become monumental once again in its emptiness.

In pagan Ireland cromlechs had been regarded as giants' graves, and people looked closely at the land, never finding it neutral but always a worry or a reassurance. Hereabouts, there were caves that had been the homes of troglodytes. And it seemed to me that there was something in the present desolation that had made the landscape important again. So the Irish had been returned to themselves in this interval, and their fears restored to them, for how could they stand amid all this towering beauty and not feel puny?

The Future in Enniskillen

Someday all cities will look like this, I had thought in Belfast; and the same thought occurred to me in Derry and now in Enniskillen. The center of these places was a "control zone," with an entrance and exit. All cars and all people were examined for weapons or bombs, and the tight security meant that inside the control zone life was fairly peaceful and the buildings generally undamaged. It was possible to control the flow of traffic and even to prevent too many people from entering. It was conceivable that this system would in time be adapted to cities that were otherwise uncontrollable. It was not hard to imagine Manhattan Island as one large control zone, with various entrances and exits; Ulster suggested to me the likely eventuality of sealed cities in the future.

In Enniskillen each car in the control zone was required to have at least one person in it. If a car was left empty or unattended, a warning siren was sounded and the town center cleared. If the driver was found, he was given a stiff fine; if no driver claimed the car, the bomb squad moved in. This system had greatly reduced the number of car bombs in Enniskillen (only ten miles from the border). The last car bomb had gone off two years ago. The nicer part of Church Street was blown to smithereens—an appropriate Gaelic word—but it was a pardonable lapse, the soldiers said. That wired-up car *seemed* to have a person in it: how were they to recognize the difference between an Ulsterman and a dummy?

Willie McComiskey, who described himself as a fruiterer, told me that Enniskillen had been pretty quiet lately—no bombs, not many fires, only a few ambushed cars.

"What they do, see, is they go to isolated farms near the border. They take the farmer and stand him up and shoot him."

He seemed rather emotionless as he spoke, and he described how the men were sometimes murdered in front of their families—the wife and children watching.

I asked him how he felt about it.

He said in the same even voice, "Why, you wouldn't do it to a dog."

"So what do you think of these gunmen?"

"I hate them," he said. He began to smile. What absurd questions I was asking! But he was uncomfortable stating the obvious. Here, such attitudes were taken for granted.

He said, "We're eighty percent British here. We couldn't have union with southern Ireland. A Protestant would have no chance. He wouldn't get a job."

So McComiskey was a Protestant; that was his emphasis. "But I don't think the IRA want union now. They don't know what they do want."

From Enniskillen I walked south to Upper Lough Erne, one of the two enormous lakes here in County Fermanagh. The sun came out as I walked, and a milkman I met said, "The weather's being kind to us." There was no sound on these country lanes except the odd squawk of a crow. I found a hotel near the village of Bellanaleck, and now the sun was shining on the green woods and the lake. It was a sixty-room hotel. I thought I was the only guest, but the next day at breakfast I saw two Frenchmen in rubber waders—fishermen.

"I have to check you for bombs," Alice, the room girl, said.

She followed me to my room and then peered uneasily into my knapsack.

"I'm not sure what a bomb looks like," she said.

"You won't find one in there," I said. "It's just old clothes—"

"And books," she said. "And letters."

"No letter bombs."

She said, "I have to check all the same."

I went for a walk. This was deep country. The pair of lakes went halfway across this part of Ulster. People spent weeks on cabin cruisers; Germans mostly. There were no English tourists here anymore.

"The English started to believe what they saw on television," Bob Ewart said. "They actually thought all that stuff about bombs and murders was true!"

He himself was from Nottingham.

"I've lived here fourteen years and I've yet to see an angry man."

That night the movie on television was *Invasion of the Body Snatchers*. I watched it with the Irish hotel workers. It was a horror movie about the world being taken over by alien germs. The Irishmen said it was frightening and of course went to bed happy. Then it struck me that a horror movie could enjoy a great popular success only if its frights were preposterous—like someone saying "Boo!" The ultimate horror was really what was happening in many Ulster towns: bombs, murders, people's hands being hacksawed off, or men having their kneecaps shot off as a punishment for disloyalty, or the tar-and-feathering of young girls for socializing with soldiers. Because this was the truth—unlike the Hollywood monster movie—it was worse than frightening: it was unbearable.

And the next day a man named Guilfoyle told me there was quite a bit of rural crime in the border areas—cattle maiming. I had no idea what he was talking about. He explained that to take revenge on farmers, some of the republican country folk sneaked into the pastures at night and knifed off the cows' udders.

Mooney's Hotel

IN BELFAST I STAYED IN A DIRTY HOTEL WITH A DAMP INTErior and wallpaper that smelled of tobacco smoke and beer and the breakfast grease. But there was no security check here. I had been searched in Enniskillen, a town that hadn't had a bomb in years; and I would have been searched at the grand Europa Hotel in Belfast—it was surrounded by a high barbed-wire fence and had sentries and guard dogs. The tourists and journalists stayed at the Europa—it was a good target for bombs. But no one of any importance stayed at Mooney's Hotel.

I called it Mooney's because it greatly resembled Mrs. Mooney's flophouse in James Joyce's story "The Boarding House." Our Mrs. Mooney also had an enormous florid face and fat arms and red hands, and she catered to traveling salesmen and drifters. The carpets were ragged, the wallpaper was peeling, there were nicks all over the woodwork. But I was free there, and I would not have been free in an expensive hotel; and I also thought that in this grubby place I was out of danger. It was Belfast logic, but it was also a pattern of life that I was sure would become more common in the cities of the future.

The bar at Mooney's was busy all night, filling the whole building with smoke and chatter.

"What time does the bar close?" I asked on my first night.

"October," a drinker told me, and laughed.

No one admitted to breaking the law in Ulster. The most they said was "Look what they make us do!" It was as if all the street violence were imaginary or else rigged by soldiers who (so it was said in Derry) coaxed children into starting riots. It was slippery, shadowy, tribal; it was all stealth. It was a folk tradition of flag waving and the most petty expression of religious bigotry west of Jerusalem: the Linfield Football Club of Belfast had a clause in its consti- . tution stipulating that no Catholic could ever play on its team. Apart from the bombing, it was not a public crime anymore. It was sneaking ambushes and doorstep murders ("I've got something for your father") and land mines in the country lanes. Some of the worst crimes took place in the prettiest rural places—the shootings and house burnings and the cattle maiming—in the green hills, with the birds singing.

People said, "There's no solution. . . . Ireland's always had troubles. . . . Maybe it'll die out. . . . I suppose we could emigrate. . . ."

I kept thinking: *This is Britain!*

It was like being shut in with a quarreling family and listening to cries of "You started it!" and "He hit me!" And I felt about Ulster as I had felt about some south coast boardinghouses on rainy days—I wanted to tiptoe to the front door and leave quietly and keep walking.

But I was grateful, too. No one had imposed on me. I had done nothing but ask questions, and I had always received interesting answers. I had met hospitable and decent people. No one had ever asked me what I did for a living. Perhaps this was tact: it was an impolite question in a place where so many people were on the dole.

I had been asked the question in England and Wales. "I'm in publishing," I always said. Publishing was respectable, harmless, and undiscussable. The conversation moved on to other matters. "I'm a writer" was a fatal admission, and certainly one of the great conversation stoppers. Anyway, with me in wet shoes and scratched leather jacket and bruised knapsack, would anyone have believed I was a writer? But no one knew what publishers looked like.

On my last night in Belfast, I was asked. I was at Mooney's talking to Mr. Doran, and I had asked too many questions about his upbringing, his mother, his ambitions, the crime rate, his job—

"And what do you do?" Doran asked, risking the question no one else had dared.

Obviously I did something. I was an alien.

"I'm in publishing," I said.

Doran's face lit up. Not once in seven weeks of my saying this had anyone responded so brightly. But this was Ireland.

"I'm working on a wee novel," Doran said, and ordered me another pint. "I've got about four hundred pages done—it's right in me room upstairs. Let's meet tomorrow and have another jar. I'll bring me novel with me. You'll love it. It's all about the troubles."

The next day I tiptoed past Doran's room. I heard the flutterblast of his snoring. I slipped out of Mooney's and shut the door on Ulster.

Cape Wrath

SOME FANTASIES PREPARE US FOR REALITY. THE SHARP STEEP Cuillins were like mountains from a storybook—they had a dramatic, fairy-tale strangeness. But Cape Wrath on the northwest coast of Scotland was unimaginable. It was one of those places where, I guessed, every traveler felt like a discoverer who was seeing it for the first time. There are not many such places in the world. I felt I had penetrated a fastness of mountains and moors, after two months of searching, and I had found something new. So even this old, overscrutinized kingdom had a secret patch of coast! I was very happy at Cape Wrath. I even liked its ambiguous name. I did not want to leave.

There were other people in the area: a hard-pressed settlement of sheep farmers and fishermen, and a community of dropouts making pots and jewelry and quilts at the edge of Balnakeil. There were anglers and campers, too, and every so often a brown plane flew overhead and dropped bombs on one of the Cape Wrath beaches, where the army had a firing range. But the size of the place easily absorbed these people. They were lost in it, and as with all people in a special place, they were secretive and a little suspicious of strangers.

Only the real natives were friendly. They were the toughest Highlanders and they did not match any Scottish stereotype I knew. They did not even have a recognizably Scottish accent. They were like white crows. They were courteous, hospitable, hard-working, and funny. They epitomized what was best in Scotland, the strong cultural pride that was separate from political nationalism. That took confidence. They were independent, too—*thrawn* was the Lowlands word for their stubborn character. I admired their sense of equality, their disregard for class, and the gentle way they treated their children and animals. They were tolerant and reliable, and none of this was related to the flummery of bagpipes and sporrans and tribalistic blood-and-thunder that Sir Walter Scott had turned into the Highland cult. What I liked most about them was that they were self-sufficient. They were the only people I had seen on the whole coast who were looking after themselves.

It was a shire full of mountains, with spaces between— some valleys and some moors—and each mountain was separate. To describe the landscape it was necessary to describe each mountain, because each one was unique. But the soil was not very good, the sheep were small, the grass thin, and I never walked very far without finding a corpse—loose wool blowing around bones, and the bared teeth of a skull.

"Look," a shepherd named Stephen said to me on one of these hillsides.

A buzzard-sized bird was circling.

"It's a hooded crow," Stephen said. "They're desperate creatures. In a place like this—no shelter, no one around for miles—they find a lamb and peck its eyes out. It's lost, it can't get to its mother, it gets weak. Then the hooded crows—so patient up there—dive low and peck it to pieces. They're a terrible bird."

He said that it was the predatory crows, not the weather, that killed the lambs. It was a cold place, but not excessively so. In winter there was little snow, though the winds were strong and the easterlies were usually freezing gales. There were always birds in the wind—crows and hawks and comic squawking oystercatchers with long orange bills and singing larks and long-necked shags and stuttering stonechats.

It could be an eerie landscape, especially on a wet day, with all the scattered bones gleaming against the dun-colored cliffs and the wind scraping against the heather. It surprised me that I was happy in a place where there were so few trees—there were none at all here. It was not picturesque and it was practically unphotographable. It was stunningly empty. It looked like a corner of another planet, and at times it seemed diabolical. But I liked it for all these reasons. And more important than these, my chief reason for being happy was that I felt safe here. The landscape was like a fierce-looking monster that offered me protection; being in Cape Wrath was like having a pet dragon.

Royal Visit

I TRIED TO HITCHHIKE IN ORDER TO GET TO ANSTRUTHER IN time to see the Queen, but no one picked me up. I fell in with a farm laborer on the road. He was coming from St. Andrews. He had gone there for the Royal Visit.

"I saw the Queen," he said, and he winced, remembering.

"How did she look?"

He winced again. His name was Dougie. He wore rubber boots. He said, "She were deep in thought."

Dougie had seen something no one else had.

"She were preoccupied. Her face were gray. She weren't happy."

I said, "I thought she was happy about her new grandson."

Dougie disagreed. "I think she were worried about something. They do worry, you know. Aye, it's a terrible job."

He began to walk slowly, as if in sympathy for the hard-pressed Queen.

I said, "Being Queen of England has its compensations."

"Some compensations and some disadvantages," Dougie said. "I say it's half a dream world and half a nightmare. It's a goldfish bowl. No privacy! She can't pick her nose without someone seeing her."

Dougie said this in an anguished way, and I thought it was curious, though I did not say so, that he was pained because the monarch could not pick her nose without being observed.

He then began to talk about television programs. He said his favorite program was "The Dukes of Hazzard," which concerned high jinks in a town in the American South. This

Scottish farm laborer in Fifeshire said that he liked it because of the way the character Roscoe talked to his boss. That was very funny. American humor was hard to understand at times, he said, but every farm laborer in Scotland would find Roscoe funny for his attitude.

At last a bus came. I flagged it down. It was empty. I said I wanted to go to Anstruther to see the Queen.

"Aye. She's having lunch there," the driver said.

I wondered where.

The driver knew. "At the Craw's Nest. It's a small hotel on the Pittenweem Road."

He dropped me farther along and I followed the bunting into Anstruther, sensing that same vibrant glow that I had felt at St. Andrews—the royal buzz. It was a holiday atmosphere. The schools were out. The shops were closed. The pubs were open. Some men were wearing kilts. People were talking in groups, seeming to remind one another of what had just happened—the Queen had already gone by, to the Craw's Nest.

I cut across the harbor sands and went up the road to what seemed a very ordinary hotel—but freshly painted and draped in lines of plastic Union Jacks. There were more men in kilts here—they had such wonderfully upright posture, the men in kilts: they never slouched and hardly ever sat down.

"She's just left," one said. His name was Hector Hay McKaye.

But there was something of her still here, like perfume that is strongest when a woman leaves suddenly. In the Queen's case it was like something overhead—still up there, an echo.

Mr. McKaye turned to his friends and said, "They had two detectives in the kitchen—"

It seemed to me that if the Queen and Prince Philip had eaten here, the food might be good. I seldom had a good meal in my traveling, not that it mattered much: food was one of the dullest subjects. I decided to stay the night at the Craw's Nest. And this hotel, which had just received the blessing of a Royal Visit, was a great deal cheaper than any hotel in Aberdeen.

"She never had a starter," the waitress Eira said. "She had the fish course, haddock Mornay. Then roast beef, broccoli, and carrots. And fresh strawberries and cream for dessert. Our own chef did it. It was a simple meal—it was good. The menu was printed and had bits of gold foil around it."

Much was made of the good plain food. It was English food—a fish course, a roast, two boiled vegetables, and fruit for the dessert course. The middle-class families in Anstruther—and everywhere else—had that every Sunday for lunch. *She's just like us,* people said of the Queen; *of course, she works a jolly sight harder!*

What was difficult for an alien to see was that this was essentially a middle-class monarchy. Decent philistines, the royal couple liked animals and country-house sports and variety shows. They never mentioned books at all, but they were famous for preferring certain television programs. Newspapers had published photographs of the Royal Television Set: it had a big screen and a sort of shawl on the top, but it was just like one you could hire for two quid a week up the High Street. Over the years the Queen had become shrewder-seeming, an even-tempered mother-in-law and a kindly gran. Prince Philip was loved for being irascible. He was noted for his grouchy remarks. He used the word *bloody* in public, and after that it was hard for anyone to find fault with him. The Queen was his opposite, growing smaller and squashier as he seemed to lengthen and grow spiky—the illusion had sprung out of his having become vocal. The Queen and the Prince were well matched, but it was less the sovereign and her consort than the double act that all successful middle-class marriages are.

In the lobby they were selling souvenirs of the Royal Visit. How had they had time to prepare these paperweights and medallions and letter openers and postcards saying CRAW'S NEST HOTEL—SOUVENIR OF THE ROYAL VISIT?

"We knew about it in January, but we had to keep it a secret until May," Eira said. "We kept praying that nothing would go wrong. We thought the Falklands might finish it."

So they had been putting the place in order and running

up souvenirs for almost seven months. The royal lunch had lasted an hour.

That night they held a celebration party in the hotel parking lot. It was a way of giving thanks. The hotel invited the whole town, or rather two—Easter Anstruther and Wester Anstruther. They had a rock band and eight pipers and some drummers. The racket was tremendous and continued until two o'clock in the morning, hundreds of people drinking and dancing. They sold sausages and fish and chips, and there were bales of hay for people to sit on. The band was bad, but no one seemed to mind. There were old people, families, drunks, and dogs. Small boys smoked cigarettes in a delighted way and sneaked beer from the hotel. Girls danced with each other, because the village boys, too embarrassed to be seen dancing, congregated in small groups and pretended to be tough. There was a good feeling in the air, hilarity and joy, something festive, but also grateful and exhausted. It wasn't faked; it was like the atmosphere of an African village enjoying itself.

The cleaning ladies were buzzing early the next morning. "I couldn't believe it," Mrs. Ross said. "It didn't seem real. It was like a dream."

I said, "What will Willie Hamilton think?"

Willie Hamilton was their Member of Parliament and noted for being in favor of abolishing the monarchy.

"Willie Hamilton can get stuffed."

Trippers

Rosalie and Hugh Mutton collected preserved railways. They had been on the Romney, Hythe, and Dymchurch; the Ravenglass; all the Welsh lines; and more. They loved steam. They would drive hundreds of miles in their

Ford Escort to take a steam train. They were members of a steam railway preservation society. This North Norfolk Railway reminded them of the line in Shepton Mallet.

Then Mrs. Mutton said, "Where's your casual top?"

"I don't have a casual top in brown, do I," Mr. Mutton said.

"Why are you wearing brown?"

Mr. Mutton said, "I can't wear blue all the time, can I."

Rhoda Gauntlett was at the window. She said, "That sea looks so lovely. And that grass. It's a golf course."

We looked at the golf course—Sheringham, so soon.

"I'd get confused going round a golf course," Mrs. Mutton said. "You walk bloody miles. How do you know which way to go?"

This was the only train in Britain today, the fifteen-minute ride from Weybourne. It was sunny in Shering ham—a thousand people on the sandy beach, but only two people in the water. Because of the railway strike all these trippers had come by car.

There were three old ladies walking along the Promenade. They had strong country accents, probably Norfolk. I could never place these burrs and haws.

"I should have worn my blooming hat."

"The air's fresh, but it's making my eyes water."

"We can look round Woolworth's after we've had our tea."

It was a day at the seaside, and then back to their cottages in Great Snoring. They were not like the others, who had come to sit behind canvas windbreaks ("eighty pence per day or any portion thereof") and read FOUR KILLED BY RUNAWAY LORRY or WIFE KILLER GIVEN THREE YEARS (she had taunted him about money; he did not earn much; he bashed her brains out with a hammer; "You've suffered enough," the judge said) or BLUNDESTON CHILD BATTERED (bruised tot with broken leg; "He fell off a chair," the mother said; one year, pending psychiatric report). They crouched on the groins, smoking cigarettes. They lay in the bright sunshine wearing raincoats. They stood in their bathing suits. Their skin was the veiny white of raw sausage casings.

The tide was out, so I walked to Cromer along the sand.

The crumbly yellow-dirt cliffs were like the banks of a quarry, high and scooped out and raked vertically by erosion. Halfway between Sheringham and Cromer there were no people, because, characteristically, the English never strayed far from their cars, and even the most crowded parts of the English coast were empty between the parking lots. Only one man was here, Collie Wylie, a rock collector. He was hacking amber-colored tubes out of the chalk slabs on the shore. Belamites, he called them. "Take that one," he said. "Now that one is between five and eight million years old."

I saw a pillbox down the beach. It had once been on top of the cliff, and inside it the men from "Dad's Army" had conned for Germans. "Jerry would love to catch us on the hop." But the soft cliffs were constantly falling, and the pillbox had slipped a hundred feet and was now sinking into the sand, a cute little artifact from the war, buried to its gunholes.

I came to Cromer. An old man in a greasy coat sat on a wooden groin on the beach, reading a comic book about war in outer space.

SEASIDE SPECIAL '82 WAS PLAYING AT THE PAVILION THEATRE, at the end of the pier at Cromer. It was the summer show, July to September, every day except Sunday, and two matinées. I had not gone to any of these end-of-the-pier shows. I was nearing the end of my circular tour, so I decided to stay in Cromer and see the show. I found a hotel. Cromer was very empty. It had a sort of atrophied charm, a high, round-shouldered, Edwardian look, red brick terraces and red brick hotels and the loudest seagulls in Norfolk.

There were not more than thirty people in the audience that night at the Pavilion Theatre, which was pathetic, because there were nine people in the show. But seeing the show was like observing England's secret life—its anxiety in the dismal jokes, its sadness in the old songs.

"Hands up, all those who aren't working," one comedian said.

A number of hands went up—eight or ten—but this was

a terrible admission, and down they went before I could count them properly.

The comedian was already laughing. "Have some Beecham Pills," he said. "They'll get you 'working' again!"

There were more jokes, awful ones like this, and then a lady singer came out and in a sweet voice sang "The Russian Nightingale." She encouraged the audience to join in the chorus of the next one, and they offered timid voices, singing,

> Let him go, let him tarry,
> Let him sink, or let him swim.
> He doesn't care for me
> And I don't care for him.

The comedians returned. They had changed their costumes. They had worn floppy hats the first time; now they wore bowler hats and squirting flowers.

"We used to put manure on our rhubarb."

"We used to put custard on ours!"

No one laughed.

"Got any matches?"

"Yes, and they're good British ones."

"How do you know?"

"Because they're all strikers!"

A child in the first row began to cry.

The dancers came on. They were pretty girls and they danced well. They were billed as "Our Disco Dollies" on the poster. More singers appeared and "A Tribute to Al Jolson" was announced: nine minstrel show numbers, done in blackface. Entertainers in the United States could be run out of town for this sort of thing; in Cromer the audience applauded. Al Jolson was a fond memory and his rendition of "Mammy" was a special favorite in musical revues. No one had ever tired of minstrel shows in England, and they persisted on British television well into the 1970s.

It had been less than a month since the end of the Falklands War, but in the second half of *Seaside Special* there was a comedy routine in which an Argentine general appeared—goofy dago in ill-fitting khaki uniform—"How dare you insult me!"

I could hear the surf sloshing against the iron struts of the pier.

"And you come and pour yourself on me," a man was singing. It was a love song. The audience seemed embarrassed by it. They preferred "California Here I Come" and "When I Grow Too Old to Dream," sung by a man named Derick, from Johannesburg. The program said that he had "appeared in every top night spot in South Africa and Rhodesia." Say "top night spot in Zimbabwe" and it does not sound the same—it brings to mind drums and thick foliage.

One of the comedians reappeared. I had come to dread this man. I had reason. Now he played "The Warsaw Concerto" and cracked jokes as he played. "It's going to be eighty tomorrow," he said. "Forty in the morning and forty in the afternoon!"

His jokes were flat, but the music was pleasant and the singers had excellent voices. In fact, most of the performers were talented, and they pretended to be playing to a full house—not the thirty of us who sat so silently in the echoing theater. The show people conveyed the impression that they were enjoying themselves. But it can't have been much fun, looking at those empty seats. Cromer itself was very dull. And I imagined these performers were miserably paid. I wanted to know more about them. I played with the idea of sending a message backstage to one of the chorus girls. I'd get her name out of the program. Millie Plackett, the one whose thighs jiggled. "Millie, it's for you! Maybe it's your big break!" *Meet me after the show at the Hotel de Paris. . . .* That was actually the name of my hotel, an enjoyable pile of brick-and-plaster splendor. But I didn't look the part. In my scratched leather jacket and torn dungarees and oily, hiking shoes, I thought Millie Plackett might misunderstand my intentions.

I stayed until the end of the show, finally admitting that I was enjoying myself. One act was of a kind I found irresistible—the magician whose tricks go wrong, leaving him with broken eggs in his hat and the wrong deck of cards. There was always an elaborate buildup and then a sudden collapse. "Presto," he said as the trick failed. And then the last trick, the one that looked dangerous, worked like a charm and was completely baffling.

They saved the saddest song for the end. It was a love song, but in the circumstances it sounded nationalistic. It was sentimental hope, Ivor Novello gush, at the end of the pier that was trembling on the tide. I had heard it elsewhere on the coast. It was anything but new, but it was the most popular number on the seaside that year:

> We'll gather lilacs in the spring agine,
> And walk together down a shady linc . . .

Typical

ON MY LAST LONG TRUDGE, CURVING DOWN THE RUMP OF England on the Norfolk coast and into Suffolk, I thought: *Every British bulge is different and every mile has its own mood.* I said Blackpool, and people said, "Naturally!" I said Worthing, and they said, "Of all places!" The character was fixed, and though few coastal places matched their reputation, each was unique. It made my circular tour a pleasure, because it was always worth setting off in the morning. It might be bad ahead, but at least it was different; and the dreariest and most defoliated harbor town might be five minutes from a green sweep of bay.

This was the reason *typical* was regarded as such an unfair word in England. And yet there *was* such a thing as typical on the coast—but to an alien, something typical could seem just as fascinating as the mosques of the Golden Horn.

There was always an Esplanade, and always a Bandstand

on it; always a War Memorial and a Rose Garden and a bench bearing a small stained plaque that said TO THE MEMORY OF ARTHUR WETHERUP. There was always a Lifeboat Station and a Lighthouse and a Pier, a Putting Green, a Bowling Green, a Cricket Pitch, a Boating Lake, and a church the guidebook said was Perpendicular. The newsagent sold two GREETINGS FROM picture postcards, one with kittens and the other with two plump girls in surf, and he had a selection of cartoon postcards with mildly filthy captions; the souvenir stall sold rock candy; and the local real estate agent advertised a dismal cottage as "chalet-bungalow, bags of character, on bus route, superb sea views, suit retired couple." There was always a funfair and it was never fun, and the video machines were always busier than the pinball machines or the one-armed bandits. There was always an Indian restaurant and it was always called the Taj Mahal and the owners were always from Bangladesh. Of the three fish-and-chips shops, two were owned by Greeks and the third was always closed. The Chinese restaurant, Hong Kong Gardens, was always empty; FOOD TO TAKE AWAY, its sign said. There were four pubs, one was the Red Lion, and the largest one was owned by a bad-tempered Londoner—"He's a real Cockney," people said, he had been in the army.

TO TOWN CENTRE, said a sign on Marine Parade, where there was a tub of geraniums. GOLF LINKS, said another, and a third, PUBLIC CONVENIENCES. A man stood just inside the door of GENTS and tried to catch your eye as you entered, but he never said a word. The man with the mop stood at the door of LADIES. Outside town was a housing estate called Happy Valley. Yanks had camped there in the war. Beyond it was a trailer park called Golden Sands. The best hotel was the Grand, the poorest the Marine, and there was a guest house called Bellavista. The best place to stay was at a bed and breakfast called the Blodgetts. Charles Dickens had spent a night in the Grand; Wordsworth had hiked in the nearby hills; Tennyson had spent a summer in a huge house near the sandy stretch that was called the Strand; and an obscure politician had died at the Rookery. A famous murderer (he had slowly poisoned his wife) had been arrested on the Front, where he had been strolling with his young mistress.

The muddy part of the shore was called the Flats, the marshy part the Levels, the stony part the Shingles, the pebbly part the Reach, and something a mile away was always called the Crumbles. The Manor, once very grand, was now a children's home. Every Easter two gangs from London fought on Marine Parade. The town had a long history of smuggling, a bay called Smugglers' Cove, and a pub called the Smugglers' Inn.

Of the four headlands nearby, the first was part of a private golf course; the second was owned by the National Trust and had a muddy path and wooden steps on the steep bits; the third—the really magnificent one—was owned by the Ministry of Defense and used as a firing range and labeled DANGER AREA on the Ordnance Survey Maps; the fourth headland was all rocks and called the Cobbler and His Dwarfs.

The Pier had been condemned. It was threatened with demolition. A society had been formed to save it, but it would be blown up next year just the same. There was now a parking lot where the Romans had landed. The discotheque was called Spangles. The Museum was shut that day, the Swimming Pool was closed for repairs, the Baptist church was open, there were nine motor coaches parked in front of the broken boulders and ruined walls called the Castle. At the café near the entrance to the Castle a fourteen-year-old girl served tea in cracked mugs, and cellophane-wrapped cookies, stale fruitcake, and cold pork pies. She said, "We don't do sandwiches" and "We're all out of spoons," and when you asked for potato chips she said, "What flavor crisps?" and listed five, including prawn, Bovril, cheese and onion, and bacon. There was a film of sticky marmalade on the tables of the café, and you left with a patch of it on your elbow.

The railway had been closed down in 1964, and the fishing industry had folded five years ago. The art deco cinema was now a bingo hall, and what had been a ship's chandler was the Cinema Club, where Swedish pornographic films were shown all day (MEMBERS ONLY). There was an American radar station—or was it a missile base? No one knew—it was a few miles away; but the Americans had kept a low profile ever since one American soldier had raped a local lass in his car at the Reach (she had been hitchhiking in her bathing suit after dark that summer night). A nuclear power station quaintly named Thorncliffe was planned for the near future a mile south of the Cobbler. Bill Haley and the Comets had once sung at the Lido. The new shopping precinct was a failure. The dog was a Jack Russell terrier named Andy. The new bus shelter had been vandalized. It was famous for its whelks. It was raining.

Riding the
Iron Rooster

Belles du Jour

I WALKED TO ST. BASIL'S, AND TO THE METROPOLE HOTEL, where I had stayed in 1968—it was now a sort of monument—and I strolled through the GUM store, looking at the merchandise.

While I was staring at some very inferior-looking alarm clocks, I realized that the woman on my right and the one on my left were sidling nearer to me.

"Is nice clock? You like clock?"

I said, "Alarm clocks wake you up. That's why I hate them."

"Is funny," the woman on my right said. She was dark, in her early twenties. "You want to change rubles?"

The surprising thing to me was that one of these young women was pushing a little boy in a pram, and the other had a bag of what looked like old laundry. They were pretty women, but obviously preoccupied with domestic chores—airing the baby, doing the wash. I invited them to the ballet—I had bought pairs of tickets. They said no, they had to cook dinner for their husbands and do the housework, but what about changing some money? The rate was seventy-two cents to the ruble: they offered me ten times that.

"What would I do with all those rubles?"

"So many things."

The dark one was Olga, the blonde Natasha—a ballet dancer, she said. Olga spoke Italian; Natasha spoke only Russian, and had a dancer's slimness and pallor and china-blue eyes with a Slavic slant and an expensive Russian mouth.

I said I was walking—I needed the exercise.

"We will go with you!"

That was why, about ten minutes later, I came to be walking with a Russian woman on each arm, and carrying Natasha's laundry—Olga pushing little Boris in his pram—down Karl Marx Prospekt. Olga was chatting to me in Italian and Natasha laughing.

"You seem to be doing all right for yourself, Paul!"

It was a group of people from the tour, heading back to the bus. I was delighted that they saw me—what would they make of it?

We stopped at a café and had a hot chocolate and they said they wanted to see me again—"We can talk!" They made a fuss about the time, probably because they were deceiving their husbands, but we agreed on a time when they would call me.

There was a message waiting for me when I got back to the Hotel Ukraine: "Olga will call tomorrow at twelve." She called on the stroke of noon the next day to say she would call again at two. At two she said she would meet me at three-thirty. These phone calls had the effect of making our meeting seem necessary and inevitable. It was only when I was waiting on the hotel steps that it occurred to me that I had no idea why I was seeing them at all.

Natasha walked by but did not greet me. She was wearing old clothes and carrying a shopping basket. She winked at me; I followed her to a taxi, in which Olga was already sitting and smoking. When I got in, Olga gave the driver an order and he drove off. After that they intermittently quarreled over whether this was the right direction or the quickest way.

After twenty minutes of this—we were now deep in the highrise Moscow suburbs—I said, "Where are we going?"

"Not far."

There were people raking leaves and picking up litter from the streets. I had never seen so many street sweepers. I asked what was going on.

Olga said that this was the one day in the year when people worked for nothing—tidying up the city. The day was called *subodnik* and this work was given free to honor Lenin—his birthday was two days away.

"Don't you think you should be out there with a shovel, Olga?"

"I am too busy," she said, and her laugh said *Not on your life!*

"Are we going to a house?"

Olga gave more directions to the driver. He turned right, entered a side street, and then cut down a dirt road and cursed. That bad road connected one housing estate with another. He kept driving on these back roads among tall bare blocks of flats and then he stopped the car and babbled angrily.

"We can walk the rest of the way," Olga said. "You can pay him."

The driver snatched my rubles and drove off as we walked toward a sixteen-story building, through children playing and their parents sweeping the pavements in a good *subodnik* spirit.

No one took any notice of me. I was merely a man in a raincoat following two women down a muddy pavement, past walls that had been scribbled on, past broken windows and through a smashed door to a hallway where three prams were parked and some of the floor tiles were missing. It could have been a housing estate in south London or the Bronx. The lift had been vandalized but it still worked. It was varnished wood, with initials scratched onto it. We took it to the top floor.

"Excuse me," Olga said. "I couldn't get my friend on the phone. I must talk to her first."

But by now I had imagined that we had come to a place where I was going to be threatened and probably robbed. There were three huge Muscovites behind the door. They would seize me and empty my pockets, and then blindfold me and drop me somewhere in Moscow. They didn't go in for kidnapping. I asked myself whether I was worried, and answered: *Kind of.*

I was somewhat reassured when I saw a surprised and sluttish-looking woman answer the door. Her hair was tangled, she wore a bathrobe. It was late afternoon—she had just woken up. She whispered a little to Olga and then she let us in.

Her name was Tatyana and she was annoyed at having been disturbed—she had been watching television in bed. I asked to use the toilet, and made a quick assessment of the flat. It was large—four big rooms and a central hall with bookshelves. All the curtains were drawn. It smelled of vegetables and hair spray and that unmistakable odor that permeates places in which there are late sleepers—the smell of bedclothes and bodies and feety aromas.

"You want tea?"

I said yes, and we all sat in the small kitchen. Tatyana brushed her hair and put on makeup as she boiled the kettle and made tea.

There were magazines on the table: two oldish copies of *Vogue*, and last month's *Tatler* and *Harper's Bazaar*. Seeing them in that place gave me what I was sure would be a lasting hatred for those magazines.

"My friend from Italy brings them for me," Tatyana said.

"She has many foreign friends," Olga said. "That is why I wanted you to meet her. Because you are our foreign friend. You want to change rubles?"

I said no—there was nothing I wanted to buy.

"We can find something for you," Olga said, "and you can give us U.S. dollars."

"What are you going to find?"

"You like Natasha. Natasha likes you. Why don't you make love to her?"

I stood up and went to the window. The three women stared at me, and when I looked at Natasha she smiled demurely and batted her eyelashes. Beside her was her shopping basket with a box of detergent, some fresh spinach wrapped in newspaper, some cans of food, a pack of plastic clothespins, and a box of disposable diapers.

"Here?" I said. "Now?"

They all smiled at me. Out of the window people were sweeping the pavements, and raking leaves, and shoveling up piles of rubbish—a little unselfish demonstration of civic pride for Lenin's birthday.

"How much will it cost me to make love to Natasha?"

"It will cost one hundred and seventy U.S. dollars."

"That's rather a precise figure," I said. "How did you arrive at that price?"

"That's how much a cassette recorder costs at the Berioska shop."

"I'll think about it."

"You have to decide now," Olga said sternly. "Do you have a credit card?"

"You take credit cards?"

"No, the Berioska shop can."

"That's an awful lot of money, Olga."

"Hah!" Tatyana jeered. "My boyfriends give me radios, tape recorders, cassettes, clothes—thousands of dollars. And you're arguing about a few hundred dollars."

"Listen, I'm not boasting—believe me. But if I like someone I don't usually buy her before we go to bed. In America we do it for fun."

Olga said, "If we don't have dollars we can't buy radios at the Berioska. It closes at six o'clock. What's wrong?"

"I don't like being hurried."

"All this talk! You could have finished by now!"

I hated this and had a strong desire to get away from the nagging. It was hot in the kitchen, the tea was bitter, all those people raking leaves sixteen floors down depressed me.

I said, "Why don't we go to the Berioska shop first?"

Tatyana dressed and we found a taxi. It was a twenty-minute ride and well after five by the time we arrived. But for me it was simply a way of saving face—and saving money. I had been disgusted with myself back there in the flat.

Before we went into the shop the three women started bickering. Olga said that it was all my fault for not making love to Natasha when I should have. Tatyana had to meet her daughter at school, Natasha was due home because she was going to the Black Sea tomorrow with her husband and small child—and was counting on having a cassette recorder; and Olga herself had to be home to cook dinner. *"Vremya,"* Natasha said, *"vremya."* Time, time.

I had never seen such expensive electronic equipment—

overpriced radios and tape decks, a Sony Walkman for $300.

"Natasha wants one of those."

Olga was pointing to a $200 cassette machine.

"That's a ridiculous price."

"It's a good cassette. Japanese."

I was looking at Natasha and thinking how thoroughly out of touch these people were with market forces.

"Vremya," Natasha said urgently.

"These are nice." I began trying on the fur hats. "Wouldn't you like one of these?"

Olga said, "You must buy something now. Then we go."

And I imagined it—the cassette recorder in a Berioska bag, and the dash to Tatyana's and the fumble upstairs with Natasha panting *"Vremya, vremya,"* and then off I'd go, saying to myself: *You've just been screwed.*

I said, "Tatyana, your daughter's waiting at school. Olga, your husband's going to want his dinner on time. And Natasha, you're very nice, but if you don't go home and pack you'll never make it to the Black Sea with your husband."

"What are you doing?"

"I have an appointment," I said, and left, as the Berioska shop was closing.

I went to the Bolshoi, and I noticed at the cloakroom and the buffet and the bar Russian women gave me frank looks. It was not lust or romance, merely curiosity because they had spotted a man who probably had hard currency. It was not the sort of look women usually offered. It was an unambiguous lingering gaze, a half smile that said: *Maybe we can work something out.*

Mongols

THE MONGOLS REACHED THE EASTERN LIMITS OF CHINA. They rode to Afghanistan. They rode to Poland. They sacked Moscow, Warsaw, and Vienna. They had stirrups—they introduced stirrups to Europe (and in that made jousting possible and perhaps started the Age of Chivalry). They rode for years, in all seasons. When the Russians retired from their campaigns for the winter, the Mongols kept riding and recruiting in the snow. They devised an ingenious tactic for their winter raids: they waited for rivers to freeze and then they rode on the ice. In this way they could go anywhere and they surprised their enemies. They were tough and patient and by the year 1280 they had conquered half the world.

But they were not fearless, and looking at these great open spaces you could almost imagine what it was that spooked them. They had a dread of thunder and lightning. It was so easy to be struck by lightning here! When an electric storm started, they made for their tents and burrowed into layers of black felt. If there were strangers among them they sent these people outside, considering them unlucky. They would not eat an animal that had been struck by lightning—they wouldn't go near it. Anything that would conduct lightning they avoided—even between storms; and one of their aims in life, along with plundering and marauding and pillaging, was propitiating lightning.

As I was watching this wilderness of low hills, the city of Ulaanbaatar materialized in the distance, and a road hove into view, and dusty buses and trucks. My first impression of the city was that it was a military garrison, and that impression stayed with me. Every block of flats looked like a barracks, every parking lot like a motor pool, every street in the city looked as though it had been designed for a parade. Most of the vehicles were in fact Soviet army vehicles. Buildings were fenced in, with barbed wire on the especially important ones. A cynic might have said that the city resembled a prison, but if so the Mongolians were very cheery prisoners—it was a youthful, well-fed, well-dressed population. They had red cheeks, and wore mittens and boots; in this brown country they favored bright colors—it was not unusual to see an old man with a red hat and a purple frock coat and blue trousers stuck into his multicolored boots. But that way of dressing meant that the Russians were more conspicuous, even when they weren't soldiers. I say the city looked like a garrison, but it was clearly not a Mongolian one—it was Russian, and there was little to distinguish it from any other military garrison I had seen in Central Asia. We had been passing such big, dull places all the way from Irkútsk: barracks, radar dishes, unclimbable fences, batteries, ammo dumps, and surely those mounds that looked like tumuli were missile silos?

The hotel was bare and smelled of mutton fat. That was the smell of Ulaanbaatar. Mutton was in the air. If there had been a menu, it would have been on the menu. It was served at every meal: mutton and potatoes—but gristly mutton and cold potatoes. The Mongolians had a way of making food inedible or disgusting, and they could transform even the most inoffensive meal into garbage, by serving it cold, or sprinkling it with black carrots, or garnishing it with a goat's ear. I made a point of visiting food shops, just to see what was available. I found fat black sausages, shriveled potatoes and turnips, black carrots, trays of grated cabbage, basins of yellow goats' ears, chunks of rancid mutton and chicken feet. The most appetizing thing I saw turned out to be a large bin of brown unwrapped laundry soap.

Chinese Inventions

THE CHINESE ARE THE LAST PEOPLE IN THE WORLD STILL manufacturing spittoons, chamber pots, treadle sewing machines, bed warmers, claw hammers, "quill" pens (steel nibs, dunk and-write), wooden yokes for oxen, iron plows, sit-up-and-beg bicycles, and steam engines.

They still make grandfather clocks—the chain-driven mechanical kind that go *tick-tock!* and *bong!* Is this interesting? I think it is, because the Chinese invented the world's first mechanical clock in the late Tang Dynasty. Like many other Chinese inventions, it was forgotten about; they lost the idea, and the clock was reintroduced to China from Europe. The Chinese were the first to make cast iron, and soon after invented the iron plow. Chinese metallurgists were the first to make steel ("great iron"). The Chinese invented the crossbow in the fourth century B.C. and were still using it in 1895. They were the first to notice that all snowflakes have six sides. They invented the umbrella, the seismograph, phosphorescent paint, the spinning wheel, sliding calipers, porcelain, the magic lantern (or zoetrope), and the stink bomb (one recipe called for fifteen pounds of human shit, as well as arsenic, wolfsbane, and cantharides beetles). They invented the chain pump in the first century A.D. and are still using it. They made the first kite, two thousand years before one was flown in Europe. They invented movable type and devised the first printed book—the Buddhist text the *Diamond Sutra*, in the year A.D. 868. They had printing presses in the eleventh century, and there is clear evidence that Gutenberg got his technology from the Portuguese, who in turn had learned it from the Chinese. They constructed the first suspension bridge and the first bridge with a segmented arch (this first one, built in 610, is still in use). They invented playing cards, fishing reels, and whisky.

In the year 1192, a Chinese man jumped from a minaret in Guangzhou using a parachute, but the Chinese had been experimenting with parachutes since the second century B.C. The Emperor Gao Yang (reigned 550–559) tested "man-flying kites"—an early form of hang glider—by throwing condemned prisoners from a tall tower, clinging to bamboo contraptions; one flew for two miles before crash-landing. The Chinese were the first sailors in the world to use rudders; westerners relied on steering oars until they borrowed the rudder from the Chinese in about 1100. Every school-boy knows that the Chinese invented paper money, fire-works, and lacquer. They were also the first people in the world to use wallpaper (French missionaries brought the wallpaper idea to Europe from China in the fifteenth century). They went mad with paper. An excavation in Turfan yielded a paper hat, a paper belt, and a paper shoe, from the fifth century A.D. I have already mentioned toilet paper. They also made paper curtains and military armor made of paper—its pleats made it impervious to arrows. Paper was not manufactured until the twelfth century in Europe, about fifteen hundred years after its invention in China. They made the first wheelbarrows, and some of the best Chinese wheelbarrow designs have yet to be used in the West. There is much more. When Professor Needham's *Science and Civilization in China* is complete, it will run to twenty-five volumes.

It was the Chinese who came up with the first design of the steam engine in about A.D. 600. And the Datong Locomotive Works is the last factory in the world that still manufactures steam locomotives. China makes big black choo-choo trains, and not only that—none of the factory is automated. Everything is handmade, hammered out of iron, from the huge boilers to the little brass whis-tles. China had always imported its steam locomotives—first from Britain, then from Germany, Japan, and Russia. In the late 1950s, with Soviet help, the Chinese built this factory in Datong, and the first locomotive was produced in 1959. There are now nine thousand workers, turning out three or four engines a month, of what is essentially a nineteenth-century vehicle, with a few refinements. Like the spittoons, the sewing machines, the washboards, the yokes, and the plows, these steam engines are built to last. They are the primary means of power in Chinese railways at the moment, and although there is an official plan to phase them out by the year 2000, the Datong Locomotive Works will remain in business. All over the world, sentimental steam railway enthusiasts are using Chinese steam engines, and in some countries—like Thailand and Pakistan—most trains are hauled by Datong engines. There is nothing Chinese about them, though. They are the same gasping locomotives I saw shunting in Medford, Massachusetts, in 1948, when I stood by the tracks and wished I was on board.

Public Bathhouse

I FOUND OUT THAT PEKING WAS FULL OF PUBLIC BATH-houses—about thirty of them, subsidized by the government. They are one of the cheapest outings in China: for 60 fen (15 cents) a person is admitted and given a piece of soap, a towel, and a bed; and he is allowed to stay all day, washing himself in the steamy public pool and resting.

The one I found was called Xing Hua Yuan. It was open from eight-thirty in the morning until eight o'clock at night. Many people who use it are travelers who have just arrived in Peking after a long journey and want to look presentable for their friends and relatives—and of course who don't want to impose on them for a bath.

The beds were in little cubicles, and men wrapped in towels were resting or walking around talking. It was like a Roman bath—social, with the scalded Chinese, pinkish in the heat, sloshing themselves and yelling at each other in a friendly way. It was also possible to get a private room, for about double the ordinary rate.

I was thinking how Roman and Victorian the bathhouse looked (there was a women's bathhouse next door), how useful for travelers and bathless residents, how like a club it was and how congenial, when a homosexual Chinese man set me straight.

"Most people go there to take a bath," he said. "But it is also a good place to go if you want to meet a boy and do things with him."

"What sort of things?"

He didn't flinch. He said, "One day I was in Xing Hua Yuan and saw two men in a private room, and one had the other one's cock in his mouth. That sort of thing."

Shanghai

SHANGHAI IS AN OLD BROWN RIVERSIDE CITY WITH THE LOOK of Brooklyn, and the Chinese—who are comforted by crowds—like it for its mobs and its street life. It has a reputation for city slickers and stylishness. Most of China's successful fashion designers work in Shanghai, and if you utter the words *Yifu Sheng Luolang*, the Shanghainese will know you are speaking the name of Yves Saint-Laurent. When I arrived in the city, there was an editor of the French magazine *Elle* prowling the streets looking for material for an article on China called "The Fashion Revolution." According to the Chinese man who accompanied her—whom I later met—this French woman was mightily impressed by the dress sense of the Shanghai women. She stopped them and took their picture and asked where they got their clothes. The majority said that they got them in the Free Market in the back streets or that they made the clothes themselves at home, basing them on pictures they saw in western magazines. Even in the days of the Cultural Revolution, the women workers showed up at their factories with bright sweaters and frilly blouses under their blue baggy suits; it was customary to meet in the women's washroom and compare the hidden sweaters before they started work.

Because it is a cosmopolitan city and has seen more foreigners—both invaders and friendly visitors—than any other Chinese city, it is a polyglot place. It is at once the most politically dogmatic ("Oppose book worship," "Political work is the lifeblood of all economic work": Mao) and the most bourgeois. When changes came to China, they appeared first in Shanghai; and when there is conflict in China, it is loudest and most violent in Shanghai. The sense of life is strong in Shanghai, and even a city hater like myself can detect Shanghai's spirit and appreciate Shanghai's atmosphere. It is not crass like Canton, but it is abrasive—and in the hot months stifling, crowded, noisy, and smelly.

It seemed to me noisy most of all, with the big-city, all-night howl that is the sound track of New York (honks, sirens, garbage trucks, shouts, death rattles). Peking was rising and would soon be a city of tall buildings, but Shanghai had been built on mud and was growing sideways and spreading into the swamps of Zhejiang. All day the pile drivers hammered steel into this soft soil to fortify it, and one was right outside my window—a cruel and dominating noise that determined the rhythm of my life. *Zhong-guo! Zhong-guo!* It affected the way I breathed and walked and ate: I moved my feet and lifted my spoon to *Zhong-guo! Zhong-guo!* It orchestrated my talking, too, it made me write in bursts, and when I brushed my teeth I discovered I did it to the pounding of this pile driver, the bang and its half echo, *Zhong-guo!* It began at seven in the morning and was still hammering at eight at night, and in Shanghai it was inescapable, because nearly every neighborhood had its own anvil clang of *Zhong-guo!*

I walked the back streets in order to keep away from the

traffic and the crowds. And I realized that it would be dishonest to complain too much about noise, the pile drivers, and the frantic energy, because on my first visit to Shanghai I felt it was dreary and moribund and demoralized. Why was it that they never knew when to stop? Even the back streets were crowded, with improvised stalls and households that served as shop fronts and markets set up in the gutters, and people mending shoes and bicycles and doing carpentry on the pavement.

Toward the Bund—Shanghai's riverbank promenade—I saw a spire behind a wall and found a way to enter. It was St. Joseph's Church, and the man I took to be the caretaker, because he was so shabbily dressed in a ragged jacket and slippers, was the pastor, a Catholic priest. He was both pious and watchful, soft-spoken and alert—it is the demeanor of a Chinese Christian who had been put through more hoops than he cares to remember. The church had been wrecked during the Cultural Revolution, daubed with slogans, and turned into a depot for machinery, and the churchyard had been a parking lot.

"*Sacramentum,*" the priest said, pointing at the flickering candle, and he smiled with satisfaction: the consecrated host was in the tabernacle.

I asked him why this was so. Was there a service today?

No, he said, and brought me to the back of the church, where there was a coffin with a white paper cross stuck to it. He said there was a funeral tomorrow.

"I take it you're busy—lots of people coming to church."

"Oh yes. And there are five churches in Shanghai. They are always full on Sundays."

He invited me to attend Mass, and out of politeness I said I might, but I knew I wouldn't. I had no business there: I was a heretic. And I was often annoyed by westerners who, although they never went to church at home, would get the churchgoing bug in China, as an assertion of their difference or perhaps a reproach to the Chinese—as if religious freedom were the test of China's tolerance. Well, it was one test, of course, but it was exasperating to see the test administered by an American unbeliever. So I didn't go to church in China, but sometimes when I saw a bird in the grass I dropped to my knees and marveled as it twitched there.

The Red Guards and the Violinist

THERE WAS A STYLISH, YOUTHFUL-LOOKING MAN NAMED Wang whom I met one day in Shanghai. It turned out that we were both born in the same year—the Year of the Snake (but Wang used the Chinese euphemism for snake, "little dragon"). He was so friendly and full of stories that I saw him often, usually for lunch at the Jin Jiang Hotel. He was a sensitive soul, but had a sense of irony, too, and said he had never been happier than when he was walking the streets of San Francisco on his one trip to America—he hinted that he was eager to emigrate to the United States, but he never became a bore on the subject and did not ask me for help. He was unusual, even in Shanghai, for his clothes—a canary-yellow French jacket and pale blue slacks, a gold watch, a chain around his neck, and expensive sunglasses.

"I like bright clothes," he said.

"Could you wear them during the Cultural Revolution?" He laughed and said, "What a mess that was!"

"Were you criticized?"

"I was under arrest. That's when I started smoking. I discovered that if you smoked it gave you time to think. They had me in a room—the Red Guards. They said, 'You called Mao's wife, Jiang Qing, a crazy lady.' She was a crazy lady! But I just lit a cigarette and puffed on it so that I could think of something to say."

"What did you say?"

"The wrong thing! They made me write essays. Self-criticism!"

"Describe the essays."

"They gave me subjects. 'Why I Like Charles Dickens,' 'Why I Like Shakespeare.' "

"I thought you were supposed to say why you didn't like them."

"They wouldn't believe that," he said. "They called me a reactionary. Therefore, I had to say why I liked them. It was awful. Six pages every night, after work unit, and then they said, 'This is dog shit—write six more pages.' "

"What work did you do?"

"Played the violin in the Red Orchestra. Always the same tunes. 'The East Is Red,' 'Long Live the Thoughts of Mao,' 'Sailing the Seas Depends on the Helmsman,' all that stuff. They made me play in the rain. I said, 'I can't—the violin will fall apart.' They don't know that a violin is glued together. I played in the rain. It fell apart. They gave me another one and ordered me to play under the trees during the Four Pests Campaign—to keep sparrows from landing in the branches."

The other three pests were mosquitoes, flies, and rats.

"That's absurd," I said.

"We painted Huai Hai Lu—that's more absurd," Wang said.

"How can you paint a street?" I asked—the street he named was one of the main thoroughfares of Shanghai.

"We painted it red, out of respect for Chairman Mao," Wang said. "Isn't that stupid?"

"How much of the street did you paint?"

"Three and a half miles," Wang said, and laughed, re-membering something else. "But there were stupider things. When we went to the work unit, we always did the *qing an* [salute] to Mao's portrait on the gateway. We'd hold up the Red Book, say, 'Long Live Chairman Mao,' and salute him. Same thing when we went home. People would make things in Mao's honor, like a knitted Mao emblem, or a red star in needlepoint, and put it in the special Respect Room at the unit—it was painted red. That was for Mao. If they wanted to prove they were very loyal, they would wear the Mao badge by pinning it to their skin."

"That must have impressed the Red Guards," I said.

"It wasn't just the Red Guards—everyone blames them, but everyone was in it. That's why people are so embarrassed at the moment, because they realize they were just as stupid about Chairman Mao as everyone else. I know a banker who was given the job of fly catcher. He had to kill flies and save their little bodies in a matchbox. Every afternoon someone would come and count the dead flies and say, 'One hundred seventeen—not good enough. You must have one hundred twenty-five tomorrow.' And more the day after, you see? The government said there was going to be a war. 'The enemy is coming—be prepared.'"

"Which enemy?"

"The imperialists—Russia, India, the United States. It didn't matter which one. They were going to kill us," Wang said, and rolled his eyes. "So we had to make bricks for the war effort. Ninety bricks a month for each person. But my parents were old, so I had to make their bricks. I used to come home from the unit, write my essay 'Why I Like Western Music,' and make bricks—I had to deliver two hundred seventy a month. And they were always asking me about my hole."

"Your hole?"

"The *Shen wa dong*—Dig Deep Holes edict. That was for the war, too. Everyone had to have a hole, in case of war. Every so often the Red Guards would knock on your door and say, 'Where is your hole?'"

He said there were bomb shelters all over Shanghai, which had been built on Mao's orders ("for the coming war"), and of course they had never been used. I asked him to show me one. We found this subterranean vault—it was just like a derelict subway station—on 1157 Nanjing Road, and it had been turned into an ice-cream parlor. The fascinating thing to me was that it was now obviously a place where young folks went to kiss their girlfriends. It was full of Chinese youths locked in the half nelson they regard as an amorous embrace. The irony was not merely that these kids were making out and feeling each other up in a place that had been built by frantic and paranoid Red Guards in the 1960s, but also that it was now called the Dong Chang Coffee Shop and owned and operated by the government.

I was talking to Wang one day about my trip through the Soviet Union when I mentioned how the scarcity of consumer goods there meant they were always pestering foreigners for blue jeans, T-shirts, track shoes, and so forth.

"That never happens in China," I said.

"No," Wang said. "But that reminds me. About three years ago there was a Russian ballet dancer at the hotel in Shanghai. I went to see the ballet—fabulous! And this dancer was very handsome. I recognized him, and he smiled at me. Then he pointed to my track shoes and pointed to himself. He wanted them, I understood that. They were expensive shoes—Nike, cost me fifty yuan. But I don't care much about money. We measured feet, side by side. Exact fit. I don't speak a word of Russian, but I could tell he really wanted those shoes."

"Did you sell them to him?"

"I gave them to him," Wang said, and frowned at the triviality of it. "I felt sorry for someone who just wanted a pair of shoes. It seemed sad to me that he couldn't get them in his own country. I took them off and walked to my office barefoot! He was really happy! I thought: *He'll go back to Russia. He'll always remember this. He'll say, 'Once I was in China. I met a Chinese man and asked him for his shoes, and he gave them to me!'* "

A moment later, he said, "You can get anything you want in China. Food, clothes, shoes, bicycles, motorbikes, TVs, radios, antiques. If you want girls, you can find girls." And then in a wide-eyed way, "Or boys—if you want boys."

"Or fashion shows."

"They have fashion shows on television almost every week," Wang said. "Shanghai is famous for them."

I asked him what the old people made of these developments—hookers and high fashion in a country where just a few years ago foreign decadence was condemned and everyone wore baggy blue suits.

"The old people love life in China now," Wang said. "They are really excited by it. Very few people object. They had felt very repressed before."

Performing Animals

ON MY WALKS IN SHANGHAI I OFTEN WENT PAST THE CHI-
nese Acrobatic Theater, a domed building near the center of
the city. And I became curious and attended a performance;
and after I saw it—not only the tumblers and clowns and
contortionists, but also the man who balanced a dinner service for twelve on a chopstick that he held in his mouth—I
wanted to know more.

Mr. Liu Maoyou was in charge of the acrobats at the
Shanghai Bureau of Culture. He had started out as an assistant at the Shanghai Library, but even at the best of times
things are quiet at the city library, since it is next to
impossible—for political reasons—for anyone to borrow a
book. The librarian is little more than a custodian of the
stacks. He jumped at the chance of a transfer and joined
the Bureau of Culture, and he accompanied the Chinese
acrobats on their first tour of the United States in 1980.

"We call it a theater, because it has an artistic and dramatic element," Mr. Liu said. "It has three aspects—
acrobats, magic, and a circus."

I asked him how it started.

"Before Liberation all the acrobats were family members. They were travelers and performers. They performed
on the street or in any open space. But we thought of bringing them together and training them properly. Of course,
the Chinese had been acrobats for thousands of years. They
reached their height in the Tang Dynasty and were allowed
to perform freely."

Mr. Liu said this with such enthusiasm that I asked him
how he felt about the Tang Dynasty.

239

"It was the best period in China," he said. "The freest time—all the arts flourished during the Tang era."

So much for the Shanghai Cultural Bureau, but he was still talking.

"Before Liberation they were doing actions without art form," he said. "But they have to use mind as well as body. That's why we started the training center. We don't want these acrobats to be mind-empty, so after their morning practice they study math, history, language, and literature."

He said that in 1986 thirty candidates were chosen from three thousand applicants. They were all young—between ten and fourteen years old, but Mr. Liu said the bureau was not looking for skill but rather for potential.

"We also have a circus," he said. "Also a school for animal training."

This interested me greatly, since I have a loathing for everything associated with performing animals. I have never seen a lion tamer who did not deserve to be mauled; and when I see a little mutt, wearing a skirt and a frilly bonnet, and skittering through a hoop, I am thrilled by a desire for its tormentor (in the glittering pantsuit) to contract rabies.

"Tell me about your animal training, Mr. Liu."

"Before Liberation the only training we did was with monkeys. Now we have performing cats—"

"Household cats? Pussycats?"

"Yes. They do tricks."

It is a belief of many Chinese I met that animals such as cats and dogs do not feel pain. They are on earth to be used—trained, put to work, killed, and eaten. When you see the dumb, laborious lives that Chinese peasants live it is perhaps not so surprising that they torture animals.

"Also pigs and chickens," Mr. Liu said.

"Performing chickens?"

"Not chickens but cocks."

"What do the cocks do?"

"They stand on one leg—hand standing. And some other funny things."

God only knows how they got these pea-brained roosters to do these funny things, but I had the feeling they wired them up and zapped them until they got the point.

"What about the pigs?" I asked.

"The pigs do not perform very often, but they can walk on two legs—"

And when he said that I realized what it was that was bothering me. It was that everything he said reminded me of *Animal Farm*; and the fact that it was a fable of totalitarianism only made Mr. Liu's images worse. He had described a living example of the moment in that book when oppression is about to overtake the farm. There is terror and confusion at the unexpected sight: *It was a pig walking on his hind legs.* And Orwell goes on:

> Yes, it was Squealer. A little awkwardly, as though not quite used to supporting his considerable bulk in that position, but with perfect balance. . . . And a moment later, out from the door of the farmhouse, came a long file of pigs, all walking on their hind legs. . . .

I was thinking of this as Mr. Liu was saying, "—and lions and tigers, and the only performing panda in China."

He said that the animals and the acrobats often went on tour—even to the United States. Many of the acrobats worked in the United States. In 1985 a deal was made whereby Chinese acrobats would join Ringling Brothers Circus for a year or two at a time. In the first year there were fifteen, and in 1986 there were twenty hired-out Chinese acrobats working in America.

I asked Mr. Liu about the financial arrangement.

"I don't know exactly," he said, "but Ringling Brothers Circus pays us and we pay the acrobats."

"How much does Ringling Brothers pay you?"

"About two hundred to six hundred dollars a week, depending on the act. For each person."

"How much do you pay the acrobats?"

"About one hundred yuan."

Thirty dollars.

Talk about performing pigs! I wondered how long people would be willing to allow themselves to be treated as exportable merchandise. For some it was not long: the very week I had the conversation with Mr. Liu a man playing the role of an acrobatic lion disappeared in New York. Months later he still had not been found.

The Edge of the World

BY MIDAFTERNOON THE TRAIN WAS MOVING ACROSS A FLAT green plain between two ranges of low mountains, the Qilian Shan and the Helan Shan. In places I could see the crumbled sections of the Great Wall. Where the land was flat, it was intensively cultivated, and in places there were tall, slender, and rather redundant-looking poplars. The Chinese, averse to planting shade trees, favored the skinny symbolic tree that doubled as a fence. The idea of The Forest was alien to China. It only existed in northern Heilongjiang province—the Manchurian northeast; and I had heard that even the little that remained was being cut down and made into chopsticks and toothpicks and Ping-Pong paddles.

In most other countries, a landscape feature was a grove of trees, or a meadow, or even a desert; so you immediately associated the maple tree with Canada, the oak with England, the birch with the Soviet Union, and desert and jungle with Africa. But no such thing came to mind in China, where the most common and obvious feature of a landscape was a person—or usually many people. Every time I stared at a landscape, there was a person in it staring back at me.

Even here in the middle of nowhere there were people and settlements. The villages were walled in, and most houses had walls around them: mud smeared over bricks. They were the sort of stockades that are frequent in Afghanistan and Iran—at the far end of this Silk Road—and probably a cultural hangover from the memory of marauders and Mongol hordes, the Central Asian nightmare.

The day had turned very hot. It was now in the nineties. I saw eighteen sheep crowded into a little blot of shade under a frail hawthorn tree. Children cooled themselves by kicking water in a ditch. Farmers with lampshade hats planted crops by pushing one sprout at a time into the ground, a process that had a greater affinity to needlepoint sewing than to farming, as though they were stitching a design into the furrows. And though there were black peaks and mountain ranges on both sides of the train, the land ahead fell away, and it was as if we were approaching the ocean—the land dipped and had the smooth, stony look of the seashore. It was the hottest part of the day, but even so the land was full of people. Hours later, in an immense and stony desert I saw a man in a faded blue suit, bumping over the stones on his bike.

Then there were sand dunes near the track—big soft slopes and bright piles; but the snowy peaks in the distance still remained. I had not realized that there was anything so strange as this on this planet.

I was eating dinner in the empty dining car at about eight that night when we came to Jiayuguan. What I saw out the window is printed on my mind: in the summer dusk of the Gobi Desert, a Chinese town lay glowing in the sand, and rising above it, ten stories high, was the last gate in the Great Wall, the Jia Yu Watchtower—a fortress-like structure with pagoda roofs; and the train slowed at the Wall's end, a crumbled pile of mud bricks and ruined turrets that the wind had simplified and sucked smooth. In the fading light of day, there was this ghostly remainder of the Great Wall, and what looked like the last town in China. The Wall went straggling west, but it was so small and destroyed it looked like little more than an idea or a suggestion—the remnants of a great scheme. But my excitement also came from seeing the red paint on the gate, and the yellow roof, and the thought that this train was passing beyond it into the unknown. The sun slanted on the gray hills and the desert and blue bushes. Most of what I saw was through the blurring haze of the day's dust, and the intimation at sunset was that I would fall off the edge of the world as soon as it got dark.

Lost Cities

"THE DESERT WHICH LIES BETWEEN ANSI AND HAMI IS A howling wilderness, and the first thing which strikes the wayfarer is the dismalness of its uniform, black, pebble-strewn surface." That was Mildred Cable speaking. And reading her book reminded me that I was missing one of the glories of this region by not visiting the caves at Dunhuang—Buddhas, frescoes, holy grottoes; the sacred city in the sands. But I intended to go one better, by visiting the lost city of Gaocheng (Karakhoja) whenever this train got to Turfan.

I had gone to bed in a strange late twilight amid a rugged landscape, and I woke, slowly jogging in the train, to a flat region of sand and stones. Farther off were large humpy sand dunes, which had the appearance of having softly flowed and blown there, because there was nothing like them nearby. The dunes were like simple gigantic animals that went blobbing along through the desert, smothering whatever they encountered.

Soon a patch of green appeared—an oasis. Once there was merely a road linking the oases—but "once" meant only thirty years ago. Before then it was a rough road, what remained of the Silk Route. But these oases were not metaphors for a few trees and a stagnant pool. They were large towns, well watered from underground irrigation canals, and grapes and melons were grown in great profusion. Later in the day the train stopped at Hami. The Hami melon is famous all over China for its sweet taste and its fragrance; and Hami had been no insignificant place, although now it was what remained of the fruit-growing communes of the fifties and sixties. It had known great

244

days, and had had a khan until this century. It had been overrun by Mongols, by Uighurs, by Tibetans and Dzungars. It had been repeatedly reoccupied by the Chinese since the year A.D. 73, during the Later Han Dynasty, and had been a Chinese city from 1698 onward. Nothing of this remained. What had not been damaged in the Muslim Rebellion of 1863–73 had been flattened in the Cultural Revolution. The Chinese had a facility for literally defacing a city—taking all its characteristic features away, robbing it of its uniqueness, cutting its nose off. Now all Hami was known for was its pig iron.

The peaks beyond Hami and farther up the line had patches of snow on their ridges that lay like saddle blankets, squarish and flat. But down here in the train and on the desert it was very hot—over one hundred degrees in the train and hotter outside. The sun burned down on the sand and stones. There were a few gullies, and in the oldest and deepest ones, which were sheltered, perhaps a dead wutong tree, and here and there clumps of camel thorn, the only identifiable weed, apart from the spikes of gray lichens. We were heading toward a dusty range of hills that was surmounted by a blue range of mountains, and rising up beyond were more mountains, which were bright with snow patches and ice slides—long streaks that might have been glaciers.

They were the first sight I had of the Bogda Shan, the Mountains of God. They were very rugged and very high, but their snow was the only lively feature of this place. Beneath those mountains there was nothing but desert, "the howling wilderness," which this afternoon was too bright to stare at. Rainfall is unknown here, and most of those mountains seemed little more than a vast, poisoned massif—a lifeless pack of rock. This is the dead center of Asia.

In this oddly lighted world of snow and sand, the stone mountains reddened and rushed up to the train. In the distance was a green basin, five hundred feet below sea level, the lowest place in China, and one of the hottest. Another oasis, the town of Turfan. Round about there was nothing else but a hundred miles of blackish gravel, and Turfan itself was twenty miles from the station. I got off the train here.

TURFAN ("ONE OF THE HOTTEST PLACES ON THE FACE OF THE earth") was an extremely popular oasis about four hundred years ago. Before then it had been a desert town overrun by successive waves of nomads, Chinese, Tibetans, Uighurs, and Mongols. The Silk Road established it as a great oasis and bazaar, but after that—from about the sixteenth century—it was all downhill. And after it was finally left alone by the warlords and the Manchus, new marauders appeared in the shape of enterprising archaeologists, and the few frescoes and statues that remained after more than two thousand years of continuous civilization were snatched and carried away to places like Tokyo, Berlin, and Cambridge, Massachusetts.

Such a place seemed to me unmissable. The station was at the edge of the depression. All I could see were telephone poles in the stony desert, and the huge purply-red range called The Flaming Mountains. The town of Turfan did not reveal itself until I was almost on top of it, and even then it seemed less like a Chinese town than a Middle Eastern one—it was straight out of the Bible, with donkeys and grape arbors and mosques, and people who looked Lebanese, with brown faces and gray eyes.

The desert was almost unbelievably horrible-looking— bouldery and black, without a single green thing in it. And it seemed as though if you walked on those stones you would cut your feet. In some spots it looked like an immensity of coal ashes, with scatterings of clinkers and scorched stones. In other places it was dust, with rounded mounds piled here and there. The mounds I discovered were part of the irrigation system called the *karez*, a network of underground canals and boreholes that had been used successfully since the Western Han Dynasty, about two thousand years ago. There were also parts of this desert surrounding Turfan that had an undersea look, as of an ocean floor after the tide went out for good. Everyone called it the *gobi*: the waterless place. Rainfall is unknown in Turfan.

In this shallow green valley in the desert, in which all the water came from underground, there were no Chinese high-rises, and most of the houses were small and square. There were grape arbors suspended over most of the streets—for the shade and also for the prettiness of them. This valley is the chief source of Chinese grapes—there is even a winery in Turfan—and thirty varieties of melon grow in the area. That intensifies the relief on having come from one of the wildest deserts in the world. Turfan is the opposite of everything that lies around it, with its water and its shade and its fresh fruit.

In Turfan I bought the local raisins made from white grapes—the best in China—and apricots. And I sat in my room, eating that stuff and drinking my Dragon Well green tea and writing my notes, until Fang and the driver had had their fill of gruel, and then we set off down the dusty roads.

Turfan was often a furnace. But on overcast mornings it was pleasant, with low clouds and temperatures only in the nineties. I liked the town. It was the least Chinese place I had seen so far, and it was one of the smallest and prettiest. There were very few motor vehicles, and it was quiet and completely horizontal.

It was a Uighur town, with a few Chinese. There were also Uzbeks, Kazakhs, Tadzhiks, and Tungus around the place, bowlegged and in high boots, in the Mongolian fashion. They were leathery-faced, and some looked like Slavs and some like gypsies, and most of them looked like people who had lost their way and were just stopping briefly in this oasis before moving on. Half the women at the Turfan bazaar had the features of fortunetellers, and the others looked like Mediterranean peasants—dramatically different from anyone else in China. These brown-haired, gray-eyed, gypsy-featured women in velvet dresses—and very buxom, some of them—were quite attractive in a way that was the opposite to the oriental. You would not be surprised to learn that they were Italians or Armenians. You see those same faces in Palermo and Watertown, Massachusetts.

Their gazes lingered, too. And some women came close and reached into the velvet and withdrew rolls of bills from between their breasts and said, "Shansh marnie?"

They put this Chinese money into my hand—the money

still warm from having been in their deep bosoms—and they offered me four to one. They had gold teeth, and some looked like foxes, and they hissed at me when I said no.

It was wonderful, that market in Turfan, just what you would expect of a bazaar in Central Asia. They sold embroidered saddlebags, and leather holsters, and homemade jackknives, and baskets and belts. The meat market dealt exclusively in lamb and mutton—no pigs in this Islamic place; and there were stalls selling shish kebab. Much of the produce was the fresh fruit for which Turfan is well known—watermelons and Hami melons and tangerines. And there were about twenty varieties of dried fruit. I bought raisins and apricots, almonds and walnuts: it struck me that dried fruit and nuts were caravan food.

There were tumblers and fire eaters at the Turfan market, too, and a man doing card tricks on an overturned wheelbarrow. There was something medieval about the market—the dust and the tents, the merchandise and the entertainers, and the people who had gathered there, the men in skullcaps, the women in shawls, the shrieking children with wild hair and dirty feet.

NOTHING PUTS HUMAN EFFORT INTO BETTER PERSPECTIVE THAN a ruined city. "This was once a great capital," people say, pointing to fallen walls and broken streets and dust. Then you stand in the silence of the lifeless place and think of Ozymandias, King of Kings, covered by a sand dune and forgotten. It is very thrilling for an American to consider such a place, because we don't yet have anything that qualifies—only ghost towns and fairly insignificant small cities, but nothing like the monumental corpses of oncegreat cities that are known in the rest of the world. Probably American optimism arises from the fact that we don't have any devastated cities. There is something wearying and demoralizing about a lost city, but it can also give you a healthy disregard for real estate.

Gaocheng was perfect in its ruin and decrepitude. It had been a renowned city for well over a thousand years, and now it was a pile of dust and crumbling mud. So far it had been spared the final insult—tourists—but one day, when the Iron Rooster turned into a streamlined train, they would find even this place, east of Turfan, twenty-five miles into the desert. It had had half a dozen different names— Karakhoja, Khocho, Dakianus (from the Roman Emperor Decius), Apsus (Ephesus), Idikut-Shahri (King Idikut's Town), and Erbu (Second Stop). Gaocheng had come to be its accepted name, but it hardly mattered, because there was not much left of it. Yet enough remained for anyone to see that it really had been an enormous place, a city on a grand scale, which was why it looked so sad. It had the melancholy emptiness of all great ruins.

Its walls and fortifications were mostly gone, but the ones that still stood made it seem a remarkable citadel. It had been an ancient capital of this region, and then a Tang city, and then a Uighur city, and at last the Mongols had captured it. The Uighurs didn't want the place destroyed, so they had surrendered without a struggle and let the Mongols take charge, as they had over the rest of China. It was the period of Mongol rule, the Yuan Empire of the thirteenth and fourteenth centuries, when the first Westerners began traveling widely in China—among them, Marco Polo.

By then Gaocheng was Muslim. It had previously been Buddhist. It had also been a center of heretics—first Manichaean, then Nestorian. It is impossible to consider these heresies without reaching the conclusion that they make a certain amount of sense. The Manichaeans, followers of the Persian prophet Manes, believed that there is good and evil in all humans, and that life is a struggle between these interdependent opposites, the light and the dark, the spirit and the flesh. The Nestorians were Christians who had been declared heretics for their belief that there were two separate persons in the incarnate Christ, denying that Christ was in one person both God and man. They went on to argue that Mary was either the mother of God or the mother of the man Jesus, but she couldn't have it both ways. For this the Nestorians were persecuted and exiled, after the Council of Ephesus (in 431, in present-day Turkey), and they ended up in the seventh century, at the last stage of the Silk Road, deep in China, where the first Nestorian church was founded in 638, in Ch'ang-an (Xian).

What made this all the more fascinating to me was that there was nothing left—no church, no heretics, no books, no pictures, no city. There was only the sun beating down on the mud bricks and the broken walls, and all the religion, trade, warfare, art, money, government, and civilization had turned to dust. But there was something magnificent in the immensity of this dumb ruin. I kept on seeing this desert as a place where an ocean had been, a gigantic foreshore of smooth stones and seaside rubble; and this city of Gaocheng was quite in key with that, looking like a sandcastle that the tide had mostly floated away.

The only live things here were goats. The frescoes and statues had been stolen—and sold or else removed to museums. Farmers had dismantled many of the buildings so that they could use the bricks, and when the local people found pots or vases or amphoras (and they were good ones, for there was both Greek and Roman influence at Gaocheng), they used them in their kitchens, so that they wouldn't have to buy new ones.

I went to a nearby village of Uighurs and asked them whether they knew anything about Gaocheng. "It is an old city," they said. The people I asked were brown-faced, hawk-nosed men whose village was shady and totally off the map. They had donkeys, they had a mosque and a small market, but they didn't speak Chinese or any language other than Uighur. The place was called Flaming Mountain Commune, but that was merely a euphemism. The village had gone to sleep. The women watched me through the folds in their black shawls, and I saw one who looked exactly like my Italian grandmother.

Mr. Liu, my guide, did not speak Uighur, though he had lived not far away for twenty years. I had the impression that these desert-dwelling Uighurs did not take the Han Chinese very seriously. When we started away, there was a thump against the side of the car, and the driver slammed on the brakes and chased after the laughing kids. He made a fuss, but no one came to help—no one even listened. And then, a further insult. He stopped to ask directions to an ancient burying ground, the necropolis at Astana, and when he put his head out of the car window, two children stuck feathery reeds into his ears and tickled him. They ran away, as he got out and raged at them.

"They are very bad boys," Mr. Liu said, and he glowered at me when he saw that I was laughing.

The corpses in the underground tombs at Astana were six hundred years old, but perfectly preserved, grinning, lying side by side on a decorated slab.

"You want to take a picture of the dead people?" the caretaker asked me.

"I don't have a camera."

She paid no attention to that. She said, "Ten yuan. One picture."

Mr. Liu said, "I hate looking at dead bodies," and hurried up the stone stairs, fleeing the burial chamber.

When he was gone, the caretaker said, "Shansh marnie?"

Fear of Flying

CHINESE TRAINS COULD BE BAD. IN TWELVE MONTHS OF traveling—almost forty trains—I never saw one with a toilet that wasn't piggy. The loudspeakers plonked and nagged for eighteen hours a day—a hangover from the days of Maoist mottoes. The conductors could be tyrants, and the feeding frenzy in the dining car was often not worth the trouble. But there were compensations—the kindly conductors, the occasional good meal, the comfortable berth, the luck of the draw; and, when all else failed, there was always a chubby thermos of hot water for making tea.

Yet whatever objections I could devise against the trains, they were nothing compared with the horrors of air travel in China. I had a small doze of it when I left Urumchi for

Lanzhou—there was no point in retracing my steps on the Iron Rooster. I was told to be at the airport three hours early—that is, seven in the morning; and the plane left five hours late, at three in the afternoon. It was an old Russian jet, and its metal covering was wrinkled and cracked like the tinfoil in a used cigarette pack. The seats were jammed so closely together that my knees hurt and the circulation to my feet was cut off. Every seat was taken, and every person was heavily laden with carry-on baggage—big skull-cracking bundles that fell out of the overhead rack. Even before the plane took off, people were softly and soupily vomiting, with their heads down and their hands folded, in the solemn and prayerful way that the Chinese habitually puke. After two hours we were each given an envelope that contained three caramel candies, some gum, and three sticky boiled sweets; a piece of cellophane almost concealed a black strand of dried beef that looked like oakum and tasted like decayed rope; and (because Chinese can be optimistic) a toothpick. Two hours later a girl wearing an old postman's uniform went around with a tray. Thinking it might be better food, I snatched one of the little parcels—it was a key ring. The plane was very hot, and then so cold I could see my breath. It creaked like a schooner under sail. Another two hours passed. I said: *I am out of my mind.* An announcement was made, saying in a gargling way that we would shortly be landing. At this point everyone except the pukers stood up and began yanking their bundles out of the racks; and they remained standing, pushing, tottering, and vaguely complaining—deaf to the demands that they sit down and strap themselves in—as the plane bounced, did wheelies on the runway, and limped to Lanzhou terminal. Never again.

Handmade Landscape

WE WERE STILL IN GANSU, GOING SOUTHEAST TOWARD Shaanxi Province (not to be confused with Shanxi, a bit northeast), and we had just left the town of Tianshui. The landscape was unlike anything I had seen in Xinjiang or even the rest of Gansu. It was the carefully constructed Chinese landscape of mud mountains sculpted in terraces which held overgrown lawns of ripe rice. The only flat fields were far below, at the very bottom of the valleys. The rest had been made by the people, a whole countryside that had been put together by hand—stone walls shoring up the terraces on hillsides, paths and steps cut everywhere, sluices, drains, and carved-out furrows. There was even more wheat than rice here, and bundles of it were piled, waiting to be collected and threshed—probably by that black beast up to his nose in the buffalo wallow.

The whole landscape had been possessed and shaped and put to practical use. It was not pretty, but it was symmetrical. You couldn't say, "Look at that hillside," because it was all terraces—mud-walled ditches and fields, and mud-walled houses and roads. What the Chinese managed in miniature with a peach stone, carving it into an intricate design, they had done with these honey-colored mountains. If there was an outcrop of rock, they balanced a rice paddy on it, and the steps and terraces down the steep hills gave them the look of Mayan pyramids. There had not been much of that in the west of China. It was huge, the sort of complicated mud kingdom that insects created, and it was both impressive and appalling that everything visible in this landscape was man-made. Of course you could say that about any city in the world, but this wasn't a city—it was supposed to be the range of hills above the river Wei; and it looked as though it had been made by hand.

The Terra-cotta Warriors

THE TERRA-COTTA WARRIORS (WHICH CANNOT BE PHOTO-graphed) were not a disappointment to me. They are too bizarre for that. They are stiff, upright, life-sized men and horses, marching forward in their armor through an area as big as a football field—hundreds of them, and each one has his own face and his own hairstyle. It is said that each clay figure had a counterpart in the emperor's real army, which was scattered throughout the Qin empire. Another theory is that the individual portraiture was meant to emphasize the unity of China by exhibiting "all the physical features of the inhabitants of mainland east Asia." Whatever the reason, each head is unique, and a name is stamped on the back of every neck—perhaps the name of the soldier, perhaps that of the potter-sculptor.

It is this lifelike quality of the figures—and the enormous number of them—that makes the place wonderful, and even a little disturbing. As you watch, the figures seem to move forward. It is very hard to suggest the human form in armor, and yet even with these padded leggings and boots and heavy sleeves, the figures look agile and lithe, and the kneeling archers and crossbowmen look alert and fully human.

This buried army was very much a private thrill for the tyrant who decreed that it be created to guard his tomb. But the first emperor, Qin Shi Huangdi, was given to grand gestures. Until his time, China was fragmented into the Warring States, and bits of the Wall had been put up. As Prince Cheng, he took over from his father in 246 B.C. He was thirteen years old. Before he was forty he had subdued the whole of China. He called himself emperor. He introduced an entirely new set of standards, put one of his generals— and many of his convicts and peasants—to work building the Great Wall, abolished serfs (meaning that, for the first time, the Chinese could give themselves surnames), and burned every book that did not directly praise his achievements—it was his way of making sure that history began with him. His grandiose schemes alienated his subjects and emptied his treasury. Three attempts were made to kill him. Eventually he died on a journey to east China, and to disguise his death, his ministers covered his stinking corpse with rotten fish and carted him back to be buried here. The second emperor was murdered, and so was his successor, in what the Chinese call "the first peasant insurrection in Chinese history."

The odd thing is not how much this ancient ruler accomplished but that he managed it in so short a time. And in an even shorter time, the achievements of his dynasty were eclipsed by chaos. Two thousand years later China's rulers had remarkably similar aims—conquest, unity, and uniformity.

The rare quality of the terra-cotta warriors is that, unlike anything else on the tourist route in China, they are exactly as they were made. They were vandalized by the rebellious peasants in the year 206 B.C., when these people invaded the tomb to steal the weapons—crossbows, spears, arrows, and pikestaffs (they were all real)—that the clay warriors were holding. After that the figures lay buried until, in 1974, a man digging a well hit his shovel against a warrior's head and unearthed it and the disinterment was begun. The warriors are the one masterpiece in China that has not been repainted, faked, and further vandalized. If they had been found before the Cultural Revolution instead of after it, they would undoubtedly have been pulverized by Red Guards, along with all the other masterpieces they smashed, burned, or melted down.

Endangered Species Banquet

"IN CHINA, WE HAVE A SAYING," JIANG LE SONG SAID. *"Chule feiji zhi wai, yangyang duo chi."* Looking very pleased with himself, he added, "It rhymes!"

"We call that a half-rhyme," I said. "What does it mean? Something about eating planes?"

" 'We eat everything except planes and trains.' In China."

"I get it. You eat everything on four legs except tables and chairs."

"You are a funny man!" Mr. Jiang said. "Yes. We eat trees, grass, leaves, animals, seaweed, flowers. And in Guilin even more things. Birds, snakes, turtles, cranes, frogs, and some other things."

"What other things?"

"I don't even know their names."

"Dogs? Cats?" I looked at him closely. I had overheard a tourist objecting to the Chinese appetite for kittens. "You eat kittens?"

"Not dogs and kittens. Everybody eats those."

"Raccoons?" I had read in a guidebook that raccoons were also popular in Guilin.

"What is that?"

Raccoon was not in his pocket English-Chinese dictionary.

He became very confidential, glancing around and drawing me close to him. "Maybe not lackeys. I have never heard of eating lackeys. But many other things. We eat"— and he drew a meaningful breath—"forbidden things."

That had rather a thrilling sound. *We eat forbidden things.*

"What sort of forbidden things?"

"I only know their Chinese names—sorry."

"What are we talking about?" I asked. "Snakes?"

"Dried snakes. Snake soup. They are not forbidden. I mean an animal that eats ants with its nose."

"Scaly anteater. Pangolin. I don't want to eat that. Too many people are eating them," I said. "It's an endangered species."

"Would you like to eat forbidden things?"

"I would like to eat interesting things," I said, equivocating. "How about sparrows? Pigeons? Snakes? What about turtles?"

"Those are easy. I can arrange it."

Mr. Jiang was young. He was new to the job. He was a little too breezy. He had the joky and insincere manner of someone who has been dealing with elderly foreigners who enjoy being joshed as they are being deferred to. I felt this obsequiousness was a deliberate ploy to undermine me.

That night Mr. Jiang emerged from behind a potted palm at my hotel to introduce me to a small monkey-like man.

"Our driver," Mr. Jiang said.

"Qi," the man said, and smiled. But it was not a smile. He was only saying his name.

"I have fixed everything you requested," Mr. Jiang said. "The driver will take us to Taohua—'Peace Flower Restaurant.' "

The driver slipped on a pair of gloves and whipped the door open for me. Mr. Jiang got into the front seat, beside the driver. The driver adjusted his mirror, stuck his head out of the window to signal—although we were in a parking lot and there were no other cars in sight—and drove into the empty road. After perhaps fifty yards he stopped the car.

"Is there anything wrong?" I said.

Mr. Jiang imitated a fat man laughing: "Ho! Ho! Ho!" And then a bored voice added, "We have arrived."

"There wasn't much point in taking a car, was there?"

"You are an honored guest! You must not walk!"

I had learned that guff like this was a giveaway in China. When anyone spoke to me in this formal and facetious way, I knew I was being taken for a ride.

Before we entered the restaurant, Mr. Jiang took me aside and said, "We will have snake soup. We will have pigeon."

"Very nice."

He shook his head. "They are not unusual. They are regular."

"What else are we having?"

"I will tell you inside."

Bu inside there was a fuss over the table, a great deal of talk I did not understand, and finally Mr. Jiang said, "This is your table. A special table. Now I will leave you. The driver and I will eat in the humble dining room next door. Please, sit! Take no notice of us. Enjoy yourself!"

This was also an unmistakable cue.

"Why don't you join me?" I said.

"Oh no!" Mr. Jiang said. "We will be very comfortable at our little table in the humble dining room reserved for Chinese workers."

This was laying it on a bit thick, I thought, but I was feeling guilty about this meal, and eating food alone made me feel selfish.

I said, "There's room at my table. Please sit here."

"Okay," Mr. Jiang said, in a perfunctory way, and indicated that the driver should follow his example.

It was quite usual for the driver to be included—in fact, it is one of the pleasures of Chinese life that on a long trip the driver is one of the bunch. If there is a banquet he is invited, if there is an outing he goes along, and he is present at every meal along the road. It is a civilized practice, and thinking it should be encouraged I made no objection, even though the driver had taken me only fifty yards.

"Special meal," Mr. Jiang said. "We have crane. Maybe a kind of quail. We call it *anchun*. We have many things. Even forbidden things."

That phrase had lost its thrill for me. It was a hot night, this young man seemed unreliable to me, and I was not particularly hungry.

"Have some wine," Mr. Jiang said, pouring out three glasses. "It is osmanthus wine. Guilin means 'City of Osmanthus Trees.' "

We gulped our wine. It tasted syrupy and medicinal.

The food was brought in successive waves—many dishes, but the portions were small. Perhaps sensing that it would go quickly, the driver began tonging food onto his plate.

"That is turtle," Mr. Jiang said. "From the Li river."

"And that is forbidden," he said, lowering his voice. "*Wawa* fish—baby fish. Very rare. Very tasty. Very hard to catch. Against the law."

The fish was excellent. It was a stew of small white lumps in fragrant sauce. The driver's chopsticks were busily dredging it for the plumpest fillets.

Mr. Jiang crept closer and mumbled a word in Chinese. "This is muntjac. From the mountains. With onions. Forbidden."

"What is a muntjac?" I asked.

"It is a kind of rabbit that eats fruit."

As all the world knows, a muntjac is a small deer. They are regarded as pests. You see them on golf courses outside London. Marco Polo found them in the Kingdom of Ergunul and wrote, "The flesh of this animal is very good to eat." He brought the head and feet of a muntjac back to Venice.

I sampled the pigeon, the snake soup, the muntjac, the crane, the fish, the turtle. There was something dreadful and depressing about this food, partly because it tasted good and partly because China had so few wild animals. These creatures were all facing extinction in this country. And I had always hated the Chinese appetite for rare animals—for bear's paws and fish lips and caribou's nose. That article I had read about the Chinese killing their diminishing numbers of tigers to use—superstitiously—as remedies for impotence and rheumatism had disgusted me. I was disgusted now with myself. This sort of eating was the recreation of people who were rich and spoiled.

"What do you think of this?" I asked Mr. Jiang.

"I like the turtle with bamboo," he said. "The muntjac is a bit salty."

"You've had this before?"

"Oh yes."

"What does the driver think?" I said. I was trying to describe to myself the taste of the snake and the crane and the pigeon. I laughed, thinking that whenever someone ate something exotic they always said "chicken."

The silent driver, endlessly stuffing himself, made a dive for the turtle, tonged some into his bowl, and gobbled it. He did the same to the *wawa* fish.

"He likes the fish," Mr. Jiang said.

The driver did not glance up. He ate like a predator in the wild—he paused, very alert, his eyes flicking, and then he darted for the food and ate it in one swift movement of his claw-like chopsticks.

Afterward, slightly nauseated from the forbidden food, I felt like a Hindu who had just eaten hamburger. I said I would walk home. Mr. Jiang tried to drag me into the car, but I resisted. Then, hiding his sheepishness in hearty guffaws, he handed me the bill: 200 yuan.

That was four months' salary for these young men. It was a huge amount of money. It was the foreigner's airfare from Guilin to Peking. It was the price of two of the best bicycles in China, the Flying Pigeon Deluxe. It was more than a night at the Great Wall Sheraton. It represented a good radio. It was two years' rent of a studio apartment in Shanghai. It was the cost of an antique silver bowl in the bazaar at Turfan.

I paid Mr. Jiang. I wanted a reaction from him. There was none. That was for form's sake. The Chinese make a practice of not reacting to any sort of hospitality. But I persisted.

"Is the driver impressed with this meal?"

"Not at all," Mr. Jiang said. "He has eaten this many times before. Ha! Ha!"

It rang in my ears—one of the few genuine laughs I heard in China.

It meant, *We can always fool a foreigner.*

I was the hairy, big-nosed devil from the back of beyond, one of those foreigners *(wei-guo ren)*, whom the Chinese regard as the yokels of the world. We lived in crappy little countries that were squeezed at the edge of the Middle Kingdom. The places we inhabited were insignificant but bizarre. Once the Chinese believed that we tied ourselves into bunches so that we would not be snatched away by eagles. Some of our strange societies were composed entirely of women, who became pregnant by staring at their shadows. We had noses like anteaters. We were hairier than monkeys. We smelled like corpses. One odd fenestrated race had holes in their chests, through which poles were thrust when they carried one another around. Most of these notions were no longer current, but they had given rise to self-deceiving proverbs, which sometimes seemed true. And then the laughter was real.

Shaoshan: "Where the Sun Rises"

"Until now visitors did not come here to look at the scenery," Mr. Li had said. How true. They had come as pilgrims, first to walk the seventy-five miles west to Shaoshan, and then—after the railway line was built in the late sixties—to take the strangest train in China. They had come believing the Cultural Revolution slogan THE SUN RISES IN SHAOSHAN (TAIYANG CONG SHAOSHAN SHENGQI), which was a metaphor for Mao Zedong's having been born there. The Chinese had once named themselves "Shaoshan" in Mao's honor, and I ran into at least one Li Shaoshan.

In the sixties there were several trains every hour. Now there is one train a day. It leaves at six in the morning from Changsha and arrives three hours later at Shaoshan. It returns from Shaoshan in the evening, just an old puffer on a forgotten branch line, which had outlived its purpose.

The road had always been popular, even after the train was running regularly. It was not only the best way for Red Guards and revolutionaries to prove their ardor, but long walks were part of Mao's political program—the "Forge Good Iron Footsoles" scheme. The idea was that all Chinese citizens were to have sturdy feet during the Cultural Revolution, because when the Nameless Enemy tried to invade China the evacuation of cities might be necessary. Mao filled the people with a war paranoia—that was the reason they were required to make bricks, dig trenches and bunkers and bomb shelters. They were also ordered to have hard feet and to take twenty-mile hikes on their days off in order to give themselves "iron footsoles" ("All I got were blisters," my informant Wang told me). It was to this end that they trekked for four days on the road from Changsha to Shaoshan, sleeping in peasants' huts and singing "The East Is Red," "The Sun Rises in Shaoshan." They also sang ditties that had been set to music from the Selected Thoughts, such numbers as "People of the World, Unite and Defeat the U.S. Aggressors and All Their Running Dogs!" with its stirring last line, "Monsters of all kinds shall be destroyed." My favorite song from the Selected Thoughts, one I was assured had enlivened the marches along the Shaoshan road with its syncopation, went as follows:

> A revolution is not a dinner party,
> Or writing an essay, or painting a picture,
>   or doing embroidery;
>
> It cannot be so refined, so leisurely and gentle,
> So temperate, kind, courteous, restrained
>   and magnanimous."*
>
> A revolution is an insurrection,
> An act of violence by which one class
>   overthrows another.

They sang them on the trains, too. They flew flags. They wore Mao buttons and badges, and the red armband. It was not a trivial matter. It compared in size and fervor to

---

*"These were the virtues of Confucius, as described by one of his disciples," runs the commentary in Mao's Selected Works. So Mao was also criticizing Confucius for not being of a revolutionary spirit.

Muslims making the Hadj to Mecca. On one day in 1966, a procession of 120,000 Chinese thronged the village of Shaoshan to screech songs and perform the *qing an* with the *Little Red Book.*

Twenty years later I arrived at the station in an empty train. The station was empty. The unusually long platform was empty, and so were the sidings. There was not a soul in sight. The station was tidy, but that only made its emptiness seem much odder. It was very clean, freshly painted in a limpid shade of blue, and entirely abandoned. No cars in the parking lot, no one at the ticket windows. A large portrait of Mao hung over the station and on a billboard was the epitaph in Chinese: MAO ZEDONG WAS A GREAT MARXIST, A GREAT PROLETARIAN REVOLUTIONARY, A GREAT TACTICIAN AND THEORIST.

That was delicate: nothing about his being a great leader. Mao's dying wish (obviously ignored) was to be remembered as a teacher.

I walked through the village, reflecting on the fact that nothing looks emptier than an empty parking lot. There were many here, designed for buses; they were very large and nothing was parked in them. I went to the hotel that was built for dignitaries and I sat in the almost-empty dining room, under a Mao portrait, eating and listening to people spitting.

The tide was out in Shaoshan; it was the town that time forgot—ghostly and echoing. And so it fascinated me. It was actually a pretty place, a rural retreat, with lovely trees and green fields, and a stream running through it that topped up the lotus ponds. In any other place an atmosphere of such emptiness would seem depressing, but this was a healthy neglect—what is healthier than refusing to worship a politician?—and the few people there had come as picnickers, not as pilgrims.

Mao's house was at the far end of the village, in a glade. It was large and its yellow stucco and Hunanese design gave it the look of a hacienda—very cool and airy, with an atrium and a lovely view of its idyllic setting. Here Mao was born in December 1893. The rooms are neatly labeled: PARENTS' BEDROOM, BROTHER'S ROOM, KITCHEN, PIGSTY, and so forth. It is the house of a well-to-do family—Mao's father was "a relatively rich peasant," clever with money and mortgages, and he was a moneylender of sorts. There was plenty of space here—a big barn and roomy kitchen. Mrs. Mao's stove was preserved (DO NOT TOUCH), and a placard near it read: IN 1921 MAO ZEDONG EDUCATED HIS FAMILY IN REVOLUTION NEAR THIS STOVE. And in the sitting room: IN 1927 MEETINGS WERE HELD HERE TO DISCUSS REVOLUTIONARY ACTIVITIES.

It was not like visiting Lincoln's log cabin. It wasn't Blenheim. It wasn't Paul Revere's house. For one thing it was very empty. The few Chinese nearby seemed indifferent to the house itself. They sat under trees listening to a booming radio. There were girls in pretty dresses. Their clothes alone were a political statement. But this handful of people were hardly visible. Its emptiness meant something. Because when it was heavily visited Shaoshan had represented political piety and obedience, now that it was empty it stood for indifference. In a sense, neglect was more dramatic than destruction, because the thing still existed as a mockery of what it had been.

It had the fusty smell of an old shrine. It had outlived its usefulness, and it looked a little absurd, like a once-hallowed temple of a sect of fanatics who had run off, tearing their clothes, and had never returned. Times have changed. Toward the end of the Cultural Revolution, the pseudonymous Simon Leys visited China and in *Chinese Shadows*, his gloomy and scolding account of his trip, he wrote that Shaoshan "is visited by about three million pilgrims every year." That is eight thousand a day. Today there were none.

If Shaoshan was embarrassing to the Chinese, it was because the whole scheme had been to show Mao as more than human. There was an obnoxious religiosity in the way his old schoolhouse had been arranged to show little Mao as a sanctified student. But the building was empty, and there was no one walking down the lane, so it didn't matter. I had the impression that the Chinese were staying away in droves.

One stall sold postcards. There was only one view:

MAO'S BIRTHPLACE (the house in the glade). And there were a few Mao badges. It was the only place in China where I saw his face on sale, but even so it was just this little badge. There were also towels and dishcloths, saying SHAOSHAN.

There was a shop in the Mao Museum.

I said, "I would like to buy a Mao badge."

"We have none," the assistant said.

"How about a Mao picture?"

"We have none."

"What about a *Little Red Book*—or any Mao book?"

"None."

"Where are they?"

"Sold."

"All of them?"

"All."

"Will you get some more to sell?"

The assistant said, "I do not know."

What do they sell, then, at the shop in the Mao Museum? They sell key chains with color photographs of Hong Kong movie actresses, bars of soap, combs, razor blades, face cream, hard candy, peanut brittle, buttons, thread, cigarettes, and men's underwear.

The museum did try to show Mao as more than human, and in its eighteen rooms of hagiography Mao was presented as a sort of Christ figure, preaching very early (giving instructions in revolution by his mother's stove) and winning recruits. There were statues, flags, badges, and personal paraphernalia—his straw hat, his slippers, his ashtray. Room by room, his life is displayed in pictures and captions: his schooldays, his job, his travels, the death of his brother, the Long March, the war, his first marriage ...

And then, after such languid and detailed exposition, an odd thing happens in the last room. In Number Eighteen, time is telescoped, and the years 1949–76, his entire chairmanship, his rule, and his death, are presented with lightning speed. There is no mention of his two other marriages, nothing about Jiang Qing. Nonpersons like Jiang Qing and Lin Biao have been airbrushed out of photographs. The 1960s are shown in one picture, the mushroom cloud of

China's first atom bomb in 1964. The rest of the decade does not exist. There has been no Great Proletarian Cultural Revolution. The Mao Museum was founded in 1967, at the height of it!

But by omitting so much and showing time passing so quickly, the museum gives the viewer a bizarre potted history of Mao's final years. In the previous rooms he looks like a spoiled child, a big brat, scowling and solemn. In this final room he develops a very unusual smile and on his pumpkin face it has a disturbing effect. After 1956 he seems to be gaga. He starts wearing baggy pants and a coolie hat, and his face is drawn from a sag into a mad or senile grimace. He looks unlike his earlier self. In one picture he is lumberingly playing Ping-Pong. In 1972 and after, meeting Nixon, Prince Sihanouk, and East European leaders, he's a heffalump, he looks hugely crazy or else barely seems to recognize the visitor grinning at him. There is plenty of evidence here to support what the Chinese say about him all the time—that after 1956 he was not the same.

Mao had set out to be an enigma and had succeeded. "The anal leader of an oral people," the sinologist Richard Soloman had said. Mao can be described but not summed up. He was patient, optimistic, ruthless, pathologically antiintellectual, romantic, militaristic, patriotic, chauvinistic, rebellious in a youthful way, and deliberately contradictory.

Shaoshan said everything about Mao: his rise and fall; his position today. I loved the empty train arriving at the empty station. Was there a better image of obscurity? As for the house and village, they were like many temples in China, where no one prayed any longer—just a heap of symmetrical stones representing waste, confusion, and ruin. China was full of such places, dedicated to the memory of someone or other and, lately, just an excuse for setting up picnic tables and selling souvenirs.

The Great Wall

BECAUSE IT IS A FLAT, DRY, NORTHERN CITY, AT THE EDGE OF Mongolia, Peking has beautiful skies. They are bluest in the freezing air of winter. China's old euphemism for itself was *Tianxia*, "All beneath the sky"—and, on a good day, what a sky! It was limpid, like an ocean of air, but seamless and unwrinkled, without a single wavelet of cloud; endless uncluttered fathoms of it that grew icier through the day and then at the end of the winter afternoon turned to dust.

Thinking it would be empty, I went to see the Great Wall again. Dr. Johnson told Boswell how eager he was to go to China and see the Wall. Boswell was not so sure himself. How could he justify going to China when he had children at home to take care of?

"Sir," Dr. Johnson said, "by doing so [going to China] you would do what would be of importance in raising your children to eminence. There would be a lustre reflected upon them from your spirit and curiosity. They would be at all times regarded as the children of a man who had gone to view the wall of China. I am serious, sir."

The Wall is an intimidating thing, less a fortification than a visual statement announcing imperiously: I am the Son of Heaven and this is the proof that I can encircle the earth. It somewhat resembles, in intention, the sort of achievement of that barmy man Christo, who giftwrapped the Golden Gate Bridge. The Wall goes steeply up and down mountainsides. To what purpose? Certainly not to repel invaders, who could never cling to those cliffs. Wasn't it another example of the Chinese love of taking possession of the land and whipping it into shape?

Anyway, it was not empty. It swarmed with tourists.

They scampered on it and darkened it like fleas on a dead snake.

That gave me an idea. "Snake" was very close, but what it actually looked like was a dragon. The dragon is the favorite Chinese creature ("just after man in the hierarchy of living beings") and until fairly recently—eighty or a hundred years ago—the Chinese believed they existed. Many people reported seeing them alive—and of course fossilized dragon skeletons had been unearthed. It was a good omen and, especially, a guardian. The marauding dragon and the dragon slayer are unknown in China. It is one of China's friendliest and most enduring symbols. And I found a bewitching similarity between the Chinese dragon and the Great Wall of China—the way it flexed and slithered up and down the Mongolian mountains; the way its crenellations looked like the fins on a dragon's back, and its bricks like scales; the way it looked serpentine and protective, undulating endlessly from one end of the world to the other.

Mr. Tian

"Is it cold outside?" I asked.

"Very," said Mr. Tian. His eyeglasses were opaque with frost.

It was five-thirty on a Harbin morning, the temperature at minus thirty-five Centigrade and a light snow falling—little grains like seed pearls sifting down in the dark. When the flurry stopped, the wind picked up, and it was murderous. Full on my face it was like being slashed with a razor. We were on our way to the railway station.

"And you insist on coming with me?" I asked.

"Langxiang is forbidden," Mr. Tian said. "So I must."

"It is the Chinese way," I said.

"Very much so," he replied.

In this darkness groups of huddled people waited in the empty street for buses. That seemed a grim pastime, a long wait at a Harbin bus stop in winter. And, by the way, the buses were not heated. In his aggrieved account of his Chinese residence, the journalist Tiziano Terzani, writing about Heilongjiang ("The Kingdom of the Rats"), quotes a French traveler who said, "Although it is uncertain where God placed paradise, we can be sure that he chose some other place than this."

The wind dropped but the cold remained. It banged against my forehead and twisted my fingers and toes; it burned my lips. I felt like Sam McGee. I entered the station waiting room and a chill rolled against me, as if my face had been pressed on a cold slab. The waiting room was unheated. I asked Mr. Tian how he felt about this.

"Heat is bad," he said. "Heat makes you sleepy and slow."

"I like it," I said.

Mr. Tian said, "I once went to Canton. It was so hot I felt sick."

Mr. Tian was twenty-seven, a graduate of Harbin University. There was humor in the way he moved. He was self-assured. He didn't fuss. He was patient. He was frank. I liked him for these qualities. The fact that he was incompetent did not matter very much. Langxiang was a day's journey by train—north, into the snow. He seemed an easy companion and I did not think he would get in my way.

He had no bag. He may have had a toothbrush in his pocket, where he kept his woolly cap and his misshapen gloves. He was completely portable, without any impedimenta. He was an extreme example of Chinese austerity. He slept in his long johns and wore his coat to meals. He rarely washed. Being Chinese he did not have to shave. He seemed to have no possessions at all. He was like a desert Bedouin. This fascinated me, too.

The train pulled in, steaming and gasping, just as the sun came up. It had come from Dalian, six hundred miles away, and it stopped everywhere. So it was sensationally littered with garbage—peanut shells, apple cores, chewed chicken bones, orange peel, and greasy paper. It was very dirty and it was so cold inside that the spit had frozen on the floor into misshapen yellow-green medallions of ice. The covering between each coach was a snow tunnel, the frost on the windows was an inch thick, the doors had no locks and so they banged and thumped as a freezing draft rushed through the carriages. It was the Heilongjiang experience: I crept in out of the cold and inside I felt even colder. I found a small space and sat hunched over like everyone else, with my hat and gloves on. I was reading Lermontov's *A Hero of Our Time* and I scribbled on the flyleaf:

> In the provinces every train is like a troop train. This is like one returning from the front, with the sick and wounded.

Even with three pairs of socks and thermal-lined boots my feet were cold; nor did I feel particularly cozy in my heavy sweater, Mongolian sheepskin vest, and leather coat. I felt like an idiot in my hat and fleece-lined mittens, but it annoyed me that I was still cold, or at least not warm. How I longed for the summer trains of the south and the sweltering trip on the Iron Rooster when I had lounged in my blue pajamas.

Mr. Tian said, "You come from which city in the States?"

"Near Boston."

"Lexington is near Boston," Mr. Tian said.

"How did you know that?"

"I studied American history in middle school. All Chinese study it."

"So you know about our war of liberation, Mr. Tian?"

"Yes. There was also a Paul who was very important."

"Paul Revere."

"Exactly," Mr. Tian said. "He told the peasants that the British were coming."

"Not just the peasants. He told everyone—the peasants, the landlords, the capitalist-roaders, the stinking ninth category of intellectuals, the minorities, and the slaves."

"I think you're joking, especially about the slaves."

"No. Some of the slaves fought on the British side. They were promised their freedom if the British won. After the British surrendered these blacks were sent to Canada."

"I didn't read about that," Mr. Tian said, as the door blew open.

"I'm cold," I said.

"I'm too hot," Mr. Tian said.

The cold put me to sleep. I was wakened later by Mr. Tian, who asked me whether I wanted to have breakfast. I thought some food might warm me up so I said yes.

There was frost on the dining-car windows and ice on the dining-car floor, and a bottle of water on my table had frozen and burst. My fingers were too cold to hold any chopsticks. I hunched over with my hands up my sleeves.

"What food do they have?" I asked.

"I don't know."

"Do you want noodles?" I asked.

"Anything but noodles," Mr. Tian said.

The waiter brought us cold noodles, cold pickled onions, diced Spam, which looked like a shredded beach toy, and cold but very tasty black fungus—a specialty of the province. Mr. Tian ate his noodles. It was the Chinese way. Even if it was not to your taste, when there was nothing else on the menu you ate it.

After several hours of crossing flat snowfields this train entered a mountainous region. The settlements were small—three or four short rows of bungalows, some of brick and some of mud and logs. They were the simplest slant-roofed dwellings and looked like the sort of houses that children draw in the first grade, with a narrow door and a single window and a blunt chimney with a screw of smoke coming out of it.

The toilet on the train looked as though a child had designed it, too. It was a hole in the floor about a foot across. Well, I had seen squat toilets before, but this one was traveling at about fifty miles an hour through the ice and snow of northern China. There was no pipe or baffle. If you looked down it you saw ice streaking past. A gust of freezing air rushed out of the hole. Anyone fool enough to use this thing would be frostbitten on a part of the body that is seldom frostbitten. And yet the passengers trooped into this refrigerated bum-freezer. When they came out their eyes were tiny and their teeth were clenched, as though they had just been pinched very hard.

We were still jogging along, stopping frequently. And the doors opened and closed with the same pneumatic gasp as those on a refrigerator, each time producing a cold blast through the coach. I hated having to get up, because when I sat down again my seat froze me.

It surprised me to see children standing outside their houses, watching the train go by. They wore thin jackets, no hats or gloves. Many of them had bright red cheeks. They had spiky unwashed hair and they wore cloth slippers. They looked very hardy, and they yelled at the train as it passed their icebound villages.

The mountains in the distance were the southernmost peaks of the Lesser Khingan Range, and the foreground was all forest. Most of these settlements were simply overgrown lumber camps. One of the centers of logging activity is Langxiang. But I had also chosen it because it has a narrow-gauge railway that goes deep into the forest and carries logs back to town to be milled.

It was hardly a town. It was a sprawling one-story village with an immense lumber yard at its center and a main street where people with scarves wrapped around their faces stood all day in the cold selling meat and vegetables. One day in Langxiang I saw a man standing behind a square of cloth which held six frozen rats and a stack of rats' tails. Were things so bad in Langxiang that they ate rats and rats' tails?

"Do you eat these?" I asked.

"No, no," came the muffled voice through the frosted scarf. "I sell medicine."

"These rats are medicine?"

"No, no!" The man's skin was almost black from the cold and the dry air.

And then he began speaking again, but I had no idea what he was saying in this local dialect. As he spoke the ice crystals thawed on his scarf.

Mr. Tian said, "He doesn't sell rats. He sells rat poison. He shows these dead rats as proof that his poison is good."

We had arrived at Langxiang in the middle of the afternoon, just as it was growing dark. This was a northern latitude in winter: night came early. I stepped from the cold train onto the freezing platform, and then we went to the guest house, which was also cold—but the clammy indoor cold that I found harder to bear than the icy outdoors. With curtains over the windows and the lights dim, it was like being in an underground tomb.

"It's very cold in here," I said to Mr. Cong, the manager.

"It will get warmer."

"When?"

"In three or four months."

"I mean, in the hotel," I said.

"Yes. In the hotel. And all over Langxiang."

I was jumping up and down to restore my circulation. Mr. Tian was simply standing patiently.

"What about a room?" I said.

He said something very rapidly to Mr. Cong.

"Do you want a clean room or a regular one?" Mr. Tian asked.

"I think I'll have a clean one for a change."

He did not remark on my sarcasm. He said, "Ah, a clean one," and shook his head, as if this were a tall order. "Then you will have to wait."

The wind blew through the lobby and when it hit the curtain that had been hung across the main door it filled it like a spinnaker.

"We can have dinner," Mr. Cong said.

"It's not even five o'clock," I said.

"Five o'clock. Dinnertime. Ha-ha!" This ha-ha meant: *Rules are rules. I don't make them, so you should not be difficult.*

The dining room in the Langxiang Guesthouse was the coldest room I had entered so far in the whole of Heilongjiang Province. I yanked my hat tight and then sat on my hands and shivered. I had put my thermometer on the table: thirty-six degrees Fahrenheit.

Mr. Cong said he was used to the cold. He was not even

wearing a hat! He was from the far north, where he had gone as a settler in the fifties to work on a commune that produced corn and grain. Although he was not very old, he was something of an antique in Chinese terms. As a commune worker in one of the remotest parts of China he found the new reforms bewildering. And he had four children, now regarded as a shameful number. "They punish us for having more than two," he said, and seemed very puzzled. "You might lose your job, or be transferred, as punishment."

From the utter boredom on Mr. Tian's face—but his boredom was a form of serenity—I could tell that Mr. Cong and Mr. Tian had nothing at all in common. In China, the generation gap has a specific meaning and is something to be reckoned with.

I asked Mr. Cong what had happened to his commune.

"It was canceled," he said. "It was dissolved."

"Did the peasants go away?"

"No. Each was given his own plot to till."

"Do you think that's better?"

"Of course," he said, but it was impossible for me to tell whether he meant it. "Production is much greater. The yields are larger."

That seemed to settle it. Any policy that increased production was a good thing. I thought: *God help China if there's a recession.*

The town was in darkness. The hotel was very cold. My room was cold. What to do? Although it was only six-thirty I went to bed—anyway, I got inside with most of my clothes on, and I listened to my short-wave radio under the blankets. That was how I was to spend all of my nights in Langxiang.

I went up the logging line on the narrow-gauge railway the next day, but I was disappointed in the forest. I had expected wilderness, but this was filled with lumberjacks cutting and bulldozing trees.

"One day we will go to the primeval forest," Mr. Tian said.

"Let's go today."

"No. It is far. We will go another day."

We went to the locomotive shed, where we met Mrs. Jin, a local guide. The shed was full of smoke and steam, and it was dark; but it was also warm, because the boilers were being stoked and the fire in the forge was blazing. As I walked along Mrs. Jin threw herself at me and pushed me against the wall, and then she laughed hysterically, a kind of chattering—one of the more terrifying Chinese laughs. I saw that she had saved me from stepping into a deep hole in which I would almost certainly have broken my back.

I was so rattled by this I had to go outside and take deep breaths. All over this town the snow was packed hard. No street or pavement was clear of ice. They habitually pedaled on the ice, and they had a way of walking—a sort of shuffle—that prevented them from slipping.

"This town is forbidden," Mr. Tian boasted. "You are very lucky to be here."

All the while in Langxiang my feet and hands were frozen—stinging and painful. My eyes hurt. My muscles were knotted. There was an icy moaning in my head. Mr. Tian asked me whether I wanted to see the ski slopes. I said yes and we drove four miles outside town just as the sun slipped below the distant mountains and an even greater cold descended with the darkness.

There on the black and white mountains were ten sluices—frozen chutes cut into the slope. People hauled small boxes up the mountain—they were like little coffins; and then they placed them into a chute and went banging down, cracking from side to side and screaming. I hopped up and down in the cold and said I wasn't interested.

Mr. Tian went thrashing up the slope with a splintery coffin and came down showing his teeth. He did it again. Perhaps he was developing a taste for this.

"Don't you like skiing?" he said.

"This isn't skiing, Mr. Tian."

In a shocked voice he said, "It's *not*?"

But he kept doing it just the same.

I walked down the path and found a shed, a sort of watchman's shack. There was a stove inside. This was a vivid demonstration of heating in Langxiang. The stove was so feeble that there was half an inch of frost on the walls of the shed. The walls (wood and mud bricks) were entirely white.

I kept a record of temperatures. Minus thirty-four Centigrade on the main street, freezing in the lobby, just above freezing in the dining room. The food went cold a minute after it was plunked down, and the grease congealed. They served fatty meat, greasy potatoes, rice gruel, great uncooked chunks of green pepper. Was this Chinese food? One day I had cabbage stuffed with meat and rice, and gravy poured over it. I had eaten such dishes in Russia and Poland, when they were called *golomkis*.

It was very tiring to be cold all the time. I began to enjoy going to bed early. I listened to the BBC and the VOA under my blanket. After a few hours I took one of my sweaters off, and one layer of socks, and by morning I was so warm in the sack that I forgot where I was. Then I saw the layer of frost on the window that was so thick I could not see outside, and I remembered.

No one spoke of the cold. Well, why should they? They reveled in it—literally, dancing and sliding on the ice. I saw children in the dark one evening pushing each other off a shelf of ice onto the frozen surface of the town's river. (Other people chopped holes in this ice and drew water from it.) Those children frolicking in the darkness and the perishing cold reminded me of penguins frisking on the ice floes through the long Antarctic night.

WHEN I TRAVEL I DREAM A GREAT DEAL. PERHAPS THAT IS ONE of my main reasons for travel. It has something to do with strange rooms and odd noises and smells, with vibrations, with food, with the anxieties of travel—especially the fear of death—and with temperatures.

In Langxiang it was the low temperatures that gave me long exhausting dreams. The cold kept me from deep sleep, and so I lay just beneath the surface of consciousness, like a drifting fish. In one of my Langxiang dreams I was besieged in a house in San Francisco. I ran from the front door shooting a machine gun and wearing headphones. I escaped on a passing cable car—President Reagan was on it, strap-hanging. I was asking him whether he was having a tough time as president. He said, "Terrible." We were still talking when I woke up feeling very cold.

I went back to sleep. Mr. Tian banged on my door and woke me up.

"We are going to the primeval forest," he said.

We drove about thirty miles, and Mrs. Jin joined us. The driver's name was Ying. The road was icy and corrugated and very narrow, but there were no other vehicles except for an occasional army truck. When we arrived at a place called "Clear Spring" (Qing Yuan), where there was a cabin, we began hiking through the forest. There was snow everywhere but it was not very deep—a foot or so. The trees were huge and very close together—great fat trunks crowding each other. We kept to a narrow path.

I asked Mrs. Jin about herself. She was a pleasant person, very frank and unaffected. She was thirty-two and had a young daughter. Her husband was a clerk in a government department. This family of three lived with six other family members in a small flat in Langxiang—nine people in three rooms. Her mother-in-law did all the cooking. It seemed cruel that in a province that had wide open spaces, people should be forced to live in such cramped conditions at close quarters. But this was quite usual. And it was a family under one roof. I often had the feeling that it was the old immemorial Confucian family that had kept China orderly. Mao had attacked the family—the Cultural Revolution was intentionally an assault on the family system, when children were told to rat on their bourgeois parents. But that had faltered and failed. The family had endured, and what were emerging with Deng's reforms were family businesses and family farms.

Kicking through the forest, I asked them whether it was possible to buy Mao's little red book of Selected Thoughts.

"I have thrown mine away," Mr. Tian said. "That was all a big mistake."

"I don't agree with him," Mrs. Jin said.

"Do you read Mao's Thoughts?" I asked.

"Sometimes," she said. "Mao did many great things for China. Everyone criticizes him, but they forget the wise things he said."

"What is your favorite thought? The one that you associate with his wisdom?"

" 'Serve the People,' " Mrs. Jin said. "I can't quote it all to you, it is too long. It is very wise."

"What about 'A Revolution Is Not a Dinner Party'—can you sing it?"

"Oh yes," she said, and did so as we marched through the woods. It was not a catchy tune, but it was perfect for walking briskly, full of iambics: *Geming bushi gingke chifan* . . .

Meanwhile I was bird-watching. It was one of the few places in China where the trees were full of birds. They were tiny flitting things, and very high in the branches. My problem was that I could only use my binoculars with bare hands, so that I could adjust the focus. The temperature was in the minus thirties, which meant that after a few minutes my fingers were too cold to use for adjustments. Yet even in this bitter cold there was birdsong, and the whole forest chattered with the tapping of woodpeckers.

"Mr. Tian, can you sing something?" I asked.

"I can't sing Mao's thoughts."

"Sing something else."

He suddenly snatched his woolly cap off and shrieked:

> Oh, Carol!
> I am but a foooool!
> Don't ever leave me—
> Treat me mean and croool . . .

He sang it with extraordinary passion and energy, this old Neil Sedaka rock-and-roll song, and when he was done he said, "That's what we used to sing at Harbin University when I was a student!"

Cherry Blossom

A YOUNG CHINESE WOMAN SMILED AT ME AS I STEPPED onto the platform at Dalian. She was very modern, I could see. Her hair had been waved into a mass of springy curls. She wore sunglasses. Her green coat had a fur collar—rabbit. She said she had been sent to meet me. Her name was Miss Tan.

"But please call me Cherry."

"Okay, Cherry."

"Or Cherry Blossom."

It was hard to include those two words in an ordinary sentence. "What is the fare to Yantai, Cherry Blossom?" But I managed, and she always had a prompt reply, usually something like, "It will cost you one arm and one leg." She had a fondness for picturesque language.

She led me outdoors and as we stood on the steps of Dalian Station, she said, "So what do you think of Dalian so far?"

"I have only been here seven minutes," I said.

"Time flies when you're having fun!" Cherry Blossom said.

"But since you asked," I went on, "I am very impressed with what I see in Dalian. The people are happy and industrious, the economy is buoyant, the quality of life is superb. I can tell that morale is very high. I am sure it is the fresh air and prosperity. The port is bustling, and I'm sure the markets are filled with merchandise. What I have seen so far only makes me want to see more."

"That is good," Cherry Blossom said.

"And another thing," I said. "Dalian looks like South Boston, in Massachusetts."

It did, too. It was a decaying port, made out of bricks, with wide streets, cobblestones, and trolley tracks, and all the paraphernalia of a harbor—the warehouses, dry docks, and cranes. I had the impression that if I kept walking I would eventually come to the Shamrock Bar and Grill. It was also Boston weather—cold and partly sunny under blowing clouds—and Boston architecture. Dalian was full of big brick churches that had probably once been called St. Pat's, St. Joe's, and St. Ray's—they were now kindergartens and nurseries, and one was the Dalian Municipal Library. But reform had come to Dalian and with it such businesses as the Hot Bread Bakery and the Hong Xing (Red Star) Cut and Perma.

"And also men hurry to Hong Xing to get a perma," Cherry Blossom said. "They go lickety-split."

The streets looked like Boston's streets. Never mind that the main thoroughfare in Dalian was called Stalin Road (Sidalin Lu). It looked like Atlantic Avenue.

At the turn of the century the Russians had schemed to make Dalny (as they called it; it means "far away" in Russian) a great port for the tsar's ships. It was valuable for fighting the Japanese, because unlike Vladivostok it would not freeze in the winter. After the Russo-Japanese war, when the Japanese flew kites in Dairen (as they called it)—each kite saying THE RUSSIANS HAVE SURRENDERED!—this port city was handed to the Japanese. They simply completed the Russian plan for turning what had been a fishing village into a great port. It prospered until the Second World War, and when the Japanese were defeated the Russians were given the city under the Yalta terms. The Russians remained until well after the Chinese Liberation, when the Chinese renamed it Dalian ("Great Link"). I liked it for its salt air and seagulls.

"What desires do you entertain in Dalian?" Cherry Blossom said.

I told her that I had come here to get warm after the freeze in Dongbei, the northeast. And I needed a ticket on the ship that traveled from Dalian across the Bohai Gulf to Yantai. Could she get that for me?

"Keep your fingers crossed," she said.

She vanished after that. I found an old hotel—Japanese pre-war baronial—but I was turned away. I was accepted at the dreary new Chinese hotel, a sort of Ramada Inn with a stagnant fish pond in the lobby. I spent the day looking for an antique shop, and the only one I found was disappointing. A man tried to sell me a trophy awarded to the winner of a schoolboys' javelin competition in 1933 at a Japanese high school. "Genuine silver," he whispered. "Qing Dynasty."

The next day I saw Cherry Blossom. She had no news about my ticket.

"You will just have to keep your hopes up!"

We agreed to meet later, and when we did she was smiling.

"Any luck?" I asked.

"No!" She was smiling. And with this bad news I noticed that she had a plump and slightly pimply face. She was wearing an arsenic-green wool scarf to match the wool cap she herself had knitted in the dormitory (she had four roommates) at the Working Women's Unit.

"I have failed completely!"

Then why was she smiling? God, I hated her silly hat.

"But," she said, wiggling her fingers, "wait!"

She had a sharp way of speaking that made every sentence an exclamation. She reached into her plastic handbag.

"Here is the ticket! It has been a total success!"

Now she wagged her head at me and made her tight curls vibrate like springs.

I said, "Were you trying to fool me, Cherry Blossom?"

"Yes!"

I wanted to hit her.

"Is that a Chinese practical joke?"

"Oh yes," she said, with a giggle.

But then aren't all practical jokes exercises in sadism?

I went to the Free Market—open since 1979. Every sort of fish, shellfish, and seaweed was on display—a pound of big plump prawns was roughly $4, but that was the most expensive item. They also sold squid, abalone, oysters, conch, sea slugs, and great stacks of clams and flatfish. The fishermen did not look Chinese; they had a flatheaded

Mongolian appearance and might have been Manchus, of whom there are five or six million in this peninsula and in the north. The market gave me an appetite and that night I had abalone stir-fried in garlic sauce: delicious.

Cherry Blossom said that foreign cruise ships stopped in Dalian in the summer. The tourists stayed for half a day.

"What can you see in Dalian in half a day?"

She said they all got on a bus and visited the shell-carving factory, the glassware factory, and a model children's school (the kids sang songs from *The Sound of Music*), and then it was back to the ship and on to Yantai or Qingdao.

"I'd like to see Stalin Square," I said.

We went there. In the center of it was a statue to the Russian army, which had occupied the city after the war.

"There are no Stalin Squares in the Soviet Union, Cherry Blossom. Did you know that?"

She said no, she was surprised to hear it. She asked why.

"Because some people think he made a few mistakes," I said, though I did not mention the pogroms, the secret police, the purges, or the mustached brute's ability to plan large-scale famines in order to punish dissenting regions.

"Is there a Mao Zedong Square in Dalian, Cherry Blossom?"

"No," she said, "because he made a few mistakes. But don't cry over spilled milk!"*

I told her that I had read somewhere that the evil genius Lin Biao had lived in Dalian. She said no, this was not so. She had lived her whole life in Dalian and no one had ever mentioned Lin's connection.

But the driver was older. He said yes, Lin Biao had lived there in Dalian. Lin Biao, a great military tactician, was now maligned because he had done so much to build up Mao—it was Lin who devised the *Little Red Book* and chose all the quotations; and in the end (so it was said) he had plotted to assassinate Mao, when Mao was weak and at

---

*She was wrong. Mao was the mover of a resolution to forbid the naming of provinces, cities, towns, or squares for himself or other living leaders (*Selected Works of Mao Zedong*, vol. 4, p. 380).

his heffalump stage; and Lin in trying to flee the country ("seeking protection from his Moscow masters . . . as a defector to the Soviet revisionists in betrayal of the party and the country") had crashed in dear old Undur Khan, in the People's Republic of Mongolia. Foul play was never mentioned. It was regarded as natural justice that this heliophobe should meet an untimely death.

It was his heliophobia that made me want to see his house. This weedy little man had a horror of the sun. I thought his house might not have any windows, or perhaps special shutters; or maybe he lived in a bomb shelter in the basement.

Cherry Blossom was saying in Chinese to the driver, "I did not know that Lin Biao lived in Dalian," and then to me in English, "It's too dark to find his house. Let's go to the beach instead."

We headed for the south part of Dalian, to a place called Fu's Village Beach. Because of the cliffs and the winding road, the driver went very slowly.

Cherry Blossom said, "This car is as slow as cold molasses in January."

"You certainly know a lot of colorful expressions, Cherry."

"Yes. I am queer as a fish." And she giggled behind her hand.

"You should be as happy as a clam," I said.

"I like that one so much! I feel like a million dollars when I hear that."

These colloquial high jinks could have been tiresome, but it was such a novelty for a Chinese person to be playful I enjoyed it. And I liked her for not taking herself too seriously. She knew she was mildly excruciating.

Meanwhile we were descending to Fu's Village—great rocky cliffs and an empty beach of yellow sand with the January wind off the sea beating the waves against it. Offshore there were five blob-like islands floating blackly on the gulf. A couple was canoodling on the beach—the Chinese do it standing up, out of the wind, usually behind a rock or a building, and they hug each other very tightly. It is all smooching. These two ran away when they saw me.

A drunken fisherman staggered across the beach toward his big wooden rowboat that was straight off an ancient scroll: a sharply rockered bottom, very clumsy, the shape of a wooden shoe, probably very seaworthy.

I asked Cherry Blossom whether she took her tourists here. She said there wasn't time.

"Some of the people have funny faces," she said.

"What is the funniest face you have ever seen, Cherry?"

She shrieked, "Yours!" and clapped her hands over her eyes and laughed.

"Another of your saucy jokes, Cherry Blossom!"

She became rather grave and said, "But truly the Tibetans have the funniest faces. They are so funny I get frightened."

"What about American faces?"

"Americans are wonderful."

We had tea at a vast empty restaurant. We were the only customers. It was at the top of one of Fu's cliffs, with a panoramic view.

"Do you want to see the Dragon Cave?"

I said yes, and was taken upstairs to see a restaurant decorated to resemble a cave. It had fiberglass walls, bulging brown plastic rocks, and lights shining through plastic stalactites, and each table was fixed in a greeny-black cleft, with fake moss and boulders around it. The idea was perhaps not a bad one, but this was a vivid example of the Chinese not knowing when to stop. It was shapeless, artless, grotesquely beyond kitsch; it was a complicated disfigurement, wrinkled and stinking, like a huge plastic toy that had begun to melt and smell. You sat on those wrinkled rocks and bumped your head on the stalactites and ate fish cheeks with fresh ginger.

Cherry Blossom said, "Do you think it's romantic?"

"Some people might find it romantic," I said. And I pointed out the window. "That's what I find romantic."

The tangerine sun had settled into the Gulf of Bohai, coloring the little islands and the cliffs of Dalian, and the long stretch of empty beach.

Cherry Blossom said, "Let your imagination fly!"

We left the Dragon Cave (and I thought: *It must have a counterpart in California*). I said, "I understand there are recuperation tours. People come to this province to try out Chinese medicine."

"Yes. It is like a fat farm."

"Where did you learn that, Cherry Blossom?"

"My teachers at the institute were Americans. They taught me so many things!"

She had loved her years at the Dalian Foreign Languages Institute. She was now only twenty-two, but she intended to go on studying and working. She had no intention of getting married, and in explaining why, she lost her joky manner and became distressed.

Her decision not to marry was the result of a trip to Peking. She had taken a group of visiting doctors to see a Chinese hospital—how it worked, how the patients were treated, the progress of surgical operations, and so forth. The doctors expressed an interest in seeing a delivery. Cherry Blossom witnessed this and, so she said, almost went into shock at the sight of the baby issuing forth with its squashed head and its bloody face and streaming water. The mother had howled and so had the baby.

In all respects it was a completely normal birth.

"It was a mess," she said, and touched her plump cheeks in disgust. "I was afraid. I hated it. I would never do it—never. I will never get married."

I said, "You don't have to have babies just because you get married."

She was shaking her head. The thought was absurd—she couldn't take it in. The whole point of marriage these days was to produce one child. Even though the Party was now stressing that the best marriages were work-related, the husband and wife joint members of a work unit, a busy little team, Cherry Blossom could not overcome the horror of what she had seen in the delivery room of Capital Hospital in Peking. She said she intended to remain in the dormitory of the Working Women's Unit and go on knitting.

It was late at night when we crossed Dalian to get to the harbor, where I intended to take the ship to Yantai. We passed through the old bourgeois suburbs that had been built by the Japanese and the Russians. On the sloping streets of these neighborhoods there were seedy semidetached villas and stucco bungalows under the bare trees. I had not seen anything quite like them in China. They were appropriate to the suburban streets, the picket fences and the brick walls; and then I saw the laundry in the front yards and the Chinese at the windows.

I often passed down streets like this, seeing big gloomy villas with gables and jutting eaves and mullioned windows, but always in nightmares. They were the sort of houses which first looked familiar in the dream, and then I saw evil faces at the windows, and I realized that I was no longer safe. How often in nightmares I had been chased down streets like these.

"I am sorry to see you go," Cherry Blossom said, when we arrived at the boat.

She was the only person in China who ever said that to me. In her old-fashioned way, with her old-fashioned clichés, she was very nice. I wished her well and we shook hands. I wanted to tell her that I was grateful to her for looking after me. I started to say it but she cut me off.

"Keep the wind at your back, Paul," she said, and giggled again, delighted with her own audacity.

Driving to Tibet

GOLMUD WAS HARDLY A TOWN. IT WAS A DOZEN WIDELY scattered low buildings, some radio antennas, a water tower. One of the few cars in town was Mr. Fu's ridiculous Galant: there were some buses, but they were the most punished-looking vehicles I had seen in China—and no wonder, for they toiled up and down the Tibetan Plateau.

"Snow," Mr. Fu said—his first word.

I had not expected this snow, and it was clear from his gloomy tone that neither had he. The snow lay thinly in the town, but behind the town it was deep and dramatic— blazing in the shadows of the mountain range.

He said, "We cannot go to Lhasa tomorrow. Maybe the day after, or the day after that, or—"

I asked him why.

"The snow. It is everywhere—very deep," he said. He was driving fast through the rutted Golmud streets—too fast, but I had seen him drive in Xining and I knew this to be normal. At the best of times he was a rather frantic driver. "The snow is blocking the road."

"You are sure?"

"Yes."

"Did you see it?"

He laughed: *Ha-ha! You idiot!* "Look at it!"

"Did anyone tell you that the road was blocked with snow?"

He did not reply, so that meant no. We continued this sparring. The snow was bad news—it glittered, looking as though it were there forever. But surely someone had a road report?

"Is there a bus station in Golmud?"

He nodded. He hated my questions. He wanted to be in charge, and how could he be if I was asking all the questions? And he had so few answers.

"People say the road is bad. Look at the snow!"

"We will ask at the bus station. The bus drivers will know."

"First we go to the hotel," he said, trying to take command.

The hotel was another prison-like place with cold corridors and squawks and odd hours. I had three cactuses in my room, and a calendar and two armchairs. But there were no curtains on the windows, and there was no hot water. "Later," they said. The lobby was wet and dirty from the mud that had been tracked in. An ornamental pond behind the hotel was filled with green ice, and the snow was a foot deep on the path to the restaurant. I asked about food. "Later," they said. Some of the rooms had six or eight bunk beds. Everyone inside wore a heavy coat and fur hat, against the cold. Why hadn't my cactus plants died? The hotel cost $9 for a double room, and $2 for food.

"Now we go to the bus station," I said.

Mr. Fu said nothing.

"We will ask someone about the snow."

I had been told that buses regularly plied between Golmud and Lhasa, especially now that there were no flights—the air service to Tibet had been suspended. Surely one of these bus drivers would put us in the picture.

We drove to the bus station. On the way, I could see that Golmud was the ultimate Chinese frontier town, basically a military camp, with a few shops, a market, and wide streets. There were very few buildings, but since they were not tall, they seemed less of a disfigurement. It was a place of pioneers—of volunteers who had come out in the 1950s, as they had in Xining. They had been encouraged by Mao to develop the poor and empty parts of China; and of course, Tibet had to be invaded and subdued, and that was impossible without reliable supply lines—settlements, roads, telegraph wires, barracks. First the surveyors and engineers came, then the railway people and the soldiers, and then the teachers and traders.

"What do you think of Golmud, Mr. Fu?"

"Too small," he said, and laughed, meaning the place was insignificant.

At the bus station we were told that the snow wasn't bad on the road. A Tibetan bus had arrived just that morning—it was late, of course, but it was explained that all the buses were late, even when there was no snow.

I said, "We will go tomorrow, but we will leave early. We will drive until noon. If the snow is bad we will turn back and try again another day. If it looks okay we will go on."

There was no way that he could disagree with this, and it had the additional merit of being a face-saving plan.

We had a celebratory dinner that night—wood-ear fungus, noodles, yak slices, and the steamed buns called *mantou* that Mr. Fu said he could not live without (he had a supply for the trip to Tibet). There was a young woman at the table, sharing our meal. She said nothing until Mr. Fu introduced her.

"This is Miss Sun."

"Is she coming with us?"

"Yes. She speaks English."

Mr. Fu, who spoke no English at all, was convinced that Miss Sun was fluent in English. But at no point over the next four or five days was I able to elicit any English at all from Miss Sun. Occasionally she would say a Chinese word and ask me its English equivalent.

"How do you say *luxing* in English?"

"Travel."

Then her lips trembled and she made a choking sound, *"Trow."*

And, just as quickly, she forgot even that inaccurate little squawk.

Over the dinner, I said, "What time are we leaving tomorrow?"

"After breakfast," Mr. Fu said.

The maddening Chinese insistence on mealtimes.

"We should get an early start, because the snow will slow us down."

"We can leave at nine."

"The sun comes up at six-thirty or seven. Let's leave then."

"Breakfast," Mr. Fu said, and smiled.

We both knew that breakfast was at eight. Mr. Fu was demanding his full hour, too. I wanted to quote a Selected Thought of Mao about being flexible, meeting all obstacles and overcoming them by strength of will. But I couldn't think of one. Anyway, a Mao Thought would have cut no ice with young, skinny, frantic Mr. Fu, who played Beethoven and wore driving gloves and had a freeloading girlfriend. He was one of the new Chinese. He even had a pair of sunglasses.

"We can buy some food and eat it on the way," I said, as a last desperate plea for an early start.

"I must eat *mantou* when it is hot," Mr. Fu said.

That annoyed me, and I was more annoyed the next morning when at half past nine I was still waiting for Mr.

Fu, who was himself waiting for a receipt for his room payment. At last, near ten, we left, and I sat in the back seat, wishing I were on a train, and feeling sour at the prospect of spending the whole trip staring at the back of Miss Sun's head.

Lhasa was a thousand miles away.

Looking toward Tibet I had a glimpse of a black and vaporous steam locomotive plowing through a dazzling snowfield under the blue summits and buttresses of the Tanggula Shan. It was one of the loveliest things I saw in China—the chugging train in the snowy desert, the crystal mountains behind it, and the clear sky above.

Mr. Fu, I could see, was terrified of the snow. He did not know its effect firsthand. He had only heard scare stories. That was why he had wanted to stay in Golmud for another week, until the snow melted. He believed that there was no way through it. But the snow was not bad.

In the first passes, so narrow they were nearly always in shadow, there was ice. Mr. Fu took his time. He was a poor driver—that had been obvious in the first five minutes of driving with him—but the snow and ice slowed him and made him careful. The icy stretches looked dangerous, but by creeping along (and trying to ignore the precipitous drop into the ravine by the roadside), we managed. For miles there was slippery snow, but this too Mr. Fu negotiated. Two hours passed in this way. It was a lovely sunny day, and where the sun had struck it, some of the snow had melted. But we were climbing into the wind, and even this sun could not mask the fact that it was growing colder as we gained altitude.

We passed the first range of mountains, and behind them—though it was cold—there was less snow than on the Golmud side. Mr. Fu began to increase his speed. Whenever he saw a dry patch of road, he floored it and sped onward, slowing only when more snow or ice appeared. Twice he hit sudden frost heaves, and I was thrown out of my seat and bumped my head.

"Sorry!" Mr. Fu said, still speeding.

I sipped tea from my thermos and passed cassettes to Miss Sun, who fed them into the machine. After a hundred miles we had finished with Brahms. I debated whether to hand her the Beethoven symphonies, as I listened to Mendelssohn. I drank green tea and looked at the sunny road and snowy peaks and listened to the music, and I congratulated myself on contriving this excellent way of going to Lhasa.

There was another frost heave.

"Sorry!"

He was an awful driver. He ground the gears when he set off, he gave the thing too much gas, he steered jerkily, he went too fast; and he had what is undoubtedly the worst habit a driver can have—but one that is common in China: going downhill he always switched off the engine and put the gears into neutral, believing that he was saving gas.

I am not a retiring sort of person, and yet I said nothing. A person who is driving a car is in charge, and if you are a passenger you generally keep your mouth shut. I had an urge to say something and yet I thought: *It's going to be a long trip—no sense spoiling it at the outset with an argument.* And I wanted to see just how bad a driver Mr. Fu was.

I soon found out.

He was rounding bends at such speed that I found myself clutching the door handle in order to prevent myself from being thrown across the seat. I could not drink my tea without spilling it. He was doing ninety—I could not tell whether the dial said kilometers or miles per hour, but did it matter? And yet if I said slow down, he would lose face, his pride would be hurt, and wasn't it true that he had got us through the snow? It was now about noon, with a dry road ahead. At this rate we would get to our first destination, the town of Amdo, before nightfall.

"Play this one, Miss Sun."

Miss Sun took the Chinese cassette of Beethoven's Ninth Symphony. She rammed it into the machine and the first few bars played. The sun was streaming through the windows. The sky was clear and blue, and the ground was gravelly beneath the gray hills. There were snowy peaks to the left and right of us, just peeping over the hills. We were approaching a curve. I was a little anxious but otherwise very happy on the highest road in the world, the way to Lhasa. It was a beautiful day.

I remembered all of this clearly, because it was about two seconds later that we crashed.

There was a culvert on the curve, and a high bump in the road that was very obvious. But Mr. Fu was doing ninety, and when he hit the bump, we took off—the car leaped, I felt weightless, and when we came twisting down we were heading into an upright stone marker on the right. Mr. Fu was snatching at the steering wheel. The car skidded and changed direction, plunging to the left-hand side of the road. All this time I was aware of wind rushing against the car, a noise like a jet stream. That increased and so did the shaking of the car as it became airborne again and plowed into a powerful wind composed of dust and gravel. We had left the road and were careering sideways into the desert. Mr. Fu was battling with the wheel as the car was tossed. My clearest memory was of the terrific wind pressing against the twisted car, the windows darkened by flying dust, and of a kind of suspense. In a moment, I thought, we were going to smash and die.

I was hanging on to the door handle. My head was jammed against the front seat. I was afraid that if I let go I would be thrown out the opposite door. I thought I heard Miss Sun screaming, but the car noise and the wind were much louder.

This went on for perhaps seven seconds. That is an achingly long time in a skidding car; terror has everything to do with time passing. I had never felt so helpless or so doomed.

So I was surprised when the car finally stopped. It was on its side. Only the deep gravelly sand had prevented it from turning over completely. I had to push the door with my shoulder to open it. The dust was still settling. The rear tire on my side of the car had been torn off, and I could hear it hissing.

I staggered away to be as far as possible from the Galant and saw Mr. Fu and Miss Sun gasping and coughing. Miss Sun was twitching. Mr. Fu looked stunned and sorrowful because he saw the damage to the car. All its chrome had been torn off, the grille was smashed, the wheel rim twisted, the doors smashed, and we were fifty yards from the road, sunk in desert gravel. It seemed incredible that the sun was still shining.

Mr. Fu laughed. It was a cough of blind fear that meant, *God, what now?*

No one spoke. We were wordlessly hysterical that we had survived. Mr. Fu tramped over to me and smiled and touched my cheek. There was blood on his finger. I had got out of the car not knowing whether I was hurt—I suspected I might have been. But I checked myself. My glasses had smashed and dug into my cheek, but the wound was not bad—anyway, not too deep. I had a bump on my forehead. My neck ached. My wrist hurt. But I was all right.

It infuriated me that this had happened on a dry road, under sunny skies, so early in the trip. Now we were stuck, and it was all because of the incompetence of Mr. Fu. He had been driving too fast. But it was also my own fault for having said nothing.

Mr. Fu had unpacked a shovel and was digging around the car. What good was that? We could not go anywhere on three wheels. It seemed hopeless. I debated whether to grab my bag and start hitchhiking, but in which direction? Mr. Fu had got himself into this mess; he could get himself out of it. I could not imagine how this car could ever be dragged onto the road. I looked around and thought: *This is one of the emptiest places in the world.*

We took turns digging for a while, but this merely seemed a cosmetic endeavor, unearthing the car. And the more we saw of the car, the more wrecked it seemed.

Some brown trucks were laboring slowly down the road. We had passed them hours ago.

"Let's stop them," I said.

"No," Mr. Fu said.

Chinese pride. He shook his head and waved me away. He knew they were Tibetans. What a loss of face for him if these savages witnessed this piece of stupid driving. He had no excuses.

"Come back," Mr. Fu said. "Help me dig."

But I did not turn. I was waving to the approaching

trucks, and I was delighted to see them slowing down. It was a three-truck convoy, and when they parked, the Tibetans came flapping slowly through the desert, laughing with pleasure at the tipped-over car and Mr. Fu on his knees digging. There were seven Tibetans. They looked very greasy in their old clothes, but I was reassured by their laughter and their squashed hats and their broken shoes: their ordinariness gave them the look of rescuers.

I dug out my "List of Useful Tibetan Phrases" and consulted it. I said, *"Tashi deleg!"* (Hello—Good luck!)

They returned the greeting and laughed some more.

I pointed to the car. *"Yappo mindoo."* (That is not good.)

They nodded and replied. True, they were saying. That's not good at all.

"Nga Amayriga nay ray," I said. (I'm an American.)

They said, *"Amayriga, Amayriga!"*

I looked at my list again and put my finger on a phrase. I said, *"Nga Lhasa la drogi yin."* (I am going to Lhasa.)

By now one of them had taken the shovel from Mr. Fu, and another was digging with his hands. One was unloading the trunk—pulling boxes out, unbolting the spare tire. Several of them were touching the wound on my face and going *tsk, tsk.*

"Want a picture of the Dalai Lama?" I said.

They nodded. Yes, yes!

The others heard. They said, "Dalai Lama, Dalai Lama!"

They dropped what they were doing and surrounded me as I pulled out the roll of portraits I had brought for just such an emergency. They were tough men, but they took the pictures with great gentleness and reverence, each one touching the paper to his head and bowing to me. They marveled at the pictures, while Mr. Fu and Miss Sun stood to the side, sulking.

"Everyone gets a picture," I said. "Now you have a nice portrait of the Dalai Lama. You are very happy, right?"— they laughed, hearing me jabber in English—"And you want to help us. Now let's straighten that axle, and get the wheel on, and push this goddamned car back onto the road."

It took less than half an hour for them to fix the wheel

and dig out the car, and then, with eight of us pushing and
Mr. Fu gunning the engine, we flopped and struggled until
the car was back on the road. As the wheels spun and everyone became covered with dust, I thought: *I love these
people.*

Afterward they showed me little pictures of the Dalai
Lama and the Panchen Lama on the sun visors in the cabs
of their trucks.

"Dalai Lama, Dalai Lama," they chanted.

Mr. Fu thanked them in Chinese. It meant that he had to
swallow his pride to do that. They didn't care. They
laughed at him and waved him away.

It was now early afternoon. It had all been a shock, and
yet I was encouraged because we had survived it. It seemed
miraculous that we were still alive. But Mr. Fu said nothing. When we set off again, he seemed both dazed and
frenzied. His glasses had broken in the crash, and I could
see that he was wild-eyed. He was also very dirty. Miss
Sun was sniffing, whimpering softly.

The car was in miserable shape. It looked the way I felt.
I was surprised that it had restarted; I was amazed that its
four wheels were turning. That is another way of saying
that it seemed logical to me, a few minutes after we set off
again, that a great screeching came from the back axle. It
was the sort of sound that made me think that the car was
about to burst apart.

We stopped. We jacked up the car. We took a back wheel
off to have a closer look. The brakes were twisted, and
pieces of metal were protruding into the rim. At low speeds
this made a clackety-clack, and faster it rose to a shriek.
There was no way to fix it. We put the wheel back on, and
while Mr. Fu tightened the nuts, I looked around. I had
never in my life seen such light—the sky was like a radiant
sea, and at every edge of this blasted desert with its leathery plants were strange gray hills and snowy peaks. We
were on the plateau. It was a world I had never seen
before—of emptiness and wind-scoured rocks and dense
light. I thought: *If I have to be stranded anywhere, this is
the place I want it to be.* I was filled with joy at the thought

of being abandoned there, at the edge of the Tibetan Plateau.

"I think it is heating up," Mr. Fu said, after he had driven a hundred yards down the road.

He was breathing hard and noisily through his nose. He slammed on the brakes, ran around to the back wheel, and spat on the rim. It wasn't frustration. It was his way of determining how hot the hub was.

"It is very high here!" he cried. There was dust on his face. His hair was bristly. His color had changed, too. He looked ashen.

After that, we kept stopping. The wheel noise was dreadful. But that was not the worst of it. Mr. Fu's driving changed. Usually he went fast—and then I told him clearly to slow down. (*No one will ever make me sit still in a speeding car again*, I thought: *I will always protest*.) Mr. Fu's overcareful slow driving unnerved me almost as much as his reckless driving.

This did not last long. We came to a pass that linked the Tanggula Shan with the Kunlun Shan. It was a Chinese belief that in a valley nearby there was a trickle that rose and became the great brown torrent that ended in Shanghai, the Great River that only foreigners know as the Yangtze. The river is one of the few geographical features that the Chinese are genuinely mystical about. But they are not unusual in that. Most people are bewitched by big rivers.

This pass was just under seventeen thousand feet. Mr. Fu stopped the car, and I got out and looked at a stone tablet that gave the altitude and mentioned the mountains. The air was thin, I was a bit breathless, but the landscape was dazzling—the soft contours of the plateau, and the long folded stretches of snow, like beautiful gowns laid out all over the countryside, a gigantic version of the way Indians set out their laundry to dry. I was so captivated by the magnificence of the place I didn't mind the discomfort of the altitude.

"Look at the mountains, Mr. Fu."

"I don't feel well," he said, not looking up. "It's the height."

He rubbed his eyes. Miss Sun was still whimpering. Would she scream in a minute?

I got in and Mr. Fu drove fifty yards. His driving had worsened. He was in the wrong gear, the gearbox was hiccuping, and still the rear wheel made its hideous ratcheting.

Without warning, he stopped in the middle of the road and gasped, "I cannot drive anymore!"

He wasn't kidding. He looked ill. He kept rubbing his eyes.

"I can't see! I can't breathe!"

Miss Sun burst into tears.

I thought: *Oh, shit.*

"What do you want to do?" I asked.

He shook his head. He was too ill to contemplate the question.

I did not want to hurt his pride, especially here at a high altitude, so I said carefully, "I know how to drive a car."

"You do?" He blinked. He was very thin. He looked like a starving hamster.

"Yes, yes," I said.

He gladly got into the back. Miss Sun hardly acknowledged the fact that I was now sitting beside her. I took the wheel and off we went. In the past few hours the ridiculous little Nipponese car had been reduced to a jalopy. It was dented; it made a racket; it smoked; and the most telling of its jalopy features was that it sagged to one side—whether it was a broken spring or a cracked axle I didn't know. It had received a mortal blow, but it was still limping along. I had to hold tight to the steering wheel. The sick car kept trying to steer itself into the ditch on the right-hand side of the road.

Mr. Fu was asleep.

Miss Sun, too, was asleep. I pushed in Beethoven's Symphony No. 6 and continued toward Lhasa. I liked this. I liked listening to music. I liked the fact that the other passengers were asleep. I loved the look of Tibet. I might have died back there on the road, but I was alive. It was wonderful to be alive and doing the driving.

There were no people here that I could see. But there were yaks grazing on some of the hillsides—presumably the herds of the nomadic tent-dwelling Tibetans who were said to roam this part of the province. The yaks were black and brown, and some had white patches. They were ornamented with ribbons in their long hair, and they all had lovely tails, as thick as any horse's. In some places, herds of Tibetan gazelles grazed near the road.

Mr. Fu slept on, but Miss Sun woke up, and before I could change the cassette, she slipped in one of her own. It was the sound track of an Indian movie, in Hindi, but the title song was in English.

> I am a disco dancer!
> I am a disco dancer!

This imbecilic chant was repeated interminably with twanging from an electric guitar.

"That is Indian music," I said. "Do you like it?"

"I love it," Miss Sun said.

"Do you understand the words?"

"No," she said. "But it sounds nice."

At about four we were almost out of gas. Mr. Fu said he had spare gas in the trunk, in big cans, but just as I noticed the fuel gauge, we approached a small settlement.

"Stop here," Mr. Fu said.

He directed me to a shack, which turned out to be a gas station—old-fashioned gas nozzles on long hoses. It was, like all gas stations in Tibet, run by the People's Liberation Army.

"We should get the tire fixed, too."

Mr. Fu said, "No. They don't fix tires."

In Xining I had asked Mr. Fu to bring two spares. He had brought one, and it was being used. So we were traveling without a spare.

"Where will we get the tire fixed?"

He pointed vaguely down the road, toward Lhasa. It meant he didn't have the slightest idea.

I walked over to the soldier filling the tank.

"Where are we?"

"This is Wudaoliang."

Names look so grand on a map. But this place hardly

justified being on a map. How could a gas station, some barracks, and a barbed-wire fence even deserve a name? And the name was bad news, because Wudaoliang was not even halfway to our destination, which was Amdo.

As if to make the moment operatic, the weather suddenly changed. A wind sprang up, clouds tumbled across the sun, and the day grew very dark and cold. My map was flapping against the car roof. It would be night soon.

"When will we get to Amdo, Mr. Fu?"

"About six o'clock."

Wrong, of course. Mr. Fu's calculations were wildly inaccurate. I had stopped believing that he had ever been on this road before. It was possible that my map was misleading—it had shown roads that didn't exist, and settlements that were no more than ruins and blowing sand.

Mr. Fu had no map. He had a scrap of paper with seven towns scribbled on it, the stops between Golmud and Lhasa. The scrap of paper had become filthy from his repeatedly consulting it. He consulted it again.

"The next town is Yanshiping."

We set off. I drove; Mr. Fu dozed.

Miss Sun played "I Am a Disco Dancer."

After an hour we passed a hut, some yaks, and a ferocious dog.

"Yanshiping?"

"No."

In the fading light and freezing air this plateau no longer seemed romantic. "This country makes the Gobi seem fertile in comparison," a French traveler once wrote. It was true. *Moonscape* is the word most often applied to such a place, but this was beyond a moonscape—it was another universe entirely.

There were more settlements ahead. They were all small and all the same: huts with stained whitewashed square walls, flat roofs, and red, blue, and green pennants and flags with mantras written on them, flying from propped-up bush branches. As these prayer flags flapped, so the mantras reverberated in the air, and grace abounded around them. There were more yaks, more fierce dogs.

"Yanshiping?"

"No."

It was nearly dark when we came to it. Yanshiping was twenty houses standing in mud on a curve in the road. There were children and dogs, yaks and goats. Several of the dogs were the biggest and fiercest I had ever seen in my life. They were Tibetan mastiffs—their Tibetan name means simply "watchdogs." They lolloped and slavered and barked horribly.

"There is nowhere to stay here," Mr. Fu said, before I could ask—I was slowing down.

"What's the next town?"

He produced his filthy scrap of paper.

"Amdo. There is a hotel at Amdo."

"How far is Amdo?"

He was silent. He didn't know. After a moment, he said, "A few hours."

Hotel is a nice word, but China had taught me to distrust it. The more usual Chinese expression was "guest house." It was the sort of place I could never identify properly. It was a hospital, a madhouse, a house, a school, a prison. It was seldom a hotel. But, whatever, I longed to be there. It was now seven-thirty. We had been on the road for ten hours.

We continued in the dark. It was snowier here, higher and colder, on a winding road that was icy in places. There was another pass, choked with ice that never melts at any time in the year because of the altitude, another seventeen-thousand-footer.

Mr. Fu woke and saw the snow.

"Road! Watch the road!" he yelled. *"Lu! Lu! Looooooo!"*

The altitude put him to sleep, but each time he woke he became a terrible nag. I began to think that perhaps many Chinese in authority were nags and bores. He kept telling me to watch the road, because he was frightened. I wanted to say, You almost got us killed, Jack, but to save his face I didn't.

I often mistook the lights of distant trucks on the far side of this defile for the lights of Amdo. There was no vegetation at this altitude, and the freezing air was clear. In the darkness I saw these pinpricks of light.

"Is that Amdo?"

"Watch the road!" Mr. Fu's voice from the back seat set my teeth on edge. *Lu! Loooo!*

Now and then he would tap me on the shoulder and cry, "Toilet!"

That was the greatest euphemism of all. It was usually Miss Sun who needed to have a slash. I watched her totter to the roadside and creep into a ditch, and there just out of the wind—and it was too dark even for the yaks to see her—she found relief.

Three more hours passed in this way. I wondered whether we might not be better off just pulling off the road and sleeping in the car. Midnight on the Tibetan Plateau, in the darkness and ice and wind, was not a good time to be driving. But the problem was the narrowness of the road. There was nowhere to pull off. There was a ditch on either side. If we stopped we would be rammed by one of the big army trucks that traveled by night.

Toward midnight I saw the sign saying Amdo. In the darkness it seemed a bleak and dangerous place. I did not know then that it would look much worse in daylight.

"We are staying at the army camp," Mr. Fu said.

To save face, Mr. Fu changed places with me and drove the last twenty feet to the sentry post. Then he got out and argued with the sentry.

He returned to the car trembling.

"They are full," he said.

"What now?"

"The guest house."

Miss Sun was sobbing quietly.

We drove across a rocky field. There was no road. We came to a boarded-up house, but before we could get out, a mastiff bounded into the car lights. It had a big square head and a meaty tongue, and it was slavering and barking. It was as big as a pony, something like the Hound of the Baskervilles, but vastly more sinister.

"Are you getting out?"

"No," Mr. Fu said, hoarse with fear.

Beyond the crazed and leaping dog there were yaks sleeping, standing up.

There were more dogs. I could take the yak-meat diet; I could understand why the Tibetans didn't wash; I found the cold and the high altitude just about bearable; I could negotiate the roads. But I could not stand those fierce dogs. I was not angry or impatient. I was scared shitless.

"There is a guest house," Mr. Fu said, grinning at some dim lights ahead.

It was a dirty two-story building with bars on the windows. I guessed it was a prison, but that was all right. We checked for dogs, and while Miss Sun threw up next to the car, we went inside. A Tibetan sat on a ragged quilt on the floor, gnawing raw flesh off a yak bone. He was black with dirt, his hair was matted, he was barefoot in spite of the cold. He looked exactly like a cannibal, tearing shreds of red meat off a shank.

"We need a room," Mr. Fu said in Chinese.

The Tibetan laughed and said there was no room. He chewed with his mouth open, showing his teeth, and then with aggressive hospitality he pushed the bone into my face and demanded I take a bite.

I took out my "List of Useful Tibetan Phrases."

"Hello. I am not hungry," I said in Tibetan. "My name is Paul. What is your name? I am from America. Where are you from?"

"Bod," the cannibal said, giving me the Tibetan name for Tibet. He was grinning at my gloves. I was cold—it was way below freezing in this room. He gestured for me to sit with him on his quilt, and in the same motion he waved Mr. Fu away.

It is a Tibetan belief that all Tibetans are descended from a sexually insatiable ogress who had six children after copulating with a submissive monkey. It is just a pretty tale, of course, but looking at this man it was easy to see how the myth might have originated.

He batted away Mr. Fu's identity card, but he took a great interest in my passport. Then he put his juicy bone down and fingered the pages, leaving bloodstains on them. He laughed at my passport picture. He compared the picture with my gray, frozen face and the wound under my eye. He laughed again.

"I agree. It's not a very good likeness."

He became very attentive, hearing English spoken, like a dog listening to footsteps in the driveway.

"Do you have rooms?" I asked. I held out a picture of the Dalai Lama.

He mumbled a reply. His shaven head and big jaw made him look ape-like. I switched to Chinese, because I couldn't understand what he was saying. He took the picture gently.

"One person—six yuan," he said, clutching the portrait.

"Oh, thank you, thank you," Mr. Fu said, abasing himself.

"Tea, tea," the cannibal said, offering me a tin kettle.

I drank some salty, buttery tea, and as I did, a truck pulled up outside. Twelve Tibetans, women and children, entered the room, went into the corridor, threw quilts on the floor, and fell on them.

I paid my money, got my bag from the car, and found an empty room on the second floor. The light on the stairwell had shown me what sort of place it was. Someone had vomited on the landing. The vomit was frozen. There was worse farther on, against the wall. It was all icy, and so the smell wasn't bad. It was very dirty, a bare cement interior that was grimmer than any prison I had ever seen. But the real prison touch was that all the lights were on—not many of them, but all bare bulbs. There were no light switches. There were howls and murmurs from the other rooms. There was no water, and no bathroom. No toilet except the stairwell.

Not far away I heard Miss Sun berating Mr. Fu in an exasperated and whining sick person's voice. I closed the door. There was no lock. I jammed an iron bed against it. There were three iron bedsteads in the room, and some reeking quilts.

I realized that I was shivering. I was cold, but I was also hungry. I ate half a jar of Ma Ling orange segments, and a banana, and I made tea from the hot water in the jug I had brought. I was light-headed and somewhat breathless from the altitude, and also nauseated from the frosty vomit in the corridors. Just as I finished eating, all the lights went out: midnight.

I put on my gloves, my hat, my extra sweater, my coat, and my third pair of socks and thermal-lined shoes, and went to bed. I had been cold in my life, but I had never worn a hat with earmuffs to bed before. I had a quilt over me and a quilt under me. Even so, I could not get warm. I could not understand why. My heart palpitated. My toes were numb. I tried to imagine what it must be like to be Chris Bonington, climbing Menlungtse near Everest. After a while I could see moonlight behind the thick frost on the window.

In the middle of the night I got up to piss. I used an enamel basin that I guessed was a chamber pot. In the morning the piss was frozen solid. So were the rest of my orange segments. So were my quails' eggs. Everything that I had that could freeze had frozen.

I had hardly slept, but I was gladdened by the sunlight. I found some peanuts and ate them. I ate my frozen banana. I visited the cannibal (he looked even dirtier in daylight) and drank some of my own tea with him. He did not want Chinese tea. He made a face as if to say, *Disgusting stuff! How can you drink it?*

The frail warmth of the morning sun only made the place worse by wakening the stinks on the stairs and in the corridors. There were dark clumps and little twists of human shit throughout the building. In this heavenly country, this toilet.

Mr. Fu was up and fussing. He said Miss Sun was not at all well. And he felt sick, too.

"Then let's go," I said.

"Breakfast first."

"Oh, God!"

Another late start. But this time I did calculations on my map, estimated the distances between towns, figured an average speed, and felt much better until I remembered the tire.

"Did you get the spare tire fixed, Mr. Fu?"

He had said that he would do it this morning, before

breakfast. Although Amdo was a dump, there were garages here, and it was the only place of any size for miles.

"No. Better to get the tire fixed in Nagqu."

That was over a hundred miles away.

Mr. Fu took the wheel. A few miles down the road he stopped the car and clawed at his face.

"I cannot do it!" he shrieked. In Chinese it sounded like a pitiful surrender.

It was another attack of the wobblies. I welcomed it; I soothed Mr. Fu as he crept into the back seat. I slotted Brahms into the cassette player and drove south, under sunny skies.

I was feeling wonky myself. I had a bump on my head, a neck ache, and a deep cut on my face from the car crash. My right wrist hurt, probably a sprain, from my holding on during our careering. And the altitude affected me, too—I felt light-headed and nauseated, and my short walk in Amdo had given me heart palpitations. But this was nothing compared with Mr. Fu's agony. The color had drained from his face, his mouth gaped, and after a while he simply swooned. Miss Sun also went to sleep. Crumpled together on the seat, they looked like poisoned lovers in a suicide pact.

There were no more settlements until Nagqu, nothing except the windswept tableland, and it was so cold that even the *drongs*, the wild yaks, were squinting and the herds of wild asses did nothing but raise their heads and stare at the badly damaged Mitsubishi Galant. After a few hours the road ran out and was no more than loose rocks and boulders, and more wild asses. The boulders clunked against the chassis and hammered the tires. We had no spare tire. We were ridiculously unprepared for Tibet, but I did not mind very much. I felt, having survived that crash, that we had come through the worst of it. There is something about the very fact of survival that produces a greater vitality. And I knew I was much safer as long as I was driving. Mr. Fu was not really very good at all, and as a nervous new driver, he had no business to be in Tibet.

On some hillsides there were huts flying colored prayer flags. I was cheered by them, by the whiteness of whitewashed huts, by the smoke coming out of the chimneys, and by the clothes that people wore—fox-fur hats, silver buckles, sheepskin coats, big warm boots. Miles from any-where I saw a mother and daughter in bright, blowing skirts and bonnets climbing a cliffside path, and a handsome herdsman sitting among his yaks, wearing a wonderful red hat with huge earflaps.

Mr. Fu was very annoyed that there was nowhere to eat at Nagqu. He was stiff and cranky from the altitude, and re-luctant to stay, but I pestered him into finding someone to fix the spare. This was done in a shed, with fires and chis-els; and while this primitive vulcanizing went on, I walked around the town. John Avedon's *In Exile from the Land of Snows* (1984), which is mainly an anti-Chinese account of the recent turmoil in Tibet, and pleasantly passionate on the subject of the Dalai Lama, claims that Nagqu is the center of the Chinese nuclear industry. The gaseous diffusion plants, the warhead assembly plants, and the research labs have been moved here from the Lop Nor Desert. Some-where in this vicinity—though you'd never know it from looking at it—there was a large repository of medium-range and intermediate-range nuclear missiles. But all I saw were yaks.

Mr. Fu drove us out of Nagqu—perhaps a face-saving gesture, because a mile outside town he stopped the car and clutched his eyes.

"I cannot do it!"

And he slumped in the back seat.

I was happier than I had been since starting this trip on the Iron Rooster. I was driving, I was in charge, I was tak-ing my time, and Tibet was empty. The weather was dramatic—snow on the hills, a high wind, and black clouds, piled up on the mountains ahead.

Today, below the snowy and majestic Nyenchen Tanglha Range, nomads rode among their herds of yak, and the road was straight through the yellow plain. That tame road con-tributed to my feeling of well-being—it was wonderful to be in such a remote place and yet to feel so secure. Mr. Fu and Miss Sun were asleep in the back seat. There were no other cars on the road. I drove at a sensible speed toward

Lhasa and watched the birds—hawks and plovers and crows. There were more gazelles, and once a pale yellow fox bounded across the road.

There was a sudden snowstorm. I went from a dry sunny valley, around a corner, into a black slushy one, the large cottony flakes whipping sideways. Mr. Fu, who was terrified of snow, mercifully did not wake. The snow eased; it became a dry flurry in a valley farther ahead, and then the sun came out again. Tibetans call their country "Land of Snows," but in fact it doesn't snow much and it never rains. The gales pass quickly. The Tibetans are not bothered by any of this. I saw children playing in the sudden storm.

I had wanted at the outset to reach Lhasa quickly. But now I didn't mind a delay. I would gladly have spent more nights on the road, provided it was not in a place like the dump at Amdo.

Damxung looked promising. It was at a bend in the road; there was an army camp nearby, and half a dozen one-room restaurants. We stopped and had four dishes, which included wood-ear fungus and yak meat, and Mr. Fu revived enough to accuse the serving girl of overcharging him—or rather me, since I paid the bill.

There were six soldiers in the kitchen, warming themselves, but they fluttered away when I tried to talk with them. Travelers in China had sometimes told me that they were harassed by soldiers or officials. This was never my experience. When I approached them they always backed away.

I found Mr. Fu spitting on the wheel to see whether it was overheated. He was kneeling, spitting, smearing, examining.

"I think we should stay here," I said.

We were watched by a small boy who had a playing-card-sized picture of the Dalai Lama tucked into the front of his fur hat. When I peered at him he ran away and returned without the picture.

"We cannot stay here. Miss Sun is sick. Lhasa is only one hundred and seventy kilometers."

"Do you feel well enough to drive?"

"I am fine!"

But he looked terrible. His face was gray. He had not eaten much. He had told me he had a pain in his heart. He also said that his eyes hurt.

"This wheel is not hot," he said. "That is good."

He gasped and gave up at a place called Baicang, saying he could not do it. I took over, and in a pretty place on a riverbank called Yangbajain, we entered a narrow, rocky valley. It was the sort of valley I had been expecting ever since Golmud. I had not realized that this part of Tibet was open country, with flat, straight roads and distant snowy peaks. But this valley was steep and cold, and half in darkness it was so deep. A river ran swiftly through it, with birds darting from one wet boulder to another. I saw from my bird book that they were thrushes, and the commonest was the White-winged Redstart.

When we emerged from this valley we were higher, and among steep mountainsides and bluer, snowier peaks. We traveled along this riverside in a burst of evening sunshine. Farther south, this little river became the mighty Brahmaputra. The valley opened wider, became sunnier and very dry; and beyond the beautiful bare hills of twinkling scree there were mountains covered with frothy snow.

Ahead was a small town. I took it to be another garrison town, but it was Lhasa, for sure. In the distance was a red and white building with sloping sides—the Potala, so lovely, somewhat like a mountain and somewhat like a music box with a hammered gold lid.

I had never felt happier, rolling into a town. I decided to pay off Mr. Fu. I gave him my thermos bottle and the remainder of my provisions. He seemed embarrassed. He lingered a little. Then he reached out and put his fingers on my cheek, where there was the wound from the crash. It was scabby, the blood had dried, it looked awful, but it didn't hurt.

"I am sorry," Mr. Fu said. He laughed. It was an abject apology. His laughter said, *Forgive me!*

Lhasa

IT IS IMMEDIATELY OBVIOUS THAT LHASA IS NOT A CITY. IT IS a small friendly-looking town on a high plain surrounded by even higher mountains. There is very little traffic. There are no pavements. Everyone walks in the street. No one runs. These streets are at twelve thousand feet. You can hear children yelling and dogs barking and bells being rung, and so it seems a quiet place. It is rather dirty and very sunny. Just a few years ago the Chinese bulldozed the Chorten, a stupa which formed the entrance to the city. It was their way of violating Lhasa, which had always been forbidden to foreigners. Even so, it is not crowded. The Chinese badly damaged Lhasa and hoped to yank the whole thing down and build a city of fine ugly factories. But they did not succeed in destroying it. Much of it, and some of its finest shrines, were made out of mud bricks—easily broken but cheap to replace, like the Buddhist statues that were made anew every few years, or the yak butter sculptures that were expected to go rancid or melt in order for new ones to be fashioned. The whole of Buddhism prepared the Tibetans for cycles of destruction and rebirth: it is a religion that brilliantly teaches continuity. You can easily see the violence of the Chinese intention in Lhasa, but it was a failure, because the Tibetans are indestructible.

Lhasa is a holy place, so it is populated by pilgrims. They give it color, and because they are strangers themselves to Lhasa they don't object to foreign travelers—in fact, they welcome them and try to sell them beads and trinkets. Chinese cities are notorious for their noise and crowds. Lhasa has a small population, and because it is flat it is full of cyclists. To me that was a complete surprise. I had expected a dark, craggy city of steepnesses and fortifications overrun by Chinese and hung with slogans. I found a bright little war-torn town full of jolly monks and friendly pilgrims and dominated by the Potala, which is an ingenious and distracting shape.

Half the population of Lhasa is Chinese, but those who are not soldiers tend to stay indoors, and even the soldiers of the People's Liberation Army keep a low profile. They know that Tibet is essentially a gigantic army camp—the roads, the airports, and all the communications were a military effort—and they know that the Tibetans resent it. The Chinese feel insecure in Tibet, and so they retreat into a sort of officiousness; they look like commissars and imperialists but their swagger is mostly bravado. They know they are in a foreign country. They don't speak the language and they have not managed to teach Chinese to the Tibetans. For over thirty years they maintained the fiction that the official language of Tibet was Chinese, but then in 1987 they caved in and changed it to Tibetan.

The Chinese imply that they have a moral right to run the Tibetans' lives, but since the late seventies, when they began to despair of political solutions to Chinese problems, they have felt more uneasy about being in Tibet. They have no right to be there at all. The Tibetans themselves would probably have found a way to tax the rich families, get rid of exploiters and raise up the Ragyaba—the scavenging class and corpse handlers—and free the slaves (slavery persisted into the 1950s). But the bossy ideology of the Chinese compelled them to invade and so thoroughly meddle with the country that they alienated the majority of the population. They did not stop there. They annexed Tibet and made it part of China, and however much the Chinese talk about liberalizing their policies it is clear that they have no intention of ever allowing Tibet to become a sovereign state again.

"It feels like a foreign country," Chinese friends of mine confided to me. They were bewildered by the old-fashioned habits and clothes, and by the incomprehensible rituals of Tibetan Buddhism, celebrating the sexual mysticism of the tantric rites, and the hugging and fornicating statues illustrating the mother-father principle of *yabyum*, and the big, toothy, goggling demons that Tibetans see as protectors. Even with the Chinese watching closely and issuing decrees and building schools and initiating public works, Lhasa is a medieval-seeming place, just like Europe in the Middle Ages, complete with grinning monks and grubby peasants and open-air festivals and jugglers and tumblers. Lhasa is holy, but it is also a market town, with pushcarts and stacked-up vegetables and dirty, air-dried cuts of yak that will keep for a year (grain keeps for fifty years in the dry Tibetan climate). The most medieval touch of all is that Tibet has almost no plumbing.

The pilgrims hunker and prostrate themselves all over Lhasa, and they shuffle clockwise around every shrine. They flatten themselves on stair landings, outside the Jokhang, and all around the Potala. They do it on the road, the riverbank, the hillsides. Being Tibetan Buddhists they are good-humored, and because they are from all over Tibet, Lhasa is their meeting place—they enrich the life of the town and fill its markets. They come out of a devotion to the Dalai Lama, the incarnation of the Bodhisattva Avalokitesvara. They pray, they throw themselves to the ground, they strew tiny one-miao notes and barley grains at the shrines, and they empty blobs of yak butter into the lamps. The very pious ones blow horns made from human thigh bones—a femur like an oboe—or carry water in bowls made from the lopped-off top of a human skull. They venerate the various thrones and couches of the Dalai Lama in the Potala, and even his narrow Art Deco bed, his bathtub and toilet, his tape recorder (a gift from Nehru), and his radio. The Dalai Lama is worshipped as the Living God, but the pilgrims also pay homage to the images of Zong Kapa—founder of the Yellow Sect, and of the Lord Buddha, and other Dalai Lamas, notably the Fifth, whose great buildings dignify Lhasa. Pilgrims have made Lhasa a town of visitors who are not exactly strangers, and so even a real foreigner feels a sense of belonging there. Its chaos and dirt and its jangling bells make it seem hospitable.

Lhasa was the one place in China I eagerly entered, and enjoyed being in, and was reluctant to leave. I liked its smallness, its friendliness, the absence of traffic, the flat streets—and every street had a vista of tremendous Tibetan mountains. I liked the clear air and sunshine, the markets, the brisk trade in scarce antiques. It fascinated me to see a place for which the Chinese had no solution. They admitted that they had made grave mistakes in Tibet, but they also admitted that they did not know what to do next. They had not counted on the tenacious faith of the Tibetans, and perhaps they found it hard to believe that such dark, grinning people, who never washed, could be so passionate. The visiting party officials strolled around looking smug and hard to please. They were mostly on junkets. Tibet is a junketer's paradise: a subject people, two fairly good hotels, plenty of ceremonial functions, and so far from Peking that anything goes. The Chinese reward each other with junkets and official trips—they often take the place of bonuses—and Tibet is the ultimate junket. But it is for sight-seeing. Tibet has made no economic gains at all. It is entirely dependent on Chinese financial aid. These Chinese nearly always look physically uncomfortable in Lhasa—it is the altitude, the strange food, and the climate, but it is also the boisterous Tibetans, who seem to the Chinese a bit savage and unpredictable—superstitious primitives if not outright subhuman.

The other aspect of Lhasa—and Tibet, too—is that like Yunnan it has become the refuge of hippies. They are not the dropouts I met years ago in Afghanistan and India, but mostly middle-class, well-heeled hippies whose parents gave them the air fare to China. Some of them come by bus from Nepal. They seemed harmless to me, and they were a great deal more desirable than the rich tourists for whom Lhasa was building expensive hotels and importing ridiculous delicacies—and providing brand-new Japanese buses so that groups of tourists could set out at dawn and photograph such rituals as the Sky Burial (Tibetans deal with their dead by placing them outside for vultures to eat). As Lynn Pan remarks in her analysis of recent Chinese history, *The New Chinese Revolution*, "it is difficult to avoid the conclusion that Tibetan culture, which has survived the worst that Maoism and force could do to stamp it out, has been left to be killed by tourism." But I had my doubts. Tibet seemed too vast and inaccessible and strange for anyone to possess it. It looked wonderful to me, like the last place on earth; like a polar ice cap, but emptier.

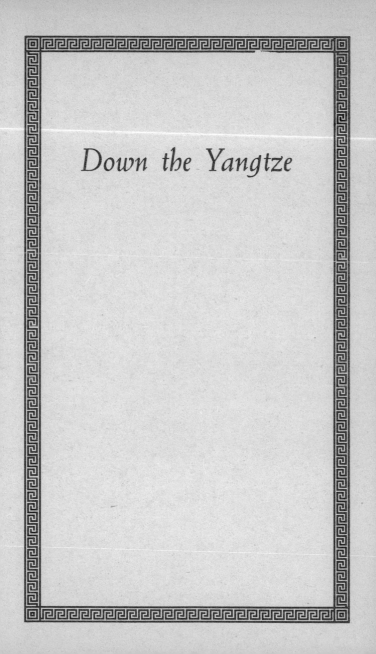

Down the Yangtze

Trackers

IT WAS NEAR CHANG SHOU, ABOUT NOON ON THAT FIRST DAY, that I saw a sailing junk steered to the bank, and the sail struck, and five men leaping onto the shore with towlines around their waists. They ran ahead, then jerked like dogs on a leash, and immediately began towing the junk against the current. These are trackers. They are mentioned by the earliest travelers on the Yangtze. They strain, leaning forward, and almost imperceptibly the sixty-foot junk begins to move upstream. There is no level towpath. The trackers are rock climbers: they scamper from boulder to boulder, moving higher until the boulders give out, and then dropping down, pulling and climbing until there is a reach on the river where the junk can sail again. The only difference—but it is a fairly large one—between trackers long ago and trackers today is that they are no longer whipped. "Often our men have to climb or jump like monkeys," wrote a Yangtze traveler, in the middle of the last century, of his trackers, "and their backs are lashed by the two chiefs, to urge them to work at critical moments. This new spectacle at first revolts and angers us, but when we see that the men do not complain about the lashings we realize that it is the custom of the country, justified by the exceptional difficulties along the route." Captain Little saw a tracker chief strip his clothes off, jump into the river, then roll himself in sand until he looked half-human, like a gritty ape; then he did a demon dance, and howled, and whipped the trackers, who—scared out of their wits—willingly pulled a junk off a sandbank.

The trackers sing or chant. There are garbled versions of what they say. Some travelers have them grunting and groaning, others are more specific and report the trackers yelling, *"Chor! Chor!"*—slang for *"Shang-chia"* or "Put your shoulder to it." I asked a boatman what the trackers were chanting. He said that they cried out, *"Hai tzo! Hai tzo!"* over and over again, which means "Number! Number!" in Szechuanese, and is uttered by trackers and oarsmen alike.

"When we institute the Four Modernizations," he added—this man was one of the minuscule number who are members of the Chinese Communist party—"there will be no more junks or trackers."

One day I was standing at the ship's rail with a man who encouraged us to call him Big Bob Brantman. We saw some trackers, six of them, pulling a junk. The men skipped from rock to rock, they climbed, they hauled the lines attached to the junk, and they struggled along the steep rocky towpath. They were barefoot.

Brantman winced. It was a wince of sagacity, of understanding: Yes, it said, I now see what this is all about. Then he spoke, still wincing a little.

"The profound cultural difference between people!"

I looked at him. He was nodding at the trackers scampering among the rocks on the shore.

"They don't care about television," he said.

I said, "That's true."

"Huh?" He was encouraged. He was smiling now. He said, "I mean, they couldn't care less if the Rams are playing tomorrow."

The Los Angeles Rams were Big Bob's favorite football team.

"Am I right, or not?"

"You're right, Bob," I said. "They don't care about television or the Rams."

The junks and these trackers will be on the river for some time to come. Stare for five minutes at any point on the Yangtze and you will see a junk, sailing upstream with its ragged, ribbed sail; or being towed by yelling, tethered men; or slipping downstream with a skinny man clinging to its rudder. There are many newfangled ships and boats on the river, but I should say that the Yangtze is a river of junks and sampans, fueled by human sweat. Still, there is nothing lovelier than a junk with a following wind (the wind blows upstream, from east to west—a piece of great meteorological luck and a shaper of Chinese history), sailing so well that the clumsy vessel looks as light as a waterbird paddling and foraging in the muddy current.

The Yangtze Gorges

IN THE DAYS THAT FOLLOWED, WE PASSED THROUGH THE gorges. Many people come to the Yangtze for the gorges alone: they excite themselves on these marvels and skip the rest of the river. The gorges are wonderful, and it is almost impossible to exaggerate their splendor, but the river is long and complicated, and much greater than its gorges, just as the Thames is more than what lies between Westminster and Greenwich.

The great gorges lie below Bai De ("White King City"), the lesser gorges just above Yichang. Bai De was as poisonous-looking as any of the other cities, but as soon as we left it the mountains rose—enormous limestone cliffs on each side of the river. There is no shore: the sheer cliffs plunge straight into the water. They were formed at the dawn of the world, when the vast inland sea in western China began to drain east and wear the mountains away. But limestone is a curious substance. It occurs in blocks, it has cracks and corners; and so the flow zigzagged, controlled by the stone, and made right angles in the river. Looking ahead through the gorges you see no exit, only the end of what looks like a blind canyon.

After seeing the great gorges of the Upper Yangtze, it is easy to believe in gods and demons and giants.

There are graffiti on the gorges. Some are political

("Mankind Unite to Smash Capitalism"), some are poetic ("Bamboos, flowers and rain purify the traveler"), while other scribbled characters give the gorge's name or its history, or they indicate a notable feature in the gorge. "Wind Box Gorge" is labeled on the limestone, and the wind boxes have painted captions. "Meng-liang's Ladder," it says, at the appropriate place. These are the zigzag holes that Captain Williamson mentioned in his notes; and they have a curious history. In the second century A.D. the Shu army was encamped on the heights of the gorge. The Hupeh general, Meng-liang, had set out to conquer this army, but they were faced with this vertical gorge wall, over seven hundred feet high. Meng-liang had his men cut the ladder holes in the stone, all the way to the top of the gorge, and his army ascended this way, and they surprised the enemy camp and overwhelmed them, ending the domination of Shu. (In 1887 Archibald Little wrote, "The days are long past since the now effeminate Chinese were capable of such exertions. . . .")

The wind blows fiercely through the gorges, as it does in New York between skyscrapers; and it is a good thing, too, because the junks can sail upstream—there is little room here for trackers. On the day I passed through, the sky was leaden, and the wind was tearing the clouds to pieces, and the river itself was yellow-brown or viscous and black, a kind of eel color. It is not only the height of the gorges but also the narrowness of the river—less than a hundred yards in places—which makes it swift, sixty meters per second in the narrower places. The scale gives it this look of strangeness, and fills it with an atmosphere of ominous splendor—the majestic cliffs, the thousand-foot gorge walls, the dagger-like pinnacles, and the dark foaming river below, and the skinny boatmen on their vessels of splinters and rags.

Archibald Little wrote, "I rejoiced that it had been my good fortune to visit the Yangtze Gorges before the coming stream of European tourists, with the inevitable introduction of Western innovation in their train, should have destroyed all their old world charm." The cities, certainly, are black and horrific, but the gorges are changeless and completely unlike anything I had ever seen before. In other landscapes I have had a sense of deterioration—the Grand Canyon looks as if it is wearing away and being sluiced, stone by orange stone, down the Colorado River. But the gorges look powerful and permanent, and make every person and artifact look puny. They will be here long after Man has destroyed himself with bombs.

It is said that every rock and cliff has a name. "The Seated Woman and the Pouncing Lion," "The Fairy Princess," and—less lyrically—"The Ox-Liver and Horse-Lung Gorge" (the organs are boulder formations, high on the cliff face). The Yangtze is a river of precise nomenclature. Only simple, wild places, like the volcanic hills of southwest Uganda, are full of nameless topography; naming is one of the features of Chinese civilization and settlement. I asked the pilot of our ship if it was so that every rock in the Yangtze had a name. He said yes.

"What is the name of that one?" I asked quickly, pointing out of the window.

"That is Pearl Number Three. Over there is Pearl Number Two. We shall be coming to Pearl Number One in a few minutes." He had not hesitated. And what was interesting was that these rocks looked rather insignificant to me.

One of the passengers said, "These gorges come up to expectations. Very few things do. The Taj Mahal did. The Pyramids didn't. But these gorges!"

We passed Wushan. There was a funeral procession making its way through the empty streets, beating drums and gongs, and at the front of the procession three people in white shrouds—white is the Chinese color of mourning—and others carrying round paper wreaths, like archery targets. And now we were in the longest gorge, twenty-five miles of cliffs and peaks, and beneath them rain-spattered junks battling the current.

At one time, this part of the Yangtze was filled with rapids. Captain Williamson's list of landmarks noted all of them. They were still in the river, breaking ships apart, in 1937. But the worst have been dynamited away. The most notorious was the Hsin Lung Tan, a low-level rapid caused by a terrific landslide in 1896. It was wild water, eighty feet wide, but blasting opened it to four hundred feet, and deepened it. Thirty years ago, only the smallest boats could travel on the river during the winter months; now it is navigable by even the largest throughout the year.

Our ship drew in below Yellow Cat Gorge, at a place called Dou Shan Tuo ("Steep Hill Village"). We walked to the road and took a bus to the top of the hill. Looking across the river at the pinnacles called "The Three Daggers," and at the sun pouring honey into the deep cliffs, one of the passengers said with gusto, "What a place for a condominium!"

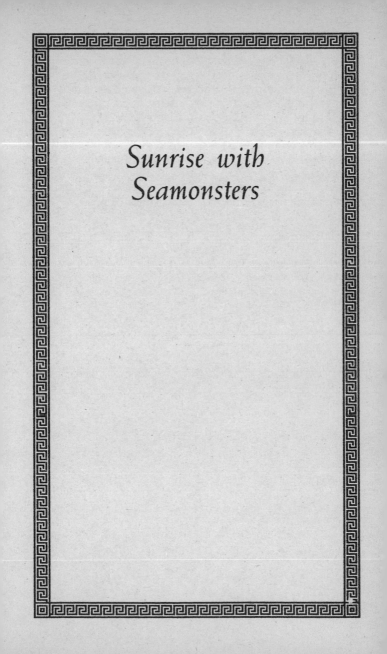

Sunrise with Seamonsters

The Edge of the Great Rift

THERE IS A CRACK IN THE EARTH THAT EXTENDS FROM THE Sea of Galilee to the coast of Mozambique, and I am living on the edge of it, in Nyasaland. This crack is the Great Rift Valley. It seems to be swallowing most of East Africa. In Nyasaland it is replacing the fishing village, the flowers, and the anthills with a nearly bottomless lake, and it shows itself in rough escarpments and troughs up and down this huge continent. It is thought that this valley was born amid great volcanic activity. The period of vulcanism had not ended in Africa. It shows itself not only in the Great Rift Valley itself, but in the people, burning, the lava of masses, the turbulence of the humans themselves who live in the Great Rift.

My schoolroom is on the Great Rift, and in this schoolroom there is a line of children, heads shaved like prisoners, muscles showing through their rags. They are waiting to peer through the tiny lens of a cheap microscope so they can see the cells in a flower petal.

Later they will ask, "Is fire alive? Is water?"

The children appear in the morning out of the slowly drifting hoops of fog wisp. It is chilly, almost cold. There is no visibility at six in the morning; only a fierce white-out where earth is the patch of dirt under their bare feet, a platform, and the sky is everything else. It becomes Africa at noon when there are no clouds and the heat is like a blazing rug thrown over everything to suffocate and scorch.

In the afternoon there are clouds, big ones, like war declared in the stratosphere. It starts to get gray as the children leave the school and begin padding down the dirt road.

There is a hill near the school. The sun approaches it by

sneaking behind the clouds until it emerges to crash into the hill and explode yellow and pink, to paint everything in its violent fire.

At night, if there is a moon, the school, the Great Rift, become a seascape of luminescent trees and grass, whispering, silver. If there is no moon you walk from a lighted house to an infinity of space, packed with darkness.

Yesterday I ducked out of a heavy downpour and waited in a small shed for the rain to let up. The rain was far too heavy for my spidery umbrella. I waited in the shed; thunder and close bursts of lightning charged all around me; the rain spat through the palm-leaf walls of the shed.

Down the road I spotted a small African child. I could not tell whether it was a boy or a girl, since it was wearing a long shirt, a yellow one, which drooped sodden to the ground. The child was carrying nothing, so I assumed it was a boy.

He dashed in and out of the puddles, hopping from side to side of the forest path, his yellow shirt bulging as he twisted under it. When he came closer I could see the look of absolute fear on his face. His only defense against the thunder and the smacking of rain were his fingers stuck firmly into his ears. He held them there as he ran.

He ran into my shed, but when he saw me he shivered into a corner where he stood shuddering under his soaked shirt. We eyed each other. There were raindrops beaded on his face. I leaned on my umbrella and fumbled a Bantu greeting. He moved against a palm leaf. After a few moments he reinserted a finger in each ear, carefully, one at a time. Then he darted out into the rain and thunder. And his dancing yellow shirt disappeared.

I stand on the grassy edge of the Great Rift. I feel it under me and I expect soon a mighty heave to send us all sprawling. The Great Rift. And whom does this rift concern? Is it perhaps a rift with the stars? Is it between earth and man, or man and man? Is there something under this African ground seething still?

We like to believe that we are riding it and that it is nothing more than an imperfection in the crust of the earth. We do not want to be captive to this rift, as if we barely belong, as if we were scrawled on the landscape by a piece of chalk.

Curfew

IT WAS NOT ODD THAT THE FIRST FEW DAYS OF OUR CURFEW were enjoyed by most people. It was a welcome change for us, like the noisy downpour that comes suddenly in January and makes a watery crackle on the street and ends the dry season. The parties, though these were now held in the afternoon, had a new topic of conversation. There were many rumors, and repeating these rumors made a kind of tennis match, a serve and return, each hit slightly more savage than the last. And the landscape of the city outside the fence of our compound was fascinating to watch. During these first days we stood in our brightly flowered shirts on our hill; we could see the palace burning, the soldiers assembling and making people scatter, and we could hear the bursts of gunfire and some shouts just outside our fence. We were teachers, all of us young, and we were in Africa. There were well-educated ones among us. One of them told me that, during the Roman Empire under the reign of Claudius, rich people and scholars could be carried in litters by *lecticarii*, usually slaves, to camp with servants at a safe distance from battles; these were curious Romans, men of high station, who, if they so wished, could be present and, between feasts, witness the slaughter.

But the curfew continued, and what were diversions for the first few days and weeks became habits. Although people usually showed up for work in the mornings, work in the afternoons almost ceased. There were too many things to be done before the curfew began at nightfall: buses had to be caught, provisions found, and some people had to collect children. We visited the bars so that we could get drunk in the company of other people; we played the slot machines and talked about the curfew, but after two weeks it was a very boring subject.

The people who never went out at night before the curfew was imposed—some Indians with large families used to matinees at the local movie houses, the Africans who did manual labor, and some settlers—felt none of the curfew's effects. And there were steady ones who refused to let the curfew get to them; they were impatient with our daily hangovers, our inefficiency, our nervous comments. Our classes were not well attended. One day I asked casually where our Congolese student was—a dashing figure, he wore a silk scarf and rode a large old motorcycle. I was told that he had been pulled off his motorcycle by a soldier and had been beaten to death with a rifle butt.

We left work early. In the afternoons it was as if everyone was on leave but couldn't afford to go to Nairobi or Mombasa, as if everyone had decided to while away his time at the local bars. At the end of the month no one was paid because the ministry was short-staffed. Some of us ran out of money. The bar owners said they were earning less and less: it was no longer possible for people to drink in bars after dark. They would only have been making the same amount as before, they said, if all the people started drinking in the middle of the morning and kept it up all day. The drinking crowd was a relatively small one, and there were no casual drinkers. Most people in the city stayed at home. They were afraid to stay out after five or so. I tried to get drunk by five-thirty. My memory is of going home drunk, with the dazzling horizontal rays of the sun in my eyes.

The dwindling of time was a strange thing. During the first weeks of the curfew we took chances; we arrived home just as the soldiers were drifting into the streets. Then we began to give ourselves more time, leaving an hour or more for going home. It might have been because we were drunker and needed more time, but we were also more worried: more people were found dead in the streets each morning when the curfew lifted. For many of us the curfew began in the middle of the afternoon when we hurried to a bar; and it was the drinkers who, soaked into a state of slow motion, took the most chances.

Different prostitutes appeared in the bars. Before the curfew there were ten or fifteen in each bar, most of them young and from the outskirts of Kampala. But the curfew was imposed after two tribes fought; most of the prostitutes had been from these tribes and so went into hiding. Others took their places. Now there were ones from the Coast, there were half-castes, Rwandans, Somalis. I remember the Somalis. There was said to be an Ethiopian at the Crested Crane, but I never saw her; in any case, she would have been very popular. All these women were old and hard, and there were fewer than before. They sat in the bars, futile and left alone, slumped on the broken chairs, waiting, as they had been waiting ever since the curfew started. Whatever other talents a prostitute may have she is still unmatched by any other person in her genius for killing time and staying on the alert for customers. The girls held their glasses in two hands and followed the stumbling drinkers with their eyes. Most of us were not interested in complicating the curfew further by taking one of these girls home. I am sure they never had to wait so long with such dull men.

One afternoon a girl put her hand on mine. Her palm was very rough; she rubbed it on my wrist and when I did not turn away she put it on my leg and asked me if I wanted to go in the back. I said I didn't mind, and she led me out past the toilets to the back of the bar where there was a little shed. She scuffed across the shed's dirt floor, then stood in a corner and lifted her skirt. Here, she said, come here. I asked her if we had to remain standing up. She said yes. I started to embrace her; she let her head fall back until it touched the wood wall. She still held the hem of her skirt in her hand. Then I said no, I couldn't nail her against the wall. I saw that the door was still open. She argued for a while and said in Swahili, "Talk, talk, we could have finished by now!" I stepped away, but gave her ten shillings just the same. She spat on it and looked at me fiercely.

Rats in Rangoon

IN ASIA A CITY SHOULD BE JUDGED NOT BY THE NUMBER OF rats scuttling in its streets but on the rats' cunning and condition. In Singapore the rats are potbellied and as sleek as housepets; they crouch patiently near noodle stalls, certain of a feed; they are quick, with bright eyes, and hard to trap.

In Rangoon I sat in an outdoor café toying with a glass of beer and heard the hedge near me rustle; four enfeebled, scabby rats, straight off the pages of *La Peste*, tottered out and looked around. I stamped my foot. They moved back into the hedge; and now everyone in the café was staring at me. It happened twice. I drank quickly and left, and glancing back saw the rats emerge once more and sniff at the legs of the chair where I had been sitting.

At five-thirty one morning in Rangoon, I dozed in the hot, dark compartment of a crowded train, waiting for it to pull out of the station. A person entered the toilet; there was a splash outside; the door banged. Another entered. This went on for twenty minutes, until dawn, and I saw that outside splashing and pools of excrement had stained the tracks and a litter of crumpled newspapers—*The Working People's Daily*—a bright yellow. A rat crept over to the splashed paper and nibbled, then tugged; two more rats, mottled with mange, licked, tugged, and hopped in the muck. Another splash, and the rats withdrew; they returned, gnawing. There was a hawker's voice, a man selling Burmese books with bright covers. He shouted and walked briskly, not stopping to sell, simply walking alongside the train, crying out. The rats withdrew again; the hawker, glancing down, lengthened his stride and walked on, his heel yellow. Then the rats returned.

Cheroots are handy in such a situation. Around me in the compartment smiling Burmese puffed away on thick green cheroots and didn't seem to notice the stink of the growing yellow pool just outside. At the Shwe Dagon Pagoda I saw a very old lady, hands clasped in prayer. She knelt near a begging leper whose disease had withered his feet and abraded his body and given him a bat's face. He had a terrible smell, but the granny prayed with a Churchillian-sized cheroot in her mouth. On Mandalay Hill, doorless outhouses stand beside the rising steps, and next to the outhouses are fruit stalls. The stink of piss is powerful, but the fruitseller, who squats all day in that stink, is wreathed in smoke from his cheroot.

Writing in the Tropics

T HE BEST JOB FOR A WRITER, A JOB WITH THE FEWEST HOURS, is in the tropics. But books are hard to write in the tropics. It is not only the heat; it is the lack of privacy, the open windows, the noise. Tropical cities are deafening. In Lagos and Accra and Kampala two people walking down a city street will find they are shouting to each other to be heard over the sound of traffic and the howls of residents and radios. V. S. Naipaul is the only writer I know of who has mentioned the abrading of the nerves by tropical noise (the chapter on Trinidad in *The Middle Passage*). Shouting is the Singaporean's expression of friendliness; the Chinese shout is like a bark, sharp enough to make you jump. And if you are unfortunate enough to live near a Chinese cemetery—only foreigners live near cemeteries, the Chinese consider it unlucky to occupy those houses—you will hear them mourning with firecrackers, scattering cherrybombs over the gravestones.

Sit in a room in Singapore and try to write. Every sound is an interruption, and your mind blurs each time a motor-cycle or a plane or a funeral passes. If you live near a main road, as I do, there will be three funerals a day (Chinese funerals are truckloads of gong orchestras and brass bands playing familiar songs like "It's a Long Way to Tipperary"). The day the Bengali gardener mows the grass is a day wasted. Hawkers cycle or drive by and each stops; you learn their individual yells, the bean-curd man with his transistor and sidecar, the fish-ball man on his bike, the ice-cream seller with his town crier's bell (a midafternoon interruption), the breadman in his Austin van, leaning on the horn; the elderly Chinese lady crouching in her *sam foo* and crying, *"Yeggs!"* through the door, the Tamil newsboy, a toddy alcoholic, muttering, "Baybah, baybah." Before the British forces left there was a fish-and-chip van; it didn't beep, but there were yells. The Singaporean doesn't stir from his house. He waits in the coolness of his parlor for the deliverers to arrive. The yells and gongs, at first far off, then closer, console him. It is four-thirty, and here comes the coconut seller ringing his bicycle bell. He has a monkey, a macaque the size of a four-year-old, on the crossbar. The coconut seller is crazy; the buyers make him linger and they laugh at him. A crowd gathers to jeer him; he chases some children and then goes away. After dark the grocery truck parks in front of your house; the grocer has a basket of fish, a slaughtered pig, and the whole range of Ma-Ling canned goods ("Tripe in Duck Grease," "Chicken Feet," "Lychees in Syrup"), and for an hour you will hear the yelp and gargle of bartering. You have written nothing.

The heat and light; you asked for those in coming so far, but it is hotter, though less bright, than you imagined—Singapore is usually cloudy, averaging only six hours of sunshine a day. That persistent banging and screeching is an annoyance that makes you hotter still. You are squinting at the pen which is slipping out of your slick fingers and wondering why you bothered to come.

Natives and Expatriates

THE ENGLISH SENSE OF ORDER, THE RESULT OF AN HABITUAL reflex rather than a systematic decree, gives the impression of a tremendous solidity and balance. It was carried abroad and it reassured those who could enter into it. English attitudes traveled without changing much, and to a large extent this accounts for some of the Englishman's isolation. The English overseas are accused of living a rather narrow existence, but the point is that they associate themselves deeply with a locality: in this sense all Englishmen are villagers. It shows in the special phrases they use when they are away, among "natives" or "locals."

"We've lived here for donkey's years, but we've never been invited to one of their houses," says the Englishman, adding, "though we had them around to tea."

"They're very secretive and awfully suspicious," says his wife.

"They *seem* very friendly, but they're not interested in us. They lack curiosity."

"They keep to themselves."

"An odd lot. I can't say I understand them."

You might think they are talking about Kikuyus or Malays, but they aren't. They are Londoners who moved to Dorset eight years ago and they are talking about ordinary folk in the village. I knew the locals: I was neutral—just passing through, stopping for five months. The locals had strong opinions on outsiders who had settled in that part of Dorset.

"They come down here and all the prices go up," one old man said. He might have been a Kenyan, speaking of settlers. There were other objections: the outsiders didn't bother to understand the village life, they kept to themselves, acted superior, and anyway were mostly retired people and not much use.

Expatriates and natives: the colonial pattern repeated in England. There was a scheme afoot to drill for oil on a beautiful hill near a picturesque village. The expatriates started a campaign against it; the natives said very little. I raised the subject in a pub one night with some natives of the area, asking them where they stood on the oil-drilling issue.

"That bugger——," one said, mentioning the name of a well-known man who had lived there for some years and was leading the campaign. "I'd like to talk to him."

"What would you say to him?" I asked.

"I'd tell him to pack his bags and go back where he came from."

So one understands the linguistic variations in England, the dialect that thickens among the natives when an expatriate enters a pub. No one recognizes him; the publican chats with him; the talk around the fireplace is of a broken fence or a road accident. The expatriate is discussed only after he leaves the room: Where does he live? What does he do? The natives know the answers, and later when he buys a round of drinks they will warn him about the weather ("We'll pay for these warm days!"). It is a form of village gratitude, the effort at small talk. But in England a village is a state of mind. "Are you new in the village?" a friend of mine was asked by a newsagent. This was in Notting Hill.

His Highness

THERE IS A SULTAN IN MALAYSIA WHOSE NICKNAME IS "BUF-fles" and who in his old age divides his time between watching polo and designing his own uniforms. His uniforms are very grand and resemble the outfit of a Shriner or thirty-second-degree Mason, but he was wearing a silk sports shirt the day I met him on the polo ground. The interview began badly, because his first question, on hearing I was a writer, was "Then you must know Beverley Nichols!" When I laughed, the sultan said, "Somerset Maugham came to my coronation. And next week Lord Somebody's coming—who is it?"

"Lewisham, Your Highness," said an Englishwoman on his left.

"Lewisham's coming—yes, Lewisham. Do you know *him*? No?" The sultan adjusted his sunglasses. "I just got a letter from him."

The conversation turned quite easily to big-game hunting. "A very rich American once told me that he had shot grizzly bears in Russia and elephants in Africa and tigers in India. He said that bear meat is the best, but the second best is horse meat. He said that. Yes!"

We discussed the merits of horse meat.

The sultan said, "My father said horse meat was good to eat. Yes, indeed. But it's very *heating*." The sultan placed his hands on his shirt and found his paunch and tugged it. "You can't eat too much of it. It's too heating."

"Have you ever eaten horse meat, Your Highness?"

"No, never. But the *syces* eat it all the time."

The match began with great vigor. The opposing team galloped up to the sultan's goal with their sticks flailing.

The sultan said, "Was that a goal?"

"No, Your Highness," said the woman, "but very nearly."

"Very nearly, yes! I saw that," said the sultan.

"Missed by a foot, Your Highness."

"Missed by a foot, yes!"

After that *chukka*, I asked the sultan what the Malay name of the opposing team meant in English.

The sultan shook his head. "I have no idea. I'll have to ask Zayid. It's Malay, you see. I don't speak it terribly well."

The Hotel in No-Man's-Land

"CUSTOMS OVER THERE," SAID THE MOTIONING AFGHAN. But the Customs Office was closed for the night. We could not go back to the Iranian frontier at Tayebad, we could not proceed into Herat. So we remained on a strip of earth, neither Afghanistan nor Iran. It was the sort of bedraggled oasis that features in Foreign Legion films: a few square stucco buildings, several parched trees, a dusty road. It was getting dark. I said, "What do we do now?"

"There's the No-Man's-Land Hotel," said a tall hippie, with pajamas and bangles. His name was Lopez. "I stayed there once before. With a chick. The manager turned me on."

In fact the hotel was nameless, nor did it deserve a name. It was the only hotel in the place. The manager saw us and screamed, "Restaurant!" He herded us into a candlelit room with a long table on which there was a small dish of salt and a fork with twisted tines. The manager's name was Abdul; he was clearly hysterical, suffering the effects of his Ramadan fasting. He began to argue with Lopez, who called him "a scumbag."

There was no electricity in this hotel; there was only enough water for one cup of tea apiece. There was no toilet, there was no place to wash—neither was there any water. There was no food, and there seemed to be a shortage of candles. Bobby and Lopez grumbled about this, but then became frightfully happy when Abdul told them their beds would cost thirty-five cents each.

I had bought an egg in Tayebad, but it had smashed in my jacket pocket, leaked into the material, and hardened in a stiff stain. I had drunk half my gin on the Night Mail to Meshed; I finished the bottle over a game of Hearts with Lopez, Bobby, and a tribesman who was similarly stranded at the hotel.

As we were playing cards (and the chiefs played in an unnecessarily cutthroat fashion), Abdul wandered in and said, "Nice, clean. But no light. No water for wash. No water for tea."

"Turn us on, then," said Lopez. "Hubble-bubble."

"Hash," said Bobby.

Abdul became friendly. He had eaten: his hysteria had passed. He got a piece of hashish, like a small mudpie, and presented it to Lopez, who burned a bit of it and sniffed the smoke.

"This is shit," said Lopez. "Third-quality." He prepared a cigarette. "In Europe, sure, this is good shit. But you don't come all the way to Afghanistan to smoke third-quality shit like this."

"The first time I came here, in '68," said Bobby, "the passport officer said, 'You want nice hash?' I thought it was the biggest put-on I'd ever heard. I mean, a passport officer! I said, 'No, no—it gives me big headache.' 'You no want hash?' he says. I told him no. He looks at me and shakes his head: 'So why you come to Afghanistan?' "

"Far out," said Lopez.

"So I let him turn me on."

"It's a groovy country," said Lopez. "They're all crazy here." He looked at me. "You digging it?"

"Up to a point," I said.

"You freaking out?" Bobby sucked on the hashish cigarette and passed it to me. I took a puff and gulped it and felt a light twanging on the nerves behind my eyes.

"He is, look. I saw him on the train to Meshed," said Lopez. "His head was together, but I think he's loose now."

Lopez laughed at the egg stain on my pocket. The jacket was dirty, my shirt was dirty, and so were my hands; there was a film of dust on my face.

"He's loose," said Bobby.

"He's liquefying," said Lopez. "It's a goofy place."

"I could hang out here," said Bobby.

"I could too, but they won't let me," said Lopez. "That scumbag passport shit only gave me eight days. He didn't like my passport—I admit it's shitty. I got olive oil on it in Greece. I know what I should do—really goop it up with more olive oil and get another one."

"Yeah," said Bobby. He smoked the last of the joint and made another.

With the third joint the conversation moved quickly to a discussion of time, reality, and the spiritual refuge ashrams provided. Both Lopez and Bobby had spent long periods in ashrams; once, as long as six months.

"Meditating?" I asked.

"Well, yeah, meditating and also hanging out."

"We were waiting for this chick to come back from the States."

Lopez was thirty-one. After graduation from a Brooklyn high school, he got a job as a salesman in a plastic firm. "Not really a salesman, I mean, I was the boss's right-hand man. I pick up a phone and say, 'Danny's out of town,' I pick up another one and say, 'Danny'll meet you at three-thirty.' That kind of job, you know?" He was earning a good salary; he had his own apartment, he was engaged to be married. Then one day he had a revelation: "I'm on my way to work. I get off the bus and I'm standing in front of the office. I get these flashes, a real anxiety trip: doing a job I hate, engaged to a plastic chick, all the traffic's pounding. Jesus. So I go to Hollywood. It was okay. Then I went to Mexico. Five years I was in Mexico. That's where I got the name Lopez. My name ain't Lopez, it's Morris. Mexico was good, then it turned me off. I went to

Florida, Portugal, Morocco. One day I'm in Morocco. I meet a guy. He says, 'Katmandu is where it's happening.' So I take my things, my chick, and we start going. There was no train in those days. Twelve days it took me to get to Erzurum. I was sick. It was muddy and cold, and snow—snow in Turkey! I nearly died in Erzurum, and then again in Teheran. But I knew a guy. Anyway, I made it."

I asked him to try to imagine what he would be doing at the age of sixty.

"So I'm sixty, so what? I see myself, sure, I'm sitting right here—*right here*—and probably rolling a joint." Which seemed a rash prophecy, since we were in the No-Man's-Land Hotel, in a candlelit room, without either food or water.

Somewhere at the front of the hotel a telephone rang.

"If it's for me," Lopez shouted, but he had already begun to cackle, "if it's for me, I'm not here!"

The Pathan Camp

THE CENTER OF KABUL IS NOT THE BAZAAR, BUT THE RIVER. It is black and seems bottomless, but it is only one foot deep. Some people drink from it, others shit beside it or do their washing in it. Bathers can be seen soaping themselves not far from where two buses have been driven into it to be washed. Garbage, sewage, and dirt go in; drinking water comes out. The Afghans don't mind dying this way; it's no trouble. Near the bus depot on the south bank bearded Afghans crouch at the side of a cart, three abreast, their faces against metal binoculars. This is a peep show. For about a penny they watch 8mm movies of Indian dancers.

Further up the Kabul River, in the rocky outskirts of the city, I found a Pathan camp. It was large, perhaps thirty ragged white tents, many goats and donkeys and a number of camels. Cooking fires were smoldering and children were running between the tents. I was eager to snap a picture of the place, and had raised my camera, when a stone thudded a few feet away. An old woman had thrown it. She made a threatening gesture and picked up another stone. But she did not throw it. She turned and looked behind her.

A great commotion had started in the center of the camp. A camel had collapsed; it was lying in the dust, kicking its legs and trying to raise its head. The children gave up their game, the women left their cooking pots, men crept out of tents, and all of them ran in the direction of the camel. The old woman ran, too, but when she saw I was following, she stopped and threw her stone at me.

There were shouts. A tall robed figure, brandishing a knife, ran into the crowd. The crowd made way for him and stood some distance from the camel, giving him room and allowing me to see the man raise his knife over the neck of the struggling camel and bring it down hard, making three slashes in the camel's neck. It was as if he had punctured a large toy. Immediately, the camel's head dropped to the ground, his legs ceased to kick, and blood poured out, covering a large triangle of ground and flowing five or six feet from the body, draining into the sand.

I went closer. The old woman screamed, and a half a dozen people ran toward her. They had knives and baskets. The old woman pointed at me, but I did not pause. I sprinted away in the direction of the road, and when I felt I was safe I looked back. No one had chased me. The people with the knives surrounded the camel—the whole camp had descended on it—and they had already started cutting and skinning the poor beast.

Dingle

THE NEAREST THING TO WRITING A NOVEL IS TRAVELING IN A strange country. Travel is a creative act—not simply loafing and inviting your soul, but feeding the imagination, accounting for each fresh wonder, memorizing, and moving on. The discoveries the traveler makes in broad daylight—the curious problems of the eye he solves—resemble those that thrill and sustain a novelist in his solitude. It is fatal to know too much at the outset: boredom comes as quickly to the traveler who knows his route as to the novelist who is overcertain of his plot. And the best landscapes, apparently dense or featureless, hold surprises if they are studied patiently, in the kind of discomfort one can savor afterward. Only a fool blames his bad vacation on the rain.

A strange country—but how strange? One where the sun bursts through the clouds at ten in the evening and makes a sunset as full and promising as dawn. An island which on close inspection appears to be composed entirely of rabbit droppings. Gloomy gypsies camped in hilarious clutter. People who greet you with "Nice day" in a pelting storm. Miles of fuchsia hedges, seven feet tall, with purple hanging blossoms like Chinese lanterns. Ancient perfect castles that are not inhabited; hovels that are. And dangers: hills and beach cliffs so steep you either hug them or fall off. Stone altars that were last visited by Druids, storms that break and pass in minutes, and a local language that sounds like Russian being whispered and so incomprehensible that the attentive traveler feels, in the words of a native writer, "like a dog listening to music."

It sounds as distant and bizarre as The Land Where the Jumblies Live, and yet it is the part of Europe that is closest in miles to America, the thirty-mile sausage of land on the southwest coast of Ireland that is known as the Dingle Peninsula. Beyond it is Boston and New York, where many of its people have fled. The land is not particularly fertile. Fishing is dangerous and difficult. Food is expensive, and if the Irish government did not offer financial inducements to the natives they would probably shrink inland, like the people of Great Blasket Island, who simply dropped everything and went ashore to the Dingle, deserting their huts and fields and leaving them to the rabbits and the ravens.

It is easy for the casual traveler to prettify the place with romantic hyperbole, to see in Dingle's hard weather and exhausted ground the Celtic Twilight, and in its stubborn hopeful people a version of Irishness that is to be cherished. That is the patronage of pity—the metropolitan's contempt for the peasant. The Irish coast, so enchanting for the man with the camera, is murder for the fisherman. For five of the eight days I was there the fishing boats remained anchored in Dingle Harbor, because it was too wild to set sail. The dead seagulls, splayed out like oldfangled ladies' hats below Clogher Head, testify to the furious winds; and never have I seen so many sheep skulls bleaching on hillsides, so many cracked bones beneath bushes.

Farming is done in the most clumsily primitive way, with horses and donkeys, wagons and blunt plows. The methods are traditional by necessity—modernity is expensive, gas costs more than Guinness. The stereotype of the Irishman is a person who spends every night at the local pub, jigging and swilling; in the villages of this peninsula only Sunday night is festive and the rest are observed with tea and early supper.

"I don't blame anyone for leaving here," said a farmer in Dunquin. "There's nothing for young people. There's no work, and it's getting worse."

After the talk of the high deeds of Finn MacCool and the fairies and leprechauns, the conversation turns to the price of spare parts, the cost of grain, the value of the Irish pound, which has sunk below the British one. Such an atmosphere of isolation is intensified and circumscribed by the language—there are many who speak only Gaelic. Such remoteness breeds political indifference. There is little talk of the guerrilla war in Northern Ireland, and the few people I tried to draw out on the subject said simply that Ulster should become part of Eire.

But no one mentions religion. The only indication I had of the faith was the valediction of a lady in a bar in Ballyferriter, who shouted, "God bless ye!" when I emptied my pint of Guinness.

On the rainiest day we climbed down into the cove at Coumeenoole, where—because of its unusual shape, like a ruined cathedral—there was no rain. I sent the children off for driftwood and at the mouth of a dry cave built a fire. It is the bumpkin who sees travel in terms of dancing girls and candlelight dinners on the terrace; the city slicker's triumphant holiday is finding the right mountaintop or building a fire in the rain or recognizing the wildflowers in Dingle: foxglove, heather, bluebells.

And it is the city slicker's conceit to look for untrodden ground, the five miles of unpeopled beach at Stradbally Strand, the flat magnificence of Inch Strand, or the most distant frontier of Ireland, the island off Dunquin called Great Blasket.

Each day, she and her sister islands looked different. We had seen them from the cliffside of Slea Head, and on that day they had the appearance of seamonsters—high-backed creatures making for the open sea. Like all offshore islands, seen from the mainland, their aspect changed with the light: they were lizard-like, then muscular, turned from gray to green, acquired highlights that might have been huts. At dawn they seemed small, but they grew all day into huge and fairly fierce-seeming mountains in the water, diminishing at dusk into pink beasts and finally only hindquarters disappearing in the mist.

Nudists in Corsica

Corsica is France, but it is not French. It is a mountain range moored like a great ship with a cargo of crags a hundred miles off the Riviera. In its three climates it combines the high Alps, the ruggedness of North Africa, and the choicest landscapes of Italy, but most dramatic are the peaks, which are never out of view and show in the upheaval of rock a culture that is violent and heroic. The landscape, which furnished some of the imagery for Dante's *Inferno*, has known heroes. The Latin playwright Seneca was exiled there, Napoleon was born there, and so—if local history is to be believed—was Christopher Columbus (there is a plaque in Calvi); part of the *Odyssey* takes place there—Ulysses lost most of his crew to the cannibalistic Laestrygonians in Bonifacio—and two hundred years ago, the lecherous Scot (and biographer of Dr. Johnson) James Boswell visited and reported, "I had got upon a rock in Corsica and jumped into the middle of life."

The landscape is just weird enough to be beautiful and too large to be pretty. On the west are cliffs that drop straight and red into the sea; on the south there is a true fjord; on the east a long, flat, and formerly malarial coast with the island's only straight road; on the north a populous cape; and in the center the gothic steeples of mountains, fringed by forests where wild boar are hunted. There are sandy beaches, pebbly beaches, boulder-strewn beaches; beaches with enormous waves breaking over them, and beaches that are little more than mud flats, beaches with hotels and beaches that have never known the pressure of a tourist's footprint. There are five-star hotels and hotels that are unfit for human habitation. All the roads are dangerous, many are simply the last mile to an early grave. "There are no bad drivers in Corsica," a Corsican told me. "All the bad drivers die very quickly." But he was wrong—I saw many and I still have damp palms to prove it.

On one of those terrible coast roads—bumper-scraping ruts, bottomless puddles, rocks in the middle as threatening and significant as Marxist statuary—I saw a hitchhiker. She was about eighteen, very dark and lovely, in a loose gown, barefoot, and carrying a basket. She might have been modeling the gown and awaiting the approach of a *Vogue* photographer. My car seemed to stop of its own accord, and I heard myself urging the girl to get in, which she did, thanking me first in French and then, sizing me up, in halting English. Was I going to Chiappa? I wasn't, but I agreed to take her part of the way: "And what are you going to do in Chiappa?"

"I am a *naturiste*," she said, and smiled.

"A nudist?"

She nodded and answered the rest of my questions. She had been a nudist for about five years. Her mother had been running around naked for eleven years. And Papa? No, he wasn't a nudist; he'd left home—clothed—about six years ago. She liked the nudist camp (there are nine hundred nudists at Chiappa); it was a pleasant, healthy pastime, though of course when the weather got chilly they put some clothes on. Sooner than I wished, she told me we had arrived, and she bounded toward the camp to fling her clothes off.

At Palombaggia, the tourist beach a few miles away, I hid behind a pine tree and put on my bathing trunks. I need hardly have bothered—the beach was nearly deserted. Rocks had tumbled into the sea, making natural jetties, and I decided to tramp over a dune and a rocky headland to get a view of the whole bay. There were, as far as the eye could see, groups of bathers, families, couples, children, people putting up windbreaks, strollers, rock collectors, sand-castle makers—and all of them naked. Naked mommy, naked daddy, naked kiddies, naked grandparents. Aside from the usual beach equipment, it was a happy little scene from idealized prehistory, naked Europeans amusing themselves, Cro-Magnon man at play. It was not a nudist camp. These were Germans, as bare as noodles, and apart from the absence of swimming togs, the beach resembled many I have seen on Cape Cod, even to the discarded Coke cans and candy wrappers. I stayed until rain clouds gathered and the sun was obscured. This drove the Germans behind their windbreaks and one woman put on a short jersey—no more than that—and paced the beach, squinting at the clouds and then leering at me. I suppose it was my fancy bathing trunks.

New York Subway

NEW YORKERS SAY SOME TERRIBLE THINGS ABOUT THE subway—that they hate it, or are scared stiff of it, or that it deserves to go broke. For tourists it seems just another dangerous aspect of New York, though most don't know it exists. "I haven't been down there in years" is a common enough remark from a city dweller. Even people who ride it seem to agree that there is more Original Sin among subway passengers. And more desperation, too, making you think of choruses of "O dark dark dark. They all go into the dark. . . ."

"Subway" is not its name, because strictly speaking more than half of it is elevated. But which person who has ridden it lately is going to call it by its right name, "The Rapid Transit"? You can wait a long time for some trains and, as in the section of T. S. Eliot's "East Coker," often

. . . an underground train, in the tube, stops too long between stations

And the conversation rises and slowly fades into silence
And you see behind every face the mental emptiness
  deepen
Leaving only the growing terror of nothing to think
  about . . .

It is also frightful-looking. It has paint and signatures all over its aged face. People who don't take it, who never ride the subway and have no use for it, say that these junky pictures are folk art, a protest against the metropolitan grayness, and what a wonderful sense of color these scribblers have—which is complete nonsense. The graffiti are bad, violent, and destructive, and the people who praise them are either malicious or lazy-minded. The graffiti are so extensive and so dreadful it is hard to believe that the perpetrators are not the recipients of some enormous foundation grant. The subway has been vandalized from end to end. It smells so hideous you want to put a clothespin on your nose, and it is so noisy the sound actually hurts. Is it dangerous? Ask anyone and he will tell you there are about two murders a day on the subway (though this is not true). It really is the pits, people say.

You have to ride it for a while to find out what it is and who takes it and who gets killed on it.

It is full of surprises. Three and a half million fares a day pass through it, and in 1981 the total number of murder victims on the subway amounted to thirteen. This baker's dozen does not include suicides (one a week), "man under" incidents (one a day), or "space cases"—people who quite often get themselves jammed between the train and the platform. Certainly the subway is very ugly and extremely noisy, but it only *looks* like a death trap. People ride it looking stunned and holding their breath. It's not at all like the BART system in San Francisco, where people are constantly chattering, saying, "I'm going to my father's wedding" or "I'm looking after my Mom's children" or "I've got a date with my fiancée's boyfriend." In New York, the subway is a serious matter—the rackety train, the silent passengers, the occasional scream.

* * *

WE WERE AT FLUSHING AVENUE, ON THE GG LINE, TALKING about rules for riding the subway. You need rules: the subway is like a complex—and diseased—circulatory system. Some people liken it to a sewer and others hunch their shoulders and mutter about being in the bowels of the earth. It is full of suspicious-looking people.

I said, "Keep away from isolated cars, I suppose," and my friend, a police officer, said, "Never display jewelry."

Just then, a man walked by, and he had Chinese coins—the old ones with a hole through the middle—woven somehow into his hair. There were enough coins in that man's hair for a swell night out in old Shanghai, but robbing him would have involved scalping him. There was a woman at the station, too. She was clearly crazy, and she lived in the subway the way people live in railway stations in India, with stacks of dirty bags. The police in New York call such people "skells" and are seldom harsh with them. "Wolfman Jack" is a skell, living underground at Hoyt-Schermerhorn, also on the GG line; the police in that station give him food and clothes, and if you ask him how he is, he says, "I'm getting some calls." Call them colorful characters and they don't look so dangerous or pathetic.

This crazy old lady at Flushing Avenue was saying, "I'm a member of the medical profession." She had no teeth, and plastic bags were taped around her feet. I glanced at her and made sure she kept her distance. The previous day, a crazy old lady just like her came at me and shrieked, "Ahm goon cut you up!" This was at Pelham Parkway, on the IRT-2 line in the Bronx. I left the car at the next stop, Bronx Park East, where the zoo is, though who could be blamed for thinking that, in New York City, the zoo is everywhere?

Then a Muslim unflapped his prayer mat—while we were at Flushing Avenue, talking about Rules—and spread it on the platform and knelt on it, just like that, and was soon on all fours, beseeching Allah and praising the Prophet Mohammed. This is not remarkable. You see people praying, or reading the Bible, or selling religion on the subway all the time. "Hallelujah, brothers and sisters," the man with the leaflets says on the BMT-RR line at Prospect Avenue in Brooklyn. "I love Jesus! I used to be a wino!" And Muslims beg and push their green plastic cups at passengers, and try to sell them copies of something called *Arabic Religious Classics.* It is December and Brooklyn, and the men are dressed for the Great Nafud Desert, or Jiddah or Medina—skullcap, gallabieh, sandals.

"And don't sit next to the door," the second police officer said. We were still talking about Rules. "A lot of these snatchers like to play the doors."

The first officer said, "It's a good idea to keep near the conductor. He's got a telephone. So does the man in the token booth. At night, stick around the token booth until the train comes in."

"Although, token booths . . ." the second officer said. "A few years ago, some kids filled a fire extinguisher with gasoline and pumped it into a token booth at Broad Channel. There were two ladies inside, but before they could get out the kids set the gas on fire. The booth just exploded like a bomb, and the ladies died. It was a revenge thing. One of the kids had gotten a summons for Theft of Service—not paying his fare."

Just below us, at Flushing Avenue, there was a stream running between the tracks. It gurgled and glugged down the whole length of the long platform. It gave the station the atmosphere of a sewer—dampness and a powerful smell. The water was flowing toward Myrtle and Willoughby. And there was a rat. It was only my third rat in a week of riding the subway, but this one was twice the size of rats I've seen elsewhere. I thought: *Rats as big as cats.*

"Stay with the crowds. Keep away from quiet stairways. The stairways at Forty-first and Forty-third are usually quiet, but Forty-second is always busy—that's the one to use."

So many rules! It's not like taking a subway at all; it's like walking through the woods—through dangerous jungle, rather: Do this, Don't do that . . .

"It reminds me," the first officer said. "The burning of that token booth at Broad Channel. Last May, six guys attempted to murder someone at Forest Parkway, on the J line. It was a whole gang against this one guy. Then they tried to burn the station down with Molotov cocktails. We stopped that, too."

The man who said this was six feet four, 281 pounds. He carried a .38 in a shoulder holster and wore a bulletproof vest. He had a radio, a can of Mace, and a blackjack. He was a plainclothesman.

The funny thing is that, one day, a boy—five feet six, 135 pounds—tried to mug him. The boy slapped him across the face while the plainclothesman was seated on a train. The boy said, "Give me your money," and then threatened the man in a vulgar way. The boy still punched at the man when the man stood up; he still said, "Give me all your money!" The plainclothesman then took out his badge and his pistol and said, "I'm a police officer and you're under arrest." "I was just kidding!" the boy said, but it was too late.

I laughed at the thought of someone trying to mug this well-armed giant.

"Rule one for the subway," he said. "Want to know what it is?" He looked up and down the Flushing Avenue platform, at the old lady and the Muslim and the running water and the vandalized signs. "Rule one is—don't ride the subway if you don't have to."

Rowing Around the Cape

THE BOAT SLID DOWN THE BANK AND WITHOUT A SPLASH into the creek, which was gray this summer morning. The air was woolly with mist. The tide had turned, but just a moment ago, so there was still no motion on the water—no current, not a ripple. The marsh grass was a deeper green for there being no sun. It was as if—this early and this dark—the day had not yet begun to breathe.

I straightened the boat and took my first stroke: the gurgle of the spoon blades and the sigh of the twisting oarlock were the only sounds. I set off, moving like a water bug through the marsh and down the bendy creek to the sea. When my strokes were regular and I was rowing at a good clip, my mind started to work, and I thought: *I'm not coming back tonight.* And so the day seemed long enough and full of possibilities. I had no plans except to keep on harbor-hopping around the Cape, and it was easy now going out with the tide.

This was Scorton Creek, in East Sandwich, and our hill—one of the few on the low, lumpy terminal moraine of the Cape—was once an Indian fort. Wampanoags. The local farmers plowed this hill until recently, when the houses went up, and their plow blades always struck flints and ax heads and beads. I splashed past a boathouse the size of a garage. When they dug the foundation for that boathouse less than twenty years ago, they unearthed a large male Wampanoag who had been buried in a sitting position, his skin turned to leather and his bones sticking through. They slung him out and put the boathouse there.

Three more bends in the creek and I could see the current stirring more strongly around me. A quarter of a mile away in the marsh was a Great Blue Heron—five feet high and moving in a slow prayerful way, like a narrow-shouldered priest in gray vestments. The boat slipped along, carrying itself between strokes. Up ahead on the beach was a person with a dog—one of those energetic early risers who boasts, "I only need four hours' sleep!" and is probably hell to live with. Nothing else around—only the terns screeching over their eggs, and a few boats motionless at their moorings, and a rather crummy clutter of beach houses and NO TRESPASSING signs, and the ghosts of dead Indians. The current was so swift in the creek I couldn't have gone back if I tried, and as I approached the shore it shot me into the sea. And now light was dazzling in the mist, as on the magnificent Turner *Sunrise with Sea-monsters*.

AFTER AN HOUR I WAS AT SANDY NECK PUBLIC BEACH— about four miles. This bay side of the upper Cape has a low duney shore and notoriously shallow water in places. The half a dozen harbors are spread over seventy miles and most have dangerous bars. It is not a coast for easy cruising and in many areas there is hardly enough water for wind-surfing. There are sand bars in the oddest places. Most sail-boats can't approach any of the harbors unless the tide is high. So the little boats stay near shore and watch the tides, and the deep draft boats stay miles offshore. I was in be-tween and I was alone. In two months of this I never saw another rowboat more than fifty yards from the shore. In-deed, I seldom saw anyone rowing at all.

Sandy Neck proper, an eight-mile peninsula of Arabian-style dunes, was today a panorama of empty beach; the only life stirring was the gulls and more distantly the hov-ering marsh hawks. A breeze had come up; it had fresh-ened; it was now a light wind. I got stuck on a sand bar, then hopped out and dragged the boat into deeper water. I was trying to get around Beach Point to have my lunch in Barnstable Harbor—my forward locker contained provi-sions. I was frustrated by the shoals. But I should have known—there were seagulls all over the ocean here and they were not swimming but standing. I grew to recognize low water from the posture of seagulls.

When I drew level with Barnstable Harbor I was spun around by the strong current. I had to fight it for half an hour before I got ashore. Even then I was only at Beach Point. This was the channel into the harbor, and the water in it was narrow and swiftly moving—a deep river flowing through a shallow sea, its banks just submerged.

I tied the boat to a rock, and while I rested a Ranger drove up in his Chevy Bronco.

He said, "That wind's picking up. I think we're in for a storm." He pointed toward Barnstable Harbor. "See the clouds building up over there? The forecast said showers but that looks like more than showers. Might be a thunderstorm. Where are you headed?"

"Just up the coast."

He nodded at the swiftly rushing channel and said, "You'll have to get across that thing first."

"Why is it so choppy?"

His explanation was simple, and it accounted for a great deal of the rough water I was to see in the weeks to come. He said that when the wind was blowing in the opposite direction to a tide, a chop of hard, irregular waves was whipped up. It could become very fierce very quickly.

Then he pointed across the harbor mouth toward Bass Hole and told me to look at how the ebbing tide had uncovered a mile of sand flats. "At low tide people just walk around over there," he said. So, beyond the vicious channel the sea was slipping down—white water here, none there.

After the Ranger drove off, I made myself a cheese sandwich, swigged some coffee from my thermos bottle, and decided to rush the channel. My skiff's sides were lapstrake—like clapboards—and rounded, which stabilized the boat in high waves, but this short breaking chop was a different matter. Instead of rowing at right angles to the current I turned the bow against it, and steadied the skiff by rowing. The skiff rocked wildly—the current slicing the bow, the wind-driven chop smacking the stern. A few minutes later I was across. And then I ran aground. After the channel were miles of watery shore; but it was only a few inches deep—and the tide was still dropping.

The wind was blowing, the sky was dark, the shoreline was distant; and now the water was not deep enough for this rowboat. I got out and—-watched by strolling seagulls—dragged the boat through the shallow water that lay over the sand bar. The boat skidded and sometimes floated, but it was not really buoyant until I had splashed along for about an hour. To anyone on the beach I must have seemed a bizarre figure—alone, far from shore, walking on the water.

It was midafternoon by the time I had dragged the boat to deeper water, and I got in and began to row. The wind seemed to be blowing now from the west; it gathered at the stern and gave me a following sea, lifting me in the direction I wanted to go. I rowed past Chapin Beach and the bluffs, and around the black rocks at Nobscusset Harbor, marking my progress on my flapping chart by glancing again and again at a water tower like a stovepipe in Dennis.

At about five o'clock I turned into Sesuit Harbor, still pulling hard. I had rowed about sixteen miles. My hands were blistered but I had made a good start. And I had made a discovery: the sea was unpredictable, and the shore looked foreign. I was used to finding familiar things in exotic places, but the unfamiliar at home was new to me. It had been a disorienting day. At times I had been afraid. It was a taste of something strange in a place I had known my whole life. It was a shock and a satisfaction.

Mrs. Coffin at Sesuit Harbor advised me not to go out the next day. Anyone with a name out of *Moby-Dick* is worth listening to on the subject of the sea. The wind was blowing from the northeast, making Mrs. Coffin's flag snap and beating the sea into whitecaps.

I said, "I'm only going to Rock Harbor."

It was about nine miles.

She said, "You'll be pulling your guts out."

I decided to go, thinking: *I would rather struggle in a heavy sea and get wet than sit in the harbor and wait for the weather to improve.*

But as soon as I had rowed beyond the breakwater I was hit hard by the waves and tipped by the wind. I unscrewed my sliding seat and jammed the thwart into place; and I tried again. I couldn't maneuver the boat. I changed oars, lashing the long ones down and using the seven-and-a-half-foot ones. I made some progress, but the wind was punching me toward shore. This was West Brewster, off Quivett Neck. The chart showed church spires. I rowed for another few hours and saw that I had gone hardly any distance at all. But there was no point in turning back. I didn't need a harbor. I knew I could beach the boat anywhere—pull it up over there at that ramp, or between those rocks, or at that public beach. I had plenty of time and I felt all right. This was like walking uphill, but so what?

So I struggled all day. I hated the banging waves, and the way they leaped over the sides when the wind pushed me sideways into the troughs of the swell. There was a few inches of water sloshing in the bottom, and my chart was soaked. At noon a motorboat came near me and asked me if I was in trouble. I said no and told him where I was going. The man said, "Rock Harbor's real far!" and pointed east. Some of the seawater dried on the boat, leaving the lace of crystallized salt shimmering on the mahogany. I pulled on, passing a sailboat in the middle of the afternoon.

"Where's Rock Harbor?" I asked.

"Look for the trees!"

But I looked in the wrong place. The trees weren't on shore, they were in the water, about twelve of them planted in two rows—tall dead limbless pines—like lampposts. They marked the harbor entrance; they also marked the Brewster Flats, for at low tide there was no water here at all, and Rock Harbor was just a creek draining into a desert of sand. You could drive a car across the harbor mouth at low tide.

I had arranged to meet my father here. My brother Joseph was with him. He had just arrived from the Pacific islands of Samoa. I showed him the boat.

He touched the oarlocks. He said, "They're all tarnished." Then he frowned at the salt-smeared wood and his gaze made the boat seem small and rather puny.

I said, "I just rowed from Sesuit with the wind against me. It took me the whole goddamned day!"

He said, "Don't get excited."

"What do you know about boats?" I said.

He went silent. We got into the car—two boys and their father. I had not seen Joe for several years. Perhaps he was sulking because I hadn't asked about Samoa. But had he asked about my rowing? It didn't seem like much, because it was travel at home. Yet I felt the day had been full of risks.

"How the hell," I said, "can you live in Samoa for eight years and not know anything about boats?"

"*Sah*-moa," he said, correcting my pronunciation. It was a family joke.

My brother Alex was waiting with my mother, and he smiled as I entered the house.

"Here he comes," Alex said.

My face was burned, the blisters had broken on my hands and left them raw, my back ached, and so did the muscle strings in my forearm; there was sea salt in my eyes.

"Ishmael," Alex said. He was sitting compactly on a chair glancing narrowly at me and smoking. " 'And I only am escaped alone to tell thee.' "

My mother said, "We're almost ready to eat—you must be starving! God, look at you!"

Alex was behind her. He made a face at me, then silently mimicked a laugh at the absurdity of a forty-two-year-old man taking consolation from his mother.

"Home is the sailor, home from the sea," Alex said and imitated my voice, "Pass the spaghetti, Mom!"

Joe had started to relax. Now he had an ally, and I was being mocked. We were not writers, husbands, or fathers. We were three big boys fooling in front of their parents. Home is so often the simple past.

"What's he been telling you, Joe?" Alex asked.

I went to wash my face.

"He said I don't know anything about boats."

Just before we sat down to eat, I said, "It's pretty rough out there."

Alex seized on this, looking delighted. He made the sound of a strong wind, by whistling and clearing his throat. He squinted and in a harsh whisper said, "Aye, it's rough out there, and you can hardly"—he stood up, banging the dining table with his thigh—"you can hardly see the bowsprit. Aye, and the wind's shifting, too. But never mind,

Mr. Christian! Give him twenty lashes—that'll take the strut out of him! And hoist the mainsail—we're miles from anywhere. None of you swabbies knows anything about boats. But I know, because I've sailed from Pitcairn Island to Rock Harbor by dead reckoning—in the roughest water known to man. Just me against the elements, with the waves threatening to pitch-pole my frail craft . . ."

"Your supper's getting cold," Father said.

"How long did it take you?" Mother said to me.

"All day," I said.

"Aye, captain," Alex said. "Aw, it's pretty rough out there, what with the wind and the rising sea."

"What will you write about?" my father asked.

"He'll write about ocean's roar and how he just went around the Horn. You're looking at Francis Chichester! The foam beating against the wheelhouse, the mainsheet screaming, the wind and the rising waves. Hark! Thunder and lightning over *The Gypsy Moth*!"

Declaiming made Alex imaginative, and stirred his memory. He had an actor's gift for sudden shouts and whispers and for giving himself wholly to the speech. It was as if he was on an instant touched with lucid insanity, the exalted chaos of creation. He was triumphant.

"But look at him now—Peter Freuchen of the seven seas, the old tar in his clinker-built boat. He's home asking his mother to pass the spaghetti! 'Thanks, Mom, I'd love another helping, Mom.' After a day in the deep sea, he's with his mother and father, reaching for the meatballs!"

Joseph was laughing hard, his whole body swelling as he tried to suppress it.

"He's not going to write about that. No, nothing about the spaghetti. It'll just be Captain Bligh, all alone, bending at his oars, and picking oakum through the long tumultuous nights at sea. And the wind and the murderous waves . . ."

"Dry up," Father said, still eating.

Then they all turned their big sympathetic faces at me across the cluttered dining table. Alex looked slightly sheepish, and the others apprehensive, fearing that I might be offended, that Alex had gone too far.

"What will you write about?" Mother asked.

I shook my head and tried not to smile—because I was thinking: *That.*

PAUL THEROUX

Available in your local bookstore.